Chicken Soup for the Soul®

What I Learned from the Dog

*Chicken Soup for the Soul: What I Learned from the Dog*
*101 Stories about Life, Love, and Lessons*
Jack Canfield, Mark Victor Hansen, Amy Newmark

Published by Chicken Soup for the Soul Publishing, LLC    www.chickensoup.com

*Front cover photo courtesy of Punchstock. Back cover photo courtesy photograph courtesy of*
*iStockphoto.com/ Fotosmurf03. Interior photograph courtesy of iStockphoto.com/ IGlobalP*

*Cover and Interior Design & Layout by Pneuma Books, LLC*
For more info on Pneuma Books, visit www.pneumabooks.com

Distributed to the booktrade by Simon & Schuster. SAN: 200-2442

**Publisher's Cataloging-in-Publication Data**
*(Prepared by The Donohue Group)*

Chicken soup for the soul : what I learned from the dog : 101 stories about
 life, love, and lessons / [compiled by] Jack Canfield, Mark Victor Hansen,
 [and] Amy Newmark.

   p. ; cm.

 ISBN: 978-1-935096-38-2

1. Dogs--Literary collections.  2. Dogs--Anecdotes.  3. Dog owners--Literary collections.  4. Dog owners--Anecdotes.  5. Human-animal relationships--Anecdotes.  I.
Canfield, Jack, 1944-  II. Hansen, Mark Victor.  III. Newmark, Amy.  IV. Title: What I
learned from the dog

PN6071.D6 C455 2009
810.8/02/03629772                    2009933200

PRINTED IN THE UNITED STATES OF AMERICA
on acid∞free paper
18 17 16 15 14 13 12 11 10        04 05 06 07 08 09 10

# Chicken Soup for the Soul®
## What I Learned from the Dog

101 Stories about Life, Love, and Lessons

Jack Canfield
Mark Victor Hansen
Amy Newmark

CSS

Chicken Soup for the Soul Publishing, LLC
Cos Cob, CT

www.chickensoup.com

# Contents

**❶**

## ~Learning about Family~

**❷**

## ~Learning to Have Courage~

❸

## ~Learning to Listen~

❹

## ~Learning to Overcome Adversity~

# ❺
## ~Learning to Heal~

# ❻
## ~Learning to Say Goodbye~

## ❼
## ~Learning to Put Things in Perspective~

## ❽
## ~Learning to Be Kinder~

**❾**

## ~Learning about Unconditional Love~

# Foreword

**W**hat have I learned from my dog?

Everything.

I live my life side by side with my pets—they are an integral part of everything that I do—and yet after all these years (animal or human), I still learn from them every day. Dogs can be the best teachers and the best teachers make learning painless and fun, heartwarming and always rewarding. That's what my dog does. I don't remember my fourth grade teacher, Mrs. Googleman, making learning that fun.

I love my dog, and I love yours too. I've spent my whole career trying to keep all of them safe and happy. A reward for all the love they've given us. I am so excited that Chicken Soup for the Soul has put together another one of their fabulous books for dog lovers, and this one is on such a special topic, with 101 true tales offering insights about life, love, and the fundamental wisdom we can learn from our dogs. It's a real-life, dog-lovers Holy Grail! This book makes me smile, laugh out loud, cry, and pick up the phone to share my favorite stories. Lucky likes the extra hugs she is getting too and is trying to get me to help her pen our very own.

What do we learn from our dogs? Perhaps the most important thing is to enjoy life and take each day as it comes. Victorian novelist Samuel Butler said, "All of the animals except man know that the principal business of life is to enjoy it." Although times have changed since the Victorian era, humans are still slowing figuring this out.

That's what this book is for. You will read about Elizabeth Cutting, who reluctantly took over the care of her grandmother's Golden Retriever. She had no idea that the dog would change her life by teaching her about integrating her "inner dog." But over the years, through the ups and downs of her life, that priceless dog taught her through example, showing her how to approach every day with "gusto," "live in the moment," "forget the bad, remember the good," and most important, "forgive mistakes—every one of them, every time."

Our dogs help us put things in perspective and give us a reason to keep going. Their love is unconditional for us. Do dogs ever have a "bad day?" In Sean Sellers' story, he details his experience after personally witnessing the events of September 11th, and says, "I might have gone out of my mind if it wasn't for that dog... she has taught me to concentrate on the rhythm of my heart and to remove the wishing, the wondering, and the worrying from my head."

Carla Andrews-O'Hara's dog helped her live through chemo. In the depths of her sickness, Chaco was "a constant reminder of the wonders of life... Chaco is blessed with the knowledge that the world is magic. His heart overflows with unconditional love. I'd reject him and he kept coming back—determined to help me fight. It's almost as though he'd look at me and say, 'Get up. Don't give in. Let's go for a walk.'"

Stacy Murphy has a powerful story in this book about overcoming her alcoholism after adopting the "runt" of a purebred Labrador Retriever litter. Ruby was destined for the pound, but Stacy took her home and writes that "with Ruby by my side, taking those first steps towards a fulfilling life was no longer such a daunting prospect... she taught me to love myself. To Ruby, I was always beautiful and fun, always smart and strong. Her love was unwavering even when I didn't feel deserving of it...In my darkest of days, I hung on for no other reason than for the love of Ruby."

That brings me to the subject of pounds and adoption. You all know how passionate I am about animal rescue. I rescued my Maltese, sidekick, lap-dog, partner-in-crime, Lucky, and my Russian Blue, Pasha, from pounds. I proudly support many animal rescue organizations and am happy to report that the tragedy of abandoned dogs and cats is steadily being addressed. Chicken Soup for the Soul shares in this passion, and this book is filled with stories of rescued dogs... and rescued people!

Belle, a long-hair Chihuahua born with a curved spine, was destined for euthanasia at the pound when Al Seradell rescued her. Belle had clearly been abused, but despite her fear she turned right around and rescued Al! He writes that "a slew of personal and career disappointments had left me depressed and very distrustful" and points out "Who says a therapist has to be human? Inspired by Belle's renewed faith, I have abandoned my own reticence and no longer wait until someone shows me a bit of kindness. I now feel confident that I can trust again. Because of Belle, I am back in the game, ready to take risks and enjoy life to its fullest."

The lessons learned in this book range in size and scope, just like the dogs. Do you feel you need to look perfect all the time? "Pooper scooping" is the great leveler, as Nancy Berk points out when she says, "Ever since the dogs came into my life, my flawed self has been on display for the world, or at least the neighborhood to see. I've been half dressed, overdressed and badly dressed, all for the sake of two sets of big sad eyes... I like to think that God made dogs so that we could escape our self-absorbed lives." I couldn't agree with Berk more. Ever since rescuing Lucky, I ditched all my expensive bags for the only one that could hold Lucky.

I hope you will enjoy this book as much as I have. The Chicken Soup for the Soul team is so dedicated to our dogs and their wellbeing, and it is a pleasure and a privilege to introduce this book to you. As Amy Newmark, Chicken Soup for the Soul publisher and co-author, says "Our dogs teach us so much about how to live our lives — sometimes we just have to stop and listen."

So live large, love your dog, love yourself, and learn from each other, whether four paws or two.

~Wendy Diamond

# Canine Lessons

If I was anything like my dog
I'd greet everyone I know
With sheer enthusiasm.
I'd consistently react with joy
to a smiling face
or a simple treat.
And I'd ride through life
With the window wide open
And gleefully welcome the breezes of experience in my face!

~Beverly F. Walker

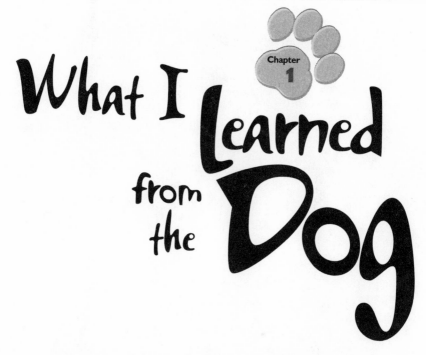

# What I Learned from the Dog

## Chapter 1

## Learning about Family

*Call it a clan, call it a network, call it a tribe, call it a family.
Whatever you call it, whoever you are, you need one.*

*~Jane Howard*

# The Rescued

*The hunger for love is much more difficult to remove
than the hunger for bread.*
*~Mother Teresa*

Panda was not an ordinary dog. He was the favorite Border Collie of our rancher friends, Pat and Sharon. Panda was much more than a favorite pet. He was a highly trained sheep dog that could herd a flock or a single sheep based on a series of varying, whistled commands. That made him a very valuable dog: several thousand dollars if he were sold, which he would never have been. Panda's real value went beyond his skills. Those who have loved pets know what I mean.

Pat and Sharon came to the city to visit. While staying at a relative's home, Panda disappeared. There was a frantic, ever-expanding search of the yard, the neighborhood, and a large park nearby. They called us to assist in the search, which we did, but there was no sign of Panda.

The next day we repeated the search, but Pat and Sharon had to return home that evening. Pat's sister and my wife agreed to split the duty of checking the city animal pound and Dumb Friends League each day, which they did for three months. We printed flyers and posted them throughout the neighborhood and the park, but to no avail.

As the months slipped by, the thoughts of Panda became more and more infrequent. We had long ago given up hope of finding him, and shifted our hopes to the unknowable—hoping instead that somehow he was in a new, loving home.

Nearly two years later my wife and I were driving along a parkway near the downtown area. We passed an obviously homeless man lying fifty feet away on a sunny, grassy spot. Next to him was a Border Collie. My wife shouted, "That's Panda! Go around the block!"

"What? Panda?" I said blankly.

"Panda! Pat and Sharon's Panda! Go around the block."

I said, "What? You glimpse some guy with a dog from fifty feet, and think it is a dog you've seen only a dozen times in your life, the last time two years ago? You have to be kidding!"

To humor her, I turned and we made a loop and drove by again. My wife became more certain that the dog was Panda and I became more certain that she had just made a leap into some alternate, delusional state.

When we got home, she immediately called Sharon. As luck would have it, Pat was going to be in a nearby town that weekend, and decided to drive the extra seventy miles into the city.

We explained to Pat the area where we had seen the pair. He went there and quickly spotted them. Pat parked nearby and walked over to them, stopping about twenty feet away.

So there they were—the dog, the homeless man, and the rancher, face to face. Pat whistled a command and the dog raced immediately to Pat's feet and sat, wagging his tail furiously. Even after two years of separation, Panda's reaction to the command was instantaneous. Panda had been found!

The homeless man was clearly surprised at the dog's response, as evidenced by his shocked look, which quickly turned into a concerned look.

Pat said, "Is this your dog?"

"Yeah, I found him a couple of years ago," the man said. "But he looks like he knows you."

"Yep, and I know him," Pat said.

There were a few seconds of awkward silence. The grizzled man cleared his throat and rubbed his chin as Pat knelt down and stroked

Panda's muzzle and shoulder. Panda wiggled from the tip of his tail to his middle, licking Pat's hand and arm.

"I know that dog is yours," the man said, "but you gotta know that he is my life. He is my only friend in this world. I found a vet who gives him free care, and the store downtown gives me dog food for him. I take care of him and he takes care of me."

"I'm sure that is true," Pat replied. "Where did you find him?"

"Down by the park. He wasn't very streetwise. He almost got hit in traffic, so I rescued him."

Panda then wandered back over to the man and sat beside him, but didn't take his eyes off Pat.

"What are you gonna do," the man asked?

"I don't know," Pat said. "Panda's a great dog, and great with the sheep. He and I traveled a lot of miles together."

"I knew he was smart and well trained," the man said.

Another long and awkward silence followed. Pat stood up, and Panda immediately came to him and sat at his feet, looking up expectantly.

Far too many dogs have no one to love them, while other dogs are lucky enough to have someone who does, but it is the rare dog that is truly loved by two unconnected people. Panda was fortunate enough to be one of those dogs.

We saw the homeless man walking or lying with Panda quite a few times over the following years. I am still not sure if the homeless man rescued Panda, or if Panda rescued the homeless man.

~Daniel James

# Coal

*The meeting of two personalities*
*is like the contact of two chemical substances:*
*if there is any reaction, both are transformed.*
~Carl Jung

In the spring of 2000, I met my new partner. I was one of the old guys, with eighteen years on the job in a local police department, and he was another rookie to train. On his first day I drove thirty-five miles to pick him up for work. My first thought when I met him was that he was such a skinny little guy, kind of skittish and shy. But I'd seen worse. My new partner was a two-year-old black Lab named Coal, and he was going to be trained for drug detection. The canine trainer, who was a retired police chief and a salty no-nonsense fellow, introduced me to Coal and said, "Here he is, now go give him a bath." A little different from the usual introduction to a new partner.

As we trained, Coal amazed me with his ability to do his job. I quickly learned that we were a team and that if we weren't performing up to standards, the problem was usually me. With the proper diet and exercise, Coal filled out and became a very handsome and fit animal, drawing the attention of everyone around him. He also became a friend to the community, visiting schools, church groups, and civic organizations to help build relationships with the citizens we serve. Those relationships served us well when the mayor decided he that he was going to disband the K-9 program. The townsfolk overwhelmed the municipal offices with calls and visits to ask for reconsideration. Fortunately, Coal's friends in the community did change the minds of those in charge and we spent eight years and seven months as a working team.

During our time together I realized that I had become one of those grumpy old cops who make people roll their eyes. Coal, however, became my icebreaker. He was a conversation starter, and he helped me to interact with the people I met rather than just command them. Don't get me wrong. There are still plenty of humans among us who could take behavior lessons from our pets, and they, on occasion, still need to be commanded and corrected. In retrospect I would say that my partner didn't weaken me, but he softened me. This "animal" made me a better human.

Our bond grew steadily as we spent all of our time together, and before I knew it Coal had become a huge part of me. I learned very quickly that my thoughts and emotions traveled from my head and my heart, down my arm, through the lead, and into my partner. He knew if I perceived that the person in front of me was going to be a problem or a threat, and he was immediately on guard without command. He would also sense when the person who I was interacting with was okay, and he would relax. On the rare occasion that he wasn't by my side, I would find myself talking to him, or reaching for him and getting a handful of air.

Coal retired two months ago and now he stays home while I'm at work. He is slowly getting used to it, but he has aged quickly since his retirement. Coal is not the only one having difficulty with the adjustment. Now I don't know what to do with the last bite of my lunch, and on several occasions I found myself parking by the woods where he used to run while he was on duty. I open the back door to let him out just to find that my partner is missing and there is nothing in the back of the car but a cold, empty seat.

About a month after Coal retired, we learned that he had cancer. That news was devastating for my wife and me, although Coal has no idea that he is sick. He still plays, cuddles up on the couch with me, and gets excited when he sees the old camouflage bag that we carry back and forth to the boat. With aggressive treatment he seems to be doing alright, and there is a strong chance that he will live a long and happy life.

I have learned from Coal each and every day, and I feel extremely lucky to have been blessed with an incredible teacher. He was once a skinny, skittish black Lab, and he grew into an icon of the community and the best buddy I have ever had. If we could just take an example from man's best friend and be honest and true to those around us, we would have better relationships that last a lifetime.

~Sgt. Ed Geib, MBPD K-9

# My Mother the Bear

*The world is hugged by the faithful arms of volunteers.*
*~Everett Mámor*

My wife pulled the blankets and scornfully turned her back to me when I whispered that I'd brought a kitten home and put him in the downstairs bathroom. I knew she would not appreciate my 2 A.M. announcement about a new kitten. We already had two cats—one dysfunctional cat that taxes us with her occasional "accidents" and a replacement cat for the other crazy stray cat we lost to FIP. We also have a black Lab. Oh, and three boys. We've had other pets too—fish, hamsters, other rescued dogs and cats. And we've taken in stray humans. Yes... we're a regular zoo at times.

But I hadn't been able to deny the bold kitten when he approached me and my Styrofoam to-go box as I walked to my car after a night out. Completely unafraid, the tiny kitten was begging for whatever I had. The special that night was chicken wings and he tore them apart. Clearly we were meant for each other. I had to take him home. So I settled in behind the wheel and he stood in my lap with his front paws on the steering wheel. Together we drove home from our night out.

My wife begrudged him and she let me know it every chance she had. We kept him in the garage for the first six months of his life until he was old enough to be vaccinated and neutered. That cost something like 600 bucks. Nina reminds me of that also.

The kitten was completely content in the garage, however. Leaping from the spare insulation in the rafters of the dusty old garage, he'd come to greet me and our black Lab, Bear, each morning. He was perpetually filthy and had cat acne on his chin. So we named him Smudgie. And each morning, Bear would give Smudgie a bath, cleaning him from head to toe and often swallowing Smudgie's head completely. Returning the affection, Smudgie would dig his claws into Bear's neck, grip Bear's jowls with his teeth, and allow himself to be toted around the garage.

Smudgie lives in the house now. He is an endless source of entertainment. Oddly enough, he looks like a Bulldog.

Smudgie was not more than a month old when I brought him home, and I think he believes Bear is his mother. From Bear, this cat has learned the way of the dog. Smudgie eats dog food, begs for chicken wings and roast beef, plays fetch, and challenges Bear to play tug of war with a shoelace. When he's tired, he grooms Bear and kneads him like a kitten does its mother in the deep of the night. Smudgie is always game for a windy-night adventure in the garage and an exploratory escape. Bear knows that and guards the door, herding him back inside if he sneaks out.

It is need that drives animals of different species to form strong bonds. You see the occasional news story featuring a dog nursing kittens, or even tiger cubs. Smudgie needed Bear, and Bear responded. I have always adopted strays—people and animals. It is difficult, foreign, challenging, sometimes a source of regret, but I need it. I am filled with love and reward whenever I observe my family—er, the zoo—loving and nurturing, and fighting with one another.

Speaking of fighting, Nina has long since forgiven me for that 2 A.M. announcement.

~Brian Taylor

# Bojangles' Teachings

*A dog is the only thing on earth that loves you more than he loves himself.*
*~Josh Billings*

When my stepdaughter, Amanda, was near ten years old, she and the school crossing guard discovered two abandoned puppies in hedges near the elementary school. The puppies were huddled together, scared and alone. The crossing guard was willing to rescue one of the puppies, and took both for a short period of time, giving Amanda the opportunity to plead with my husband and me to adopt the other. Once we saw the tiny little puppy fitting into the palms of our hands, and gazed into her big brown eyes, the decision was obvious. And so, Bojangles (BJ for short) became part of our family.

Two years later we were expecting a new baby... our daughter, Elizabeth. We had recently moved into a larger home to accommodate our growing family so BJ, like all of us, had some adjustments to make. What I wasn't sure of was whether the addition of a new family member would be too much adjustment for BJ to tolerate.

As Elizabeth's birth date drew near, I became anxious. I had read and heard of many instances where dogs displayed jealousy and aggression toward new babies. Simultaneously, I knew that Amanda would be devastated if we needed to find another home for BJ should she not adjust to the new addition.

Elizabeth was born on December 20th and we brought her home two days later. My husband Ted and I hesitantly walked in the door. Ted stooped down next to BJ and gently introduced Elizabeth. BJ did the courteous sniffing and then wandered away, seemingly disinterested.

I had Elizabeth by C-section and was dealing with some complications. In order to avoid multiple trips up and down the stairs, we kept a stroller next to the couch in the family room. During the day, Elizabeth and I could both rest, yet be near each other. The very first time that Elizabeth was placed in the stroller, BJ jumped on the end of the sofa, looked inside at Elizabeth resting, and laid her own head down on the edge of the stroller. And there she slept. At least, BJ slept until Elizabeth made any little sound. With that, BJ was alert and made sure that I, too, knew that my baby was stirring.

Being near Christmas, and with a brand new baby, there naturally was a parade of visitors. Family and friends would drop by to admire this miraculous new baby girl. BJ remained steadfast next to the stroller. Her beautiful brown eyes were glued on my daughter's equally beautiful blue eyes. There were visitors to whom BJ gave a nod of acceptance and those who were met at the stroller with a low growl. (While BJ probably thought she was menacing, she was merely a fifteen-pound ball of fur!)

I began to notice BJ's remarkable ability to "read" the visitors. She absolutely would not tolerate certain individuals coming near Elizabeth unless I, myself, picked Elizabeth up so that they could get a better look.

BJ was equally protective when Elizabeth was in her crib overnight or taking a nap. While we, like many parents, had installed a baby monitor, it was actually quite unnecessary. Each time Elizabeth was put up in her nursery, BJ was right there, under the crib. Since the floor was hardwood, we even placed a nice comfy bed under the crib for her. One tiny movement and BJ would quickly alert us that Elizabeth needed attention. I believe that is why Elizabeth was not much of a crier... she didn't need to be. BJ had her covered.

This protection and the adoration between BJ and Elizabeth continued as Elizabeth grew. BJ would rest in the shade of a tree next to the swing set as Elizabeth played. Many times I watched as Elizabeth ran around the backyard with BJ running right beside her. BJ even tolerated the dress-up stage, wearing Elizabeth's small purses hooked over her neck and bows stuck on the top of her furry head.

Watching BJ's protectiveness and clear love for Elizabeth, I wondered why I was even worried about any jealousy. This was pure instinct and I learned as I watched. BJ somehow showed me who to watch out for, what to watch out for, and how to meet Elizabeth's needs whenever necessary. BJ also showed me how important quality time with your kids is as I watched not only BJ and Elizabeth but BJ and Amanda grow so quickly.

Sadly, BJ began to slow in the races around the yard with the girls. She began sleeping or resting much more often, yet still while keeping one eye open on the family. BJ began needing help with stairs and rarely barked when she, herself, needed attention. I then watched both of my girls give the same loving care to BJ that BJ had given to them. I knew that I had learned some motherly instincts from BJ, and I also was learning how to grow older with pride and dignity.

In the end, as BJ slowly drifted off to eternal sleep at the ripe old age of seventeen (isn't that 120 years or so in "dog" years?), watching the gratitude in those beautiful brown eyes, I learned how to be truly grateful for my life and all those who share my life with me. BJ in her own way told me that her work was now done. Each time I pass the stepping stone in the backyard dedicated to our beloved BJ, I know that while she still watches, she trusts me to have learned her instincts, protective nature, and unconditional love.

~Lil Blosfield

# Another Door Opens

*Scratch a dog and you'll find a permanent job.*
*~Franklin P. Jones*

On a gray afternoon in September, he came limping up to me on a street near my house—completely trusting me, with his kind face, and sad brown eyes... no tags, no name, and a story he couldn't tell.

I was in my car at the time, and had stopped to reach my hand out the window and pat him on the head. He liked that, so I got out to get a better look at him, leaving the door wide open. The next thing I knew he was in the car. The big mook had known me for ten seconds and just jumped in, with no invitation, climbed over into the passenger seat, sat down and looked at me. Apparently he expected me to take him to his home, but since I didn't know where that was, I really didn't know what to do.

First we sat on the lawn in front of my house for awhile. Surely someone would come rushing up, so glad to find him and take him home.... No one came. Then we walked around the neighborhood. Then we drove around in the car, in wider and wider circles. "Anybody lose a dog? Do you recognize this pooch? Anybody? Anybody?" Nobody. Next I tried putting "Found" ads in the newspapers, on craigslist.com... no response. What about the shelters? No, they didn't know about him. I checked the "Lost" ads everywhere, put up color pictures of him all over the neighborhood, posted information at the nearby dog park, rec center, vet clinic. Nothing.

The dog would stay with me until someone claimed him. Days went by, and I kept looking into those sad eyes, learning more and more what an extraordinary creature he was. So gentle, so very patient, and so lonely. Can you imagine finding yourself living in a different house, different neighborhood, with a different person, never hearing your name spoken, your people nowhere to be found, and having no idea how any of it happened? I want so much to know his story, to know his name....

What is your name, gentle one? What is your name?

The middle of October came, and still I had questions. How did you get separated from your family? How did you get from there all the way to here? And why—why didn't anyone call to claim you, come over and get you, take you home? Imagine the depths of his confusion. Imagine him answering—"I don't know... I don't know."

It's painfully sad to see how far a dog will go to adapt, adjust, and accept. Maybe it's an example for us, though, how an animal moves on, lets go of his past, his habits, his will. He's out there on my back porch, wishing he were inside... he looks up at me through the window, turns away, and puts his chin on his paws. A surgery has come and gone, to remove some benign lumps—he put up with days of soreness, stitches, and difficulty eating, and when I pushed the awful lampshade (the plastic collar that keeps dogs from picking out the stitches) over his head every night, he hated it vigorously, yet in time he would actually stretch his neck forward a little, to help me put it on. When we're out walking, I go right, or left, or straight, and he goes with me, whether that's the way he wants to go or not.

Ironically this species of person we call The Dog, who so gracefully accepts one disappointment after another, still manages to hope, still looks out longingly at all horizons. Although the dog endures all things, he also believes in all things, hopes for all things. By now we're going on walks around the neighborhood in the afternoons. With a front-left leg problem, and something wrong with his back (was he hit by a car in his former life?), he still lives for his walks, because that's when he gets to meet everybody. Believing, as he does, that all people are friends he hasn't met yet, he looks longingly at every passing car, every front porch, every house—no stone unturned, in his endless search for his friend and soul mate, the human. He sees a mom and dad up ahead, pushing baby in the stroller. Away we go, me in tow. He greets them with wild affection, and they are immediately won over. He is everybody's buddy... ninety-two pounds of unconditional love—pretty hard to turn away from that. Pretty hard to... how could anybody just... well, I guess we'll never know.

Eventually it was time for him to have a name. I guess I liked how people often greet an animal they don't know by saying, "Hi, Buddy." So "Buddy" it is. Now this lost dog whose name nobody knew has a name everybody seems to know: "Hey, Buddy? How ya doin', Buddy?" the strangers say, trying to get out of their cars while he charges up and smothers them.

Weeks went by and I gave up finding his former home for him. I tried to find him a new one. It was getting harder and harder to think of giving him away, but my house and yard were not right for him, and with me being the only one here... I just couldn't. But his new family would have to be just right... they would really have to love him, and have the perfect house and yard for a dog. A difficult search began. We met with many people, made lots of phone calls, sent lots of e-mails. I sent his picture all over the place. No takers.

Then one late-October evening we walked over to a pet adoption event held by the nice folks at Planet Pethood a couple blocks from my house. They put a bright orange vest on him that said "Adopt Me," in big black letters. Dozens of people came by to see all the dogs, and Buddy had the time of his life. He wagged and nuzzled and looked everyone in the eye. Everybody loved him. Nobody took him.

Let us all learn from the unshaken faith, the quiet perseverance of the dog, for on this day Buddy would find a place he could call "Home." He had trusted me from the moment I opened that car door when we first met. Now, standing in a crowd of nice people who didn't want him, this sad, sweet animal, this long-suffering friend of humanity, pressed his soft muzzle into my hand and looked up. I couldn't take it any more. Good night, everyone. The adoption event was over for us.

I hooked the leash to Buddy's collar, and he shuffled down the sidewalk and around the corner, leading me gently. He knew the way, and the look on the face of this accepting, trusting animal told me he was happy—happy to be going home.

~Marty McGovern

# When Teenage Years Hit...
# Try Puppy Love

*Adolescence is perhaps nature's way of preparing parents*
*to welcome the empty nest.*
~Karen Savage and Patricia Adams

My daughter entered high school this fall, and she has started showing signs of independence. Hugs and kisses are few and far between. It's no longer "cool" to be seen in a movie theater with one's parents.

Even shopping in the mall turns ugly. "You can't wear that," she tells me. "It's so 1970s." "Don't greet me next time... just wait in the car." "You treat me like a baby." "Don't talk to my friends." "You don't listen." "I know how to iron; I just don't want to."

The dreaded curse is upon me. I am the mother of a teenage daughter. Suddenly, I'm a total embarrassment.

In order to feel appreciated and loved once again, I must find a substitute, possibly a pet.

My husband isn't particularly pet-friendly and I attribute this to the fact that as a child, he never had a dog. Years ago, when I brought home a parakeet for my daughter, he took one look at the bird and asked, "How long do they live?"

Three days of the cold shoulder routine. That's all it took to convince my husband that we needed a new addition to our family.

Not to show disrespect, I did give him three choices in the

decision-making process. They were: an affair, a divorce, or a pet. Being a wise man, he opted for a dog, and that's how Tanner, a cross between a Golden Retriever and Standard Poodle, came into our lives.

What I failed to realize is that raising a puppy is much like raising a child. They come with advantages and disadvantages.

I get barking instead of crying in the middle of the night. Fortunately, the food preparation technique and cleanup time is a lot easier with pets. Food goes from bag to bowl and is devoured in thirty seconds. There aren't any sterility concerns—no boiling of bottles and nipples, no fixing of formulas. Best of all, breast feeding isn't an option.

Not only does a puppy lick his plate clean, but also the floor. On the contrary, babies have to be hand-fed. They leave morsels of leftovers smeared everywhere; on the high chair, under the high chair, in their hair and in every orifice. And I never have to ask, "Did Tanner eat his squash today?"

Puppies and babies pee and poop quite frequently, like it or not. Babies need their diapers changed but potty training Tanner involves taking him out, day and night, in all sorts of inclement weather.

And there's nothing like a puppy to take my mind off world troubles. I have more pressing issues to contend with, such as: take the puppy out, feed the puppy, tire out the puppy, take the puppy out again. I remember reading books as a child that read, "See Spot run. Go Spot go." Now, when the puppy pees on the carpet, I yell, "Here's a spot, there's a spot, everywhere a spot spot."

The greatest advantage is that Tanner, unlike my daughter, is always happy to see me. I can kiss and pet him all day. He follows me from room to room. He seeks my affection and gives unconditional love.

Will this last forever? To my dismay, I heard that dogs go through a teenage phase themselves. Will he be ashamed to be seen on the other end of a leash with me? Can he get too sexy for his tail? Doggone-it, I guess I'll have to wait and see.

~Karen Adragna Walsh

"Where's the dog?"

Chicken Soup
for the Soul

# Unrealistic Expectations

*Just because somebody doesn't love you the way you want them to,*
*doesn't mean they don't love you with all they have.*
*~Author Unknown*

I love dogs! I have had either one or two or three at a time around me since I was a little girl. They have always been a part of my family. There have only been a few times when our house has been dog-less, and that happened to be the case when the call came that night.

The voice on the other end of the phone line was desperate. "Mom, I need you. Summer and Ernie got into a terrible fight. They can't stay together. Please, please let me bring Summer over to your house to stay for a few days until we figure out what to do."

Summer and Ernie are my granddogs; they belong to my son, Mike, and his wife, Crescent. Although Mike has always had dogs around, Summer was the first dog that he got on his own after he and Crescent got married. He absolutely loves that dog like he has loved no other one. She has a special place in his heart. And my husband and I love Mike and Crescent and would do anything for them. So of course I told him that he could bring Summer to us that night.

She arrived around midnight looking like she had been in a fight. Mike didn't look too good either. He had to literally throw himself in the middle of the fight to break it up because neither Summer nor Ernie would back down. We know it would have been a fight to the death. Even though Ernie is bigger than Summer, Summer is the more agile of the two so I'm not sure who would have won.

Summer is a Jindo. We had never heard of the breed until Summer came into our family. She is a medium-sized dog that originated in Korea. The breed has only been in the United States since the 1980s but is known to be very protective and have a high prey drive instinct. What that means is — don't have a Jindo around other animals or those other animals will wind up dead! That instinct has been bred into them and is almost impossible to change. Jindos do get along well with people and are not at all aggressive towards them. Summer is very smart and her sense of hearing is amazing.

Summer has settled into our home and since we were dog-less when she came, she fills a void for us and we are happy to have her around. Her needs are few and she is a very easy dog to care for. But it seems as if something is missing. Every other dog we ever had was loving and affectionate. Summer is very solitary. She is happy and excited to see us when we come home but that happiness only lasts for about thirty seconds. And then she's done. She wants to be where the people are — but not in the same room. When we are upstairs, she is upstairs, but in a different room. When we go downstairs she follows us. But does she lie at our feet and look at us with adoring eyes? No. She is usually in the next room... all by herself. Near, but not too close.

She isn't terribly fond of being groomed or loved either. When we want to hold her, she tolerates us, just barely, and then gets up, shakes and leaves at the earliest opportunity. Mike says she shakes because she is shaking off our cuddles! Why doesn't she act like every other dog we have ever had? She is very much like a cat. We think that maybe she is really a cat in a dog suit!

Summer is territorial and protective. If someone parks in front of the house she lets me know it. If someone is walking a dog, even if it's across the street from our house, Summer goes into protective mode and barks and barks. We will never, ever be attacked by birds or butterflies; Summer is constantly on guard to make sure that doesn't happen. I know when the mailman is three houses away because Summer starts her mailman bark to alert me. Guests coming into our home get barked at and inspected and then she leaves the room and has nothing more to do with them. Will she fetch the ball? No. Will she play tug of war? No. Will she shake paw? Well, maybe if she feels like it. Will she lie out in the sun, by herself over there, and not pay any attention to you even if you call her and offer her a treat? Yes. That's just the way she is.

Even after all of these years of having dogs as members of my family, Summer has taught me some very basic lessons. She has taught me that not all dogs are alike, just as no two people are alike. To expect every person to behave in the same way in all situations is just unrealistic. And the same goes for dogs. You will always be disappointed if that's what you expect. Some dogs are outgoing; some are introverts. Some are outwardly affectionate; some are standoffish. Just because Summer doesn't behave in the way that I had come to expect a dog to behave doesn't mean that there is something wrong with her. It doesn't mean that she doesn't love me.

That terrible fight happened two years ago. Having her stay here for a "few days" until we could figure out what to do with her has turned into a permanent arrangement. These days many grandparents have taken on the responsibility for the care for their grandchildren. That is what has happened to us. The only difference is that our grandchild is a dog... our granddogger. She has fit into our lives and has made our house her home. We love her and have learned to accept that her behavior is just the way she is. We know that, in her own way, she loves us and that she is doing the best she can with what she has. Summer has taught us that we had unrealistic expectations about how she, or any dog, should behave. Now that we understand that, we have accepted it. We are comfortable... and so is she.

~Barbara LoMonaco

# "Daddy's Girl"

*Properly trained, a man can be a dog's best friend.*
*~Corey Ford*

It was the day before New Year's Eve and my husband Ed said, "I still need a little more time to finish grad school before starting our family." I cried for hours, unable to fall asleep. I even called the Crisis Center and poured out my emotions for about three hours. (While he snored.) We had already been married four years, my "baby hope chest" of Golden Books was full, and there was a hole in my heart.

Books do not cry, wet, sleep, cuddle, or need you. So I decided to adopt "our first baby" at the pound. Ed would just have to understand.

I expected to pick a young pup, not more than two months old. I viewed cage after cage and petted yipping, yapping, jumping, snapping puppies of all kinds. Then my eyes locked with the sweetest and saddest brown eyes I had ever seen. Brown eyes just like "Daddy Ed's." A paw squeezed through the chain link. The fur and toe pads were baby soft. My hand was repeatedly kissed. I whispered, "Don't worry, Mama's here!"

The Humane Society attendant noticed my interest and said, "That's Princess!"

Princess was a little over six months old and was nearly full grown at thirty-something pounds. She looked as if she should be wearing dangly rhinestone earrings and a diamond studded collar.

She was glamorous, with long black fur that framed her face and was crowned with upright pointed ears. Princess resembled a giant Pomeranian, but was in fact a hybrid of Spitz and Chow. When she stood up, her back hind leg haunches revealed a petticoat of whitish gray hair that continued under her tail. One could not help but smile because she looked like she had just unknowingly sat down in wet white paint and walked away.

I proudly purchased her and agreed to pick her up the next Saturday morning. I broke the news cowardly over the phone to Ed's voicemail, "We are now the proud owners of a precious puppy!" Click.

He took me first thing Saturday to buy ALL the things the new dog would need and announced them one by one in his parental tone: bowl$, lea$h, something to $leep on, collar$, $tuff to eat, chew toy$, etc. He was a natural. He smugly enjoyed watching me $quirm as I $pent about $200 on dog care purcha$e$ with my own money, which did not even include the vet and groomer vi$it$ yet to take place. I suddenly felt nauseous and had morning $ickne$$.

With the trunk packed with the pup's nursery-to-go, we arrived for our long awaited special delivery. Ed was surprised when he saw what a "big puppy" she was. She trembled as he carried her in both his arms threshold style to the car. That was the first time Daddy and his girl bonded.

That first night and every one after, she slept on the top basement step because that was as close to us as she could get once we turned in. We also soon named her Ed's favorite name for a future daughter, "Sophie." (Which can also be written: $ophie.) Sophie was often the topic of our dinner conversations. Like proud parents, we talked about her latest milestones and naughty chewing habits. We marveled at how she would walk up the driveway like a bear on back legs growling at the mailbox or recycling cart. We talked about how she loved to be held. She was amazingly quiet, probably because of the Chow in her, but the vet assured us that she had the cordial mentality of a Spitz.

I groomed her myself weekly, with tub, shampoo, and toothbrush.

Once I was blow-drying her hair as we sat on the back deck while roofers were working next door. Can you believe the hammering stopped when the "brrrrwhrrrr!" of the blowdryer started? We must have been quite a sight. Every evening, I would pull in the garage after a long day's work, and I'd see Sophie stand up with pricked ears looking out the basement door window. Her dark silhouette looked like Batman and she would jump with excitement as I approached, humming the theme, "Daaa, daaa, daaa ,daa ,daaa, daaaa... Batman!" Late at night I rocked her and sang a favorite lullaby, "You are my sunshine!" She was loving and loyal.

Until one weekend morning. Something changed. Sophie bypassed me and ran to Ed first, licking his ankles constantly. Future mornings and evenings she greeted him most affectionately and vied for his attention. I might as well have been an empty food bowl. She was acknowledging me less enthusiastically. I had no idea why... but she suddenly preferred him. I admit I was privately jealous and puzzled. After all, I was the one who rescued her, fed her, walked her, brushed her, bathed her and changed her newspaper! I told myself that the loyalty switch was just a gender thing. Girl-dogs like boys. I put my frustrations aside and unconditionally doted upon her. I still loved her tremendously even if she seemed to love Ed more.

One Saturday during dinner I nonchalantly asked, "Have you noticed how much Sophie adores you?" Ed's eyes darted away. No comment. I continued, "I can tell that she likes you better. Have you noticed?" He deflected my remarks by shrugging them off and quickly changing the subject. Obviously, he knew I was hurting and wondering. How sweet... but he didn't offer any reason why or speculate. The only thing I was certain of was that she and I had good taste in men. I just had to accept that he was her favorite parent despite the fact that he did less for her.

The next afternoon I had forgotten my wallet before running an errand and entered the kitchen through the back door because it was faster than garage entry. At the time I didn't realize it was also quieter. And there they were... caught in the act! "Grrrr! Grrrrr!" Both Ed and Sophie were growling, positioned opposite each other; on all fours, rear ends high in the air, sharing a dish towel in their mouths. They were playing tug of war!!!

I stood there watching in disbelief. Amused, amazed, and betrayed.

Then Ed's alpha male primal animal instinct sensed my presence. He turned his head and caught a glimpse of me in his peripheral vision. His end of the rag dropped from his mouth as his face full-blushed red in seconds. I believe at this point I won the dominant stare-off. Sophie jumped on him repeatedly trying to get back in the game. But the game was over. It was clear to me now why Sophie was indeed Daddy's Girl. A "Daddy's Girl" who would forever have her father's eyes and mother's heart.

~Lisa Plowman Dolensky

# Almost Human

*On the Internet, nobody knows you're a dog.*
*~Peter Steiner*

"To the parents of PHOEBE CHESLER!" the headline blared. "We want YOUR daughter for our Young Miss Preteen Pageant!!" The slick glossy mailer went on to tell us how we could prepare Phoebe for a glamorous, successful life as a model/actress/pitchwoman simply by taking advantage of this fantastic opportunity! All we would have to do, we were informed, was send in a $150 entry fee (apparently the old adage "you've got to spend money to make money" can be applied to those not yet in puberty), procure a formal "party" dress for the pageant, and have some professional headshots taken. For a nominal fee, the company hosting the pageant would be delighted to provide this service for us.

You might think that visions of my child becoming the next Brooke Shields danced tantalizingly in my head. Was I tempted, even for a minute? You bet I was. The image of someone looking in disbelief at a picture of my Border Collie wearing a taffeta petticoat made me dissolve into laughter. You see... Phoebe was a dog. A beautiful dog, yes, but a dog nonetheless. And the thought of her in a party dress still makes me smile.

We adopted Phoebe when she was just three months old from an animal shelter in Auburn, California. I took one look at the black and white puppy yapping her head off, determined not to be overlooked amidst the chaos of the shelter, and fell completely in love. She was the first dog my husband and I had together, and was as smart as they come. In retrospect, perhaps she was a little too smart, but her Mensa-level intelligence was perfectly offset by the innate sweetness of some Springer Spaniel blood. We forgave her for doing things no dog should really know how to do, like opening the door that leads from the kitchen to the garage, then leaping up and hitting the garage door opener button that allowed her to escape, on her way to freedom.

My husband and I had a good laugh over this first letter, and briefly wondered how a dog got on a mailing list obviously intended for children. We figured it was a one-time deal, and had fun sharing it with a few friends. Then, we forgot about it—until the deluge began.

"HEY!" the next mailing trumpeted. "We're looking for Hollywood's NEXT CHILD STAR! We think that child could be PHOEBE CHESLER! You owe it to HER to sign up NOW for our series of acting/modeling workshops!" All this company needed to secure my child's wildly successful future was a check for $500. They assured me it was just too good to pass up.

"To the parents of PHOEBE CHESLER! If something happened to you, do you have adequate life insurance to provide for YOUR daughter?" Somehow, I think the insurance company sending the letter would look askance at our application. Imagine the look on the adjuster's face who reads this:

Child's Full Name: Phoebe Alexandra "Feeber-Deeber-Dog" Chesler
Age: 8
Height: 2 feet on all fours, approximately 4 feet when on her hind legs.
Weight: 50 lbs.
Nationality: Border Collie/Springer Spaniel.
Hair: Black and white
Allergies: Flea spray and corn meal

Over the next few years, we received many letters asking us to consider Phoebe for modeling schools, pageants (I wonder what they would have done had I sent in the application with "herding" listed under the "talent" section?) and acting workshops. I decided to start saving them when I noticed the nature of each solicitation coincided with Phoebe's age. We had fun opening the latest ones and seeing just where Phoebe was supposed to be in her "human" life at that moment.

As she grew older, the "Preteen" offers gradually gave way to "Teen" opportunities, Army recruitment and then, lo and behold, college solicitations. How fast they grow—our "baby" was about to start college! It was around this time that the credit card applications began arriving, thick and fast. According to whatever database she was in, she was now in college, and urgently needed to start building her credit history as quickly as possible.

Up until this point, the whole thing was a great source of amusement for my husband and me, but the credit card solicitations were upsetting. I hadn't realized just how much the big card companies preyed on college students. The "offers" were amazing, and not in a good way: huge annual fees, exorbitant interest rates, and credit limits that shouldn't be offered to most adults, let alone a student. I worked myself up into a fit over it one day until my husband gently reminded me that our "daughter" could not and would never be a casualty of America's overspending. She was in fact, at that moment, enjoying a rawhide chewie. Still, I felt for all the parents and students who must have been constantly barraged with these offers.

Over the years, I have never stopped wondering why it was Phoebe who mysteriously made the leap into the human system, while none of our other dogs ever did. I'd like to think it was some sort of cosmic destiny, as she was the smartest dog I've ever known, but I seriously doubt intelligence is the criteria for most mailing lists. One person suggested it was because we had given her a "human" name. Hmm. Our other two dogs were named Chloe and Madeleine, so, no, I don't think that was it. Yet another friend jokingly suggested that perhaps our veterinarian sold his client list to marketers. It got to the point where an accountant friend dryly remarked that if we could only issue Phoebe a social security number, we could claim her as a deduction. My husband brightened considerably at that idea, until I reminded him it was illegal.

Those of us who love dogs feel that at times that they are almost human, to the point of attributing human characteristics to much of their behavior. Still, we know they are dogs, and as such are usually exempt from the annoyance we call junk mail by virtue of their species.

Phoebe lived to the ripe old age of fifteen, and after she died, the offers slowly stopped arriving. How did they know? There was no hospital death certificate, no obituary. How did they know to remove her from The List? We may never know, but I'm wondering if maybe my veterinarian is chuckling even now, enjoying his secret prank. One of these days, I'll have to ask. For Phoebe's sake... and for mine.

~Laura F. Chesler

# Six Teachers

*I make the most out of all that comes my way.*
~Sara Teasdale

I'm convinced that dogs, like people, enter your life for a reason. Some drift in, hang around, and drift out, leaving you wondering if it was something you said. Others stay and stay and stay until you start wishing that they would drift out soon, please. Some bring substance, others pure fun. And sometimes, the catastrophes prove to be the biggest blessings. With the benefit of hindsight, I have learned to appreciate the itinerants and the lightweights as much as the keepers. They are all lessons learned.

As a child, I drove my parents to distraction with my incessant pleas for a dog, but dog hair was not welcome in my mother's Spanish Provincial living room. Marriage presented a new opportunity for dog ownership. One day, my husband arrived home with the princess of cute, our Beagle, Winnie. We were like new parents and Winnie bore the brunt of our inexperience. But she forgave us our blunders.

When Winnie contracted encephalitis and died after only three months, I climbed into the shower and sobbed my way through half the daily water supply of Montreal. A friend, not known for her sentimentality, rolled her eyes and said, "For heaven's sake! Two months you had it. Go get another one." I got another friend instead.

That day I learned that the depth of one's love has little to do with the length of the relationship. That a hot shower helps soothe a broken heart. And that you never forget your first love.

Twelve years later, as I rounded a corner on my bicycle, I was knocked over by a cuddly Doberman. Boyee literally crashed her way into my life. By then, I was a divorcee, disillusioned with my not-so-swinging singles lifestyle and the teaching profession. I abandoned both for a six-month stay on a kibbutz in Israel. I had resolved to find myself before becoming entangled in any more romantic relationships. But Boyee captured my heart, as did her owner, and four months later we were a family. I learned then that love is not bound by our schedules. That the right person is more important than the right time. And that romance could be just around the corner.

Attie, our Dalmatian, was the epitome of naughty exuberance. I forgave my daughter Naomi's ripped bunny pajamas. I remained calm over the gnawed teak coffee table. I even swallowed my expletives when Attie destroyed my daughter Shelley's new running shoes. But seeing my lace designer blouse hanging in tatters on the clothesline resulted in a meltdown. I was not in a forgiving mood and Attie tried to avoid my vile temper for the rest of the day.

That evening, passing by Shelley's room, I overheard crying. Peeking in, I saw Attie gently licking Shelley's hand while my little one poured her heart out. In that moment, all was forgiven. I was reminded that "things" are cheap, no matter how expensive. That the love and loyalty of those who care about us is priceless. That a sympathetic silence is more meaningful than words. And that nothing is more powerful than a well-timed kiss.

Several years later, against my husband's better judgment and protests, we adopted Mitch, a deaf Dalmatian. He was impossible to control and destroyed our entire lawn with his obsessive hours-long digging. Despite our sincerest efforts, we never succeeded in calming him down. When the vet advised us for the eighth time to put Mitch out of his misery, we finally admitted defeat. I learned the heartbreaking way that no matter how heroic and altruistic and loving my intentions, I can't save everyone. That there is a fine line between "try, try again" and "enough is enough." And some relationships are just not meant to be.

Wolfy was on a reconnaissance mission when I first spotted

him casing out the neighborhood. How anyone could abandon this beautiful, intelligent Husky was beyond my comprehension. On the fourth day, displaying infallible instincts, he followed me home.

His fierce independence and refusal to pander to humans often elicit comments about his lack of affection. I believe that he has resolved to err on the side of caution. I'm sad for him, sad that I can't reassure him that this family would never dream of leaving him by the side of the road. But he won't risk having his heart broken again.

Yet sometimes, in the midst of a spirited romp, he forgets to be aloof and bestows a loving lick on my hand. It startles both of us and causes him to withdraw in embarrassment.

Living with Wolfy's fear and hurt, I have learned that history does not always determine or predict the future. That my love must be unconditional and given without expectations. And that those who do not plunge in with trust, deny themselves the love they seek.

And then there's Puppy, he of the cheery disposition and the optimistic tail, who loves and hugs with his entire body and soul. He has been my best teacher. Abandoned in a supermarket parking lot, he ignored the drizzling rain as he hopefully approached everyone leaving the store. His velvet brown eyes and the wrinkles of concern on his forehead melted my heart. Blocking out the reality of the very male Wolfy waiting at home, I opened my car and invited him in. For several minutes he danced a canine cha-cha-cha, with each approach-and-withdraw iteration bringing him closer. Finally, he dove into the car and settled down for a nap before I had a chance to change my mind.

Puppy's motto is "Bark with Gusto, but Compromise." It's effective. He has yet to meet a dog or human that he hasn't won over.

Watching Puppy navigate so successfully through life, I have learned that an untamed ego can ruin the most promising friendship. That it pays to keep my tongue soft and sweet. And that I must always let my tail wag with joy and abandon.

~Ryma Shohami

# His Name Is Samson

*We could have bought a small yacht with what we spent on our dog
and all the things he destroyed. Then again, how many yachts
wait by the door all day for your return?*
~John Grogan

fuzzy little Golden Retriever arrived in our driveway one cold mid-December morning as I was taking the trash to the curb. He weaved in and around my ankles as I tried to shoo him away, and then he moved back a few feet, sat down and wagged his curly tail so hard it almost toppled him over. Soft brown eyes watched me, contemplating whether I was friend or foe, and then he inched his way toward me and sat on my stocking feet, looking up wistfully with what appeared to be his best smile. When I moved, he moved, as he began to follow me back up the drive.

I kept thinking he must have wandered off from his owners. Surely, they would be out searching for him. Scanning the surrounding streets and yards and seeing no one, I placed him in our backyard for safety. Someone would probably be coming to claim him during the day, but my fear of him bounding into the street was put at ease with him secured behind a fence. A cardboard box with an old rug made a perfect bed. And a bowl of fresh water would have to satisfy him until I could decide what to do with him.

Before leaving for work, I called my husband to let him know what I had done, just in case he came home for lunch before me and discovered a "surprise." We had been talking about getting a dog for weeks, but couldn't decide on a breed. The night before, I had shared how much fun owning a Retriever would be and what a wonderful and kind pet it would make.

"Hi, it's me. You will never believe what happened. Remember how we had talked about getting a dog and I said how much I loved Retrievers?"

"Yes, I remember," he said, with hesitation in his voice.

"Well," I began, "the cutest little golden Retriever puppy I've ever seen showed up on our front porch today! I'm sure he's lost and his owners are out looking for him right now, but if they don't come, can we keep him?"

Teasingly, he said, "You went and bought a puppy, didn't you?"

After much reassurance that the puppy really did magically appear from nowhere and that I would give him to his rightful owners as soon as they came for him, we hung up and I went on to work. I kept telling myself all the time not get too attached to this puppy and to not give him a name because he wasn't mine.

This precious little puppy had survived at least one night in the frigid December air before he found me. He was small, but he appeared to be very strong. Driving by our church it suddenly hit me. "His name is Samson!"

No one ever claimed Samson, and so Samson became our dog. It was surprising to learn just how much a free dog could cost. From vet bills to dog collars to leashes to toys, and many bags of food, this cute little eight-pound puppy had many needs. And he ate and ate and ate. It didn't take long for him to graduate from a small bag of puppy food to the extra large economy-size bag. Every time we thought that he was just too much to handle, he would sit, looking up with his soft brown eyes, and give us his best grin and melt our hearts.

One fact most Retriever owners don't share is that their loveable pets seem to live to dig. Samson dug foxholes all over the yard wherever he found a soft spot that would yield to his strong paws. Tunneling long wide holes with dirt flying everywhere, I guess that somehow he just couldn't figure out how to dig down. Our yard was a disaster.

He chewed up everything... from the wooden patio furniture, a freezer cord, outside computer lines and any and all greenery that stuck up from the grass. But, after the most mischievous behavior, he would lean into us, loving us, knowing that when all was said and done, we would reach down and stroke his fuzzy ears and forgive him.

Samson has lived up to his name. He is strong in so many ways, but easily distracted. After chasing a squirrel up a tree, he ran across an open pool of water before he realized it wasn't solid. We have learned to make him sit before opening the door when he wants to go outside, after he nearly knocked us over like bowling pins many times, rushing his huge body past us to go for a walk. He still thinks he is a lap dog, climbing on top of us whenever we sit down in the recliner. He's always at our feet anticipating every move we make and causing us to trip over his bulky torso. He's ready to play, and eagerly awaits our praise and a treat for every new thing he has learned from us.

But in reality he is the one who has taught us important lessons that we find ourselves using in our everyday lives. He does not judge us and only asks that we give him love and loyalty. We love and laugh at his antics, even when we are experiencing hardships in our own lives. He has taught us patience and gentleness. When he is outside and wants to come in, he will sit outside the window peering in. Have we forgotten him? I think he would wait for us forever. He wants to be close to us and he has given us companionship when we have needed it the most. We delight in watching him squeeze his sixty-five pounds underneath his favorite hiding spot, our living room coffee table. When we move, he moves. If we leave a room, he is right beside us, wagging his huge tail and sharing more love than we could have possibly imagined.

How lucky we are that Samson found us on that cold winter morning. Our lives are so much richer for it.

~Terri Lacher

# A Grand Old Man

*We cannot direct the wind but we can adjust the sails.*
*~Author Unknown*

My friend, I remember our earlier walks
while you, in your youth, strained so at the leash.
I used to marvel at how a creature could walk so powerfully
while simultaneously being choked to death by its collar.
Today we walk together in the silence of great companions;
my pace slower now to match your own,
the leash of long ago abandoned.

Your playful antics as a pup made me laugh.
Your exuberant diligence as a watchdog in your middle years
comforted me because I knew you would hear
and alert me to every sound.
I slept peacefully for many years.

The realization that you have aged more quickly than I puzzles me
as I'm still middle-aged yet you've entered your golden years
without fanfare or much notice.
You are a grand old man,
and you are my best friend.

Now, old boy, it's your turn to lie in the sun and relax.
Let me take watchful care of you and tend to your needs.

Fear not that you have lost your usefulness
for when your gaze lights on me, still in trust
and undeserved adoration, I find unconditional love
and I am reminded to be a better person.

~Jeri Chrysong

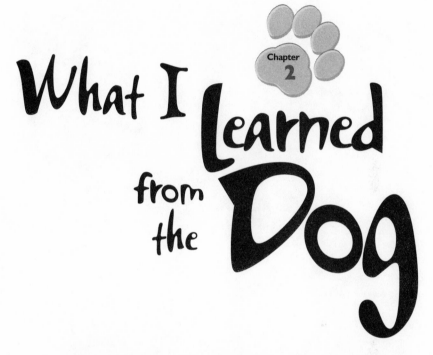

What I **Learned** from the **Dog**

Chapter 2

## Learning to Have Courage

*Courage doesn't always roar.*
*Sometimes courage is the little voice at the end of the day that says*
*I'll try again tomorrow.*

*~Mary Anne Radmacher*

# Integrating My Inner Dog

*There is deep wisdom within our very beings,*
*if we can only come to our senses and feel it.*
~Elizabeth A. Behnke

The death of my beloved dog left me grieving to the core. Surprisingly, from the depth of my pain came tremendous healing. My Golden Retriever left treasured gifts—ones that both made me feel better and made me a better person.

Looking back, Joey had been teaching me for years, talking silently to me through soulful brown eyes, demonstrating lessons of devotion and exuberance.

It was NOT love at first sight. Joey had been my grandmother's dog—Joe Dandy, she'd named him. When visiting my grandmother's country home, Joey was... obnoxious. In an impressive campaign for attention, Joey would stand outside, looking through the sliding glass doors into the living room, and bark non-stop for hours. He was long on enthusiasm and short on discipline. Years later I'd observe that little Golden Retriever puppies are better off with ten-year-old boys to play with than eighty-five-year-old women with Napoleonic control tendencies.

After my grandmother's move to an assisted living facility, I moved into her house on the rolling hills of the cattle farm where she'd lived twenty years beyond my grandfather. My family engaged in some unholy behind-my-back laughing at the thought of me putting up with Joey. I had my own doubts. Pets had not been part of my nomadic years of apartment living.

After some time, people said I'd done wonders with Joey. I think he did wonders with me.

At first I just let him be with me. He'd run to meet my car each night, the picture of animal health and happiness as he raced across the yard. He was amazingly attuned to my moods. One time, when I was in deep emotional pain (but I'm sure making no noise) from across the house I heard a scrambling of paws on hardwood floors. He was rushing to comfort me. The anguish of that day is long forgotten, however I will always remember the sound of his full-out—and successful—race to comfort.

Joey was an extraverted dog. He loved people and did anything he could to be included. One day when I was quietly rowing my grandfather's old boat in the middle of a large pond, I looked over to see Joey's nose lead a gentle wake as he dog-paddled out to join me.

As he got older, I savored my time with him. He adored being adored, and I adored him. Even though he was "all dog," he looked like a proud lion receiving his due adulation. I whispered in his ear that he could be the longest-lived-golden ever, but that wasn't to be.

One night after watching him closely, I knew the end was coming. That summer night he could not make it in the house, so I slept outside with him. It was a restless night, but I was with him. I cried and petted him and told him how much I loved him. Sometime near dawn he stuck his head on the lounge chair and looked intently at me one last time. I felt an amazing amount of love coming out of the still strong life-force in those familiar eyes. In a perfect world he'd get his young body back and be my life-long dog. I fell asleep for a while. When I awakened, he was gone.

I believe in grieving. I also know I have to function in daily life. Even with good friends, good memories and various healing methods, three weeks after Joey passed I was still not functioning. I had to find a way to move forward. The lesson that happened to help me the most was what I called "integrating my inner dog."

At first I said that as a joke. I had often heard of one's inner child, but never about inner dogs. However, to find inside myself what I had lost when I lost Joey proved to be healing. I began by listing the qualities I missed most.

The most important lesson was "Love myself like my dog loved me." My life had been lived with a regrettable amount of self-criticism. Over the years I'd accrued some self-acceptance, identified a few qualities I actually liked, and genuinely tried not to be so hard on myself. But to love myself the way my dog loved me? No way! Wag my tail in enthusiastic joy whenever I'm around myself? Uh, No! Silly though it may have seemed, the image of being so happy with myself as to joyously wag my tail (although certainly never in public) brought a short laugh and I was on my path to feeling better.

Life can be complicated, but Joey taught me to "be simple." He never "stressed out" about all the thoughts and worries that would (excuse the expression) hound me. When I came home, his simplicity brought me "home," back to myself, out of seriousness. In his own way, he made sure I heard, "Don't give the option of getting depressed—my cold, wet nose is here to remind you 'it's okay'." Just like an inner child might remind me to play or find comfort, my inner dog could remind me to find satisfaction in simple pleasures.

The memory of Joey's non-stop barking served to remind me to "Go for what I want—with gusto—and without giving up." He did not hold my bad moods of yester-minute against me, demonstrating, "Live in the moment," "Forget the bad, remember the good," and most important, "Forgive mistakes—every one of them, every time."

General dog wisdom taught: "Mark and protect your boundaries," and "Keep your wild side alive," and "Keep a keen eye on your world."

It amazed me how powerful it was to receive Joey's gifts. In a sense, when he was alive he would "do it for me." When he was young, he was a good watchdog. With him gone, I needed to be alert and watchful.

These gifts continue. I wish I could say I'd mastered all his lessons, but not so. Just making a list was a tremendous help. His gifts grow in me. As I hold within me the gifts my furry friend modeled for me, and they have become healing balm. Receiving his lessons honored his life and gave strength to go on. Joey taught me that whether we live twelve or one hundred years, it's good to sniff out what the day has to offer, to savor the good, and to hold dear the gifts he gave with his life.

~Elizabeth Cutting

# Routine

*Our perfect companions never have fewer than four feet.*
*~Colette*

our o'clock is the darkest part of the night and if I opened my eyes, my mind raced and I felt lost in my loneliness. Consumed by the emptiness of the hour, my mind spiraled out of control wondering, worrying, wishing, mentally trying to persuade the sun to peek over the horizon. I struggled to go back to sleep.

In the midst of this misery, I found myself sitting in Tompkins Square Park in the heart of the East Village of New York City watching dogs jump, run, and play. I saw people commingling and realized that we are constantly transitioning throughout life—a new job, a lost job, marriage, divorce, family obligation, birth, and death. At that moment, I woke up and I realized many of my friends had moved on but I had not.

I decided to get a dog to help me get into a better routine—to be active and get back to the business of living. Given the chance, I might sleep late; I would get a dog because I thought it would help get me up and out the door earlier. I guess I expected this dog to have a coffee fix just like me; I confused a dog with a rooster. Actually, the reality is that I was just lonely and so I decided to get my dog, Magnolia.

Then came the morning that changed everything and yet it changed very little. This particular morning I got up first as usual and took my shower while Maggie curled up in the warmest part of the bed. After my shower, I realized I was supposed to attend an event that evening requiring a tie. I ran down to the cleaners to pick up shirts and it was around 8:46 A.M. when our morning routine changed.

I was standing in the cleaner's on the ground floor of the building, dealing with Maggie's unabashed energy, which was difficult. I was supposed to be at work. Hearing an airplane, I walked out onto First Avenue and 3rd Street and witnessed for myself a nightmare in broad daylight. I kept walking from First Avenue west and closer to Second Avenue.

As I reached the last building of the block, the second plane hit one of the towers. I saw the plume of smoke and flames and glinting confetti of debris. I ran back to my apartment and called home. It was the last phone call I was able to make before the towers fell.

Then it was just my dog and me. After talking to my father, I followed our morning routine and took Maggie to the Tompkins Square dog run where I ran into several dog park regulars. We agreed to meet every two hours to keep in touch. So, throughout the day in two-hour intervals, we walked to the park and checked in, because after the towers fell we had no other means of communication.

It was at the dog run I learned the bridges and tunnels were closed. My dog park acquaintances told me to go to the store and purchase necessities. Being from south Alabama, I went into hurricane mode and bought the things I needed. Having had Maggie for such a short time, it did not occur to me in my panicked state to purchase anything other than a supply of food for myself. She was a puppy and her energy added to the overwhelming, frenetic confusion of the day.

The afternoon dragged on and in the middle of me being overwhelmed, Maggie was full of energy. Because I did not stock up on her foods, just mine, I ran out of dog treats. She was hyper, wanting to go out, and it did not help that I was feeding her the only thing I could find, a stash of Chinese fortune cookies. The two of us sat in silence in the hours before we returned to the dog park; we just sat and ate fortune cookies.

Thank goodness we were together; I might have gone out of my mind if it wasn't for that dog. That nine-month-old puppy was relentless in demanding my attention. I was dealing with so many different feelings, fear being the primary one, but she hijacked my heart. She got into my head and she kept me focused on the routine. Functioning is what one has to do in times like this. I cannot say she made me smile that day, but her nonsensical antics commanded my attention.

Our inner voice is often the voice of an inner child when we speak from our hearts, much different than speaking from the rational part of our heads. Maggie taught me how to separate the two. She helped me stay focused and functioning on that devastating day.

Four o'clock is the darkest part of the night and if I open my eyes I see Magnolia sleeping peacefully. In the darkness her silhouette is small. I caress the steadfastness of her warm chest and I am conditioned by the power of routine; she has taught me to concentrate on the rhythm of my heart and to remove the wishing, the wondering, and the worrying from my head.

~Sean Sellers

# 15

*Chicken Soup for the Soul*

# That Day on the Beach

*Courage is being afraid but going on anyhow.*
*~Dan Rather*

My husband Ben and I hadn't been in Portland, Oregon long when our friend Dan paid us a visit on a cool but sunny May weekend. The three of us decided to go to the coast for the day with our Golden Retriever mix, Gus. He was five at the time, weighed one hundred pounds, and had a dark, rusty color. We thought it would be the perfect time to introduce Gus to the ocean and to the beautiful Oregon coast.

Gus loves to go in the water—at least rivers and lakes—but he has always been a little timid when it comes to swimming. I can see the anxiety in his face much of the time, by the way his skin wrinkles heavily above his eyes and the way he holds his ears back. He often makes a quiet but high-pitched yelping noise as he swims. Every time his jaw moves to yelp, he swallows too much water, causing him to sputter and cough each time he reaches the shore.

I was always the overprotective mom and probably babied Gus too much, ever since he almost drowned when he was five months old. He had been fetching a stick from the lake over and over again. Maybe Gus was tired, or maybe it was his youth and clumsiness. I am not sure of the reason, but he slipped below the water. I jumped in and pulled him out. I could not tell if he understood what had happened. I resisted the urge to act upset about the near drowning. We were going through puppy kindergarten at the time. Our trainer stressed the importance of not reacting emotionally to a dog as it can lead to lifelong behavioral problems. Humans, apparently, are the only animals on earth that will follow an emotionally unstable leader. I always tried to follow the instructor's advice by remaining calm and nonchalant.

So yes, maybe I am overprotective and maybe Gus has always picked up on my internal apprehension when he goes swimming. Though he looks anxious at times when swimming, Gus appears to enjoy it just the same. He has short, shiny, water-repelling fur and webbed feet. I know Gus is genetically predisposed to swim, despite his early fiasco with water, and so he does—always beneath my watchful eye.

Though I did not like what happened that day, I feel that this intense episode created a bond between us. I do not believe Gus carries with him the memory of that day but rather the extreme love and affection I have for him. He follows me around constantly, watching me obsessively and involving himself in everything I do. We are such a big part of each other's lives that the thought of separation, for any reason, makes me incredibly sad.

On this beautiful day, Gus was running and jumping excitedly on the beach but it was obvious to me that he was too afraid of the water to go swimming. He approached the edge of the water many times and appeared to enjoy getting his big paws wet. However, Gus did not go any farther than that. The waves were rolling in and crashing on the shore. Gus had never seen such a mass of frothy water. We played on the beach with his ball and with whatever sticks we could find. It was a wonderful, fun day, uneventful until the end.

Dan and Ben wanted to go swimming. I felt they were a little crazy and chose to stay on the sand with Gus. They ran in together, laughing. Ben came out very fast. "The water," he said, "was very cold."

Dan swam a way out hooting and hollering because of the cold, but loving the refreshing effect. Until this time, Gus was busy chewing a stick, lying, as usual, at my feet. All of a sudden, he jumped up and ran to the edge of the water. I called after him to come back.

What was he doing? He was frantic. Dan continued to yell loudly at the cold water. I could not make out his words, if there were any; the waves were loud and the wind was blowing. A wave came in and crashed at Gus's feet. He turned back to me and started to run. He stopped. He turned back toward the water once again and ran in.

Gus swam all the way out to Dan to rescue him. He thought Dan was drowning! I was stunned. So was my husband. Occasionally, I hear on the news or read in the paper the story of a local dog that saves a drowning person. However, I never thought of Gus as "that dog." I realize Dan wasn't actually drowning. But Gus didn't know that. Gus has never had much need to be brave before—he lives a very sheltered life of being fed, loved, walked, and played with.

It all happened so quickly. Gus reached Dan and they both swam to shore and ran along the beach to where my husband and I were standing. They had a similar appearance: drenched, excited, eyes sparkling in the bright, coastal sunshine. Gus was running around, pausing only to shake the cold water from his fur. Dan was yelling, "Did you see that? Did you see him come out to save me?" Oh yes, we saw.

Gus scares easily, and when he is afraid he runs behind me, forces his snout between my knees and peers out at the world with just a few inches of his face, protected, apparently, from his strange, canine fears. Not this time though. This time was different.

Gus ignored his obvious concerns about the ocean and swam out a hundred feet, over several waves to rescue my friend. He also ignored my concerns and my yells for him to return to us. He did not behave like his typical "mama's boy" self and did what instinct, or love, or something beyond human comprehension drove him to do.

After the excitement died down, we all got in the car to head home. I sat in the backseat with Gus's head in my lap, silent. I stroked his big, soft head and looked at him intently. Was the memory of his heroic afternoon already gone? What guided him to behave so bravely today, yet be so deathly afraid of the vacuum cleaner? I felt some guilt at having judged him a sweet but spoiled, freeloading dog.

He was no longer a freeloader. He had earned his keep in many ways that day on the beach.

My dog has the heart of a hero. I now know that love, loyalty, and instinct can drive a seemingly simple being to do great things, that fears can be overcome in an instant, and that there are those that expect nothing in return.

~Sarah Retzer

Reprinted by permission of
Bruce Robinson ©2009

# 16

# The Night Lily Saved the Day

*Courage is not the absence of fear,*
*but rather the judgement that something else is more important than fear.*
*~Ambrose Redmoon*

Lily, the Australian Shepherd, came bounding into our family at five months of age. She was twenty-five wiggling pounds of pure puppy love. Lily's coat color was called blue merle, but to me she looked like sparkling silver that had been splattered with black inkblots. Bred to be a show dog, Lily was rejected from that career because of her crooked teeth. The show world's loss was our gain, as she was a perfect fit for our family of four.

The first couple of months with Lily were filled with training, housebreaking, and bonding. Lily was a quick study and soon learned to accept her new surroundings and rules. We fell more deeply in love with our puppy each day. Lily and the children bonded quickly and spent their days keeping one another busy.

Part of our daily routine included story time before bed each night. The kids and I would gather on the couch in our PJs with storybook in hand to spend some time in the land of make-believe adventure. Lily always lay at our feet to be near "her" children and listen to the sound of our voices. She seemed to enjoy the nightly ritual as much as we did.

One evening as the children, Lily, and I were deeply involved in our story, we heard loud noises coming from the house next door. We didn't pay a lot of attention to the noise at first. As I continued reading our story, the commotion got louder and sounded as if it might be getting closer to our house. I started to ask my husband to check it out, but remembered he was in the shower.

I began moving the books and children from my lap so I could get up to look outside when Lily suddenly jumped up and ran towards the front door. With the hair raised along her spine like porcupine quills, Lily stuck her head under the sheer curtain covering the window panes of the door. She rose up on her hind legs and uttered a low thunderous growl and began barking for all she was worth. I knew something had to be terribly wrong, as our sweet-tempered Lily had never growled at anyone and rarely ever barked. Trusting her judgment, I hurriedly picked up a child under each arm and ran to get my husband. I began hearing yelling and crashing noises on our front porch and heavy footsteps at the door. Glancing back over my shoulder as I left the room, I saw the face of a wild-looking man appear in the window of the door where Lily had the curtain pushed aside. Lily stood her ground barking ferociously.

I ran to get my husband, James, who had been taking a leisurely shower, oblivious to the commotion at the front of the house. As my heart raced like a runaway freight train, I quickly told James of the situation. When he got to our front door the face in the window had gone, but Lily was still standing guard. James started to go outside to check things out, and I asked him to take the dog with him. I was sure that Lily would find the wild-looking man if he were still out there. James stopped long enough to hook Lily to her Flexi-leash and they were off. I watched them until they disappeared into the darkness of the night. I then called the police who informed me they already had an officer on the way.

The minutes crept by as I sat waiting for James and Lily to return. I paced through the house from window to window, until I saw the red and blue strobe lights of police cars reflecting throughout the neighborhood. Realizing I still had a child under each arm, I sat them down at my feet and parted the blinds at our bedroom window. I noticed the flashing lights seemed to be coming from behind our house.

A little while later James and Lily returned. James told me the whole disturbance had started when a man high on drugs had tried to get in to our next-door neighbor's house. That had been the original noise I heard. That neighbor and his family, along with a deadbolt lock, had held the door closed and in place against the drug-induced, super-human strength of the wild man as he tried to yank the door open.

Failing to get into our neighbor's house, the man moved on to ours. He might have made it into our house had Lily not shown her protective instincts to him through the window in our front door. He apparently wasn't on enough drugs to want to face our much-loved loyal Aussie while she was protecting her family.

Running like a pack of wolves were after him, and yelling like a banshee, the man ended up at the house behind us. He literally yanked the locked front door from its hinges and ran screaming inside, where he found a frightened young single mother with her toddler child.

It was at that time that James and Lily burst out of our house. Without any instruction from her master, Lily knew exactly what to do. She led James straight from our front door, around both houses, and inside the missing front door of our back door neighbor's house. Finding the man inside in a crazed stupor, Lily held him in place until the police arrived, allowing our neighbor and her toddler to escape unharmed.

As if she hadn't already, Lily cemented her place forever in our family with her bravery and loyalty, and earned our undying grati-tude. We don't know what might have happened to our neighbors or to us that night had Lily not been a part of our family. The wild man could very easily have burst in our door while the children and I sat reading had Lily's instincts not caused her to protect her new fam-ily. The quick arrival at our neighbor's house by James and Lily also allowed a mother and her young child to escape possible harm from a drug-crazed and very disoriented man.

Lily grew up with our children and remained a much-loved part of our family for nine years.

~Karen Starling

# 17

# Sage

*Wherever you go, no matter what the weather,*
*always bring your own sunshine.*
~Anthony J. D'Angelo

The words, "I'm afraid I have bad news for you—your dog is going blind," coursed through me like a lightning bolt. My husband Greg and I had recently adopted Sage, a one-and-a-half-year-old Springer Spaniel, from an animal shelter, and no one said anything about blindness. But we had noticed her stumbling on the porch steps and staring at the ceiling so we took her to the vet. In addition to the traditional vaccinations, Dr. Johnson gave her a checkup and discovered progressive retinal atrophy (PRA), a genetic disease of the eye. Many dog breeds are prone to PRA, and those diagnosed are usually between the ages of three and five. Sage was much younger when she was diagnosed, and by age three, she was completely blind.

How does an owner cope? And how does a dog adjust to living with blindness? I was about to find out as Sage and I embarked upon a journey that would take us through her gradual loss of sight, several surgeries, new training, and discoveries about faith, love, and courage—lessons I never imagined I'd learn from a blind dog.

Sage did not know the terms "timid" or "disabled." She chased squirrels and treed them in the backyard. She could not fetch a ball, but she played tug of war and also swam in a nearby creek. She walked proudly and happily on a leash, through the neighborhood or on a forest path.

As her eyesight dwindled, her other senses became increasingly acute. She could smell or hear a squirrel from inside the house as it ran across a telephone wire. She cocked her head to listen to birds singing from the trees. When strolling around the neighborhood or in the woods, not one scent, whether squirrel or rabbit or person or other dog, got past that Spaniel nose. And her tail always wagged. Sage accepted her disability with grace and perseverance, and I found myself in awe of her courage and faith—courage to adjust and learn new things, and faith in herself and her caretakers.

With the help of a friend who had trained dogs in the past, we taught Sage the words "stop," "step up," "step down," and "enough." Eager to please and learn, Sage quickly caught on to the terms. "Step up" and "step down" helped her navigate stairs not only in our house but also in hotels when we traveled. Those words also came in handy when traversing the neighborhood on daily walks. "Stop" also helped her wait for traffic in order to safely cross the street. "Enough" was used to keep her from pulling on the leash and to shush her when she barked too much at squirrels in the backyard.

Also, as her vision decreased, her courage seemed to increase, and I often marveled at her fortitude. Sage's bravery would be tested, and my faith assessed, not long after the second eye surgery.

Sage, my husband, and I went camping one night on mountain property Greg and I had just purchased. The morning after arriving, I unzipped the tent and let Sage out to do her business, then, unthinking, turned around and fell back to sleep. About twenty minutes later Greg woke up, left the tent briefly, then stuck his head back in and asked, "Where's Sage?"

"Oh, I let her go out a bit ago—she's out there."

"No, Gayle, she's not," came his tense reply.

We spent the next two days looking for her. Friends helped us: walking, driving, posting flyers, visiting campgrounds and cabins. My throat became raw from calling Sage's name, talking to people, and crying. Greg's forehead furrowed like a newly planted field, worry aging his face past its forty-seven years. Neither of us spoke of our fears: Sage falling down a hillside, hit by a car, mauled by a bear or mountain lion. The third night after her disappearance a call came—someone had seen Sage nearly two miles from our property.

Early the next morning Greg and I drove to the area where Sage had been seen. We had been looking for nearly thirty minutes when I stopped at a cabin where a woman was sweeping off her porch. As I talked with the lady, my back to the road, the woman asked, "Is that the dog you're talking about?"

I turned around to see our beloved Sage running along the road. I called and called, but she did not turn; I believe her fear was too great to recognize my voice. I ran quickly to find Greg, and we briskly, yet quietly, walked the dirt road, in hopes of sneaking up on her. A light rain had fallen the night before, and we discovered her tracks, following the circular road of this forested cabin area. Twenty minutes later we found her, off the roadway, sitting in a ditch and panting heavily. Quietly, we approached, and my husband reached down and grabbed her. Her eyes reflected terror, the horror of blindly running through woods and sagebrush and the fear of uncertainty. We were thrilled to know she was back with us, but we also knew we needed to be calm, so we gently said her name over and over. Recognition soon came to her eyes, and she barked with joy! Greg and I lay our heads across her neck and cried with thanksgiving.

Sage rebounded well from her ordeal. Her continual devotion to the people who caused her such anxiety, her courage to survive alone in the forest, and her faith in living life with vigor and valor humble me to this day. Sage is now more than nine years old and is a great ambassador for disability awareness. She and I frequently visit elementary classrooms, showcasing that disability does not mean "no ability" in either people or pets. When children meet her and hear her story, they respond with admiration. Sage enjoys the attention and leans into their small hands and bodies as they pet and hug her. Through this dog, children learn about respect for others and for themselves, and about courage and facing obstacles. Sage and I share that it's okay to be different because everyone is different and everyone has value. Children understand that if Sage can be brave although she is blind, they, too, can persevere when the difficulties come their way.

When I first wondered how I'd cope living with a blind dog, little did I know the great lessons she would teach me or that together, we would teach others. I am grateful to travel this life journey with such an inspiring dog!

~Gayle M. Irwin

# Puppy Love

*God could not be everywhere, so he created mothers.*
*~Jewish Proverb*

One rainy night, I dreamed a Beagle named Sunny came into our lives. The next day, by strange happenstance, a friendly little tri-color wandered onto our farm, half-starved, with that draggy-saggy look of having recently had a litter of pups.

She looked at me with big, brown eyes.

My husband, Stephen, knelt to pet her. "We should try to find her owner."

Knowing this was the "Sunny" from my dream, I said, "But she doesn't have any identification."

Still, we ran an ad in the paper to try to find her owner. Over the next several days, I dreaded each time the phone rang.

A week later, a storm rumbled far away. We turned out the lights for the night, and rain began to patter on the roof. Within an hour, thunder rattled our front door like an impatient intruder, and lightning flashed through the windows.

As though possessed by a poltergeist, Sunny whined and cried as she frantically scurried around the bedroom; she was clearly frightened by the storm. Finally, she found her way to the closet and pushed the door open with her nose.

Though we coaxed, she refused to come out, and we decided to move her bed to her self-imposed sanctuary. There, in safe darkness and relative quiet, she slept the rest of the night.

Nobody called to claim Sunny, so we adopted her into our animal family—a dog and four cats. I took her to our veterinarian for a checkup and shots.

"No," Dr. Woody said. "She didn't just have puppies. She's about to have puppies. I'd say in about two weeks."

"She's... pregnant?!" But we were leaving for China in two weeks. I wanted to keep her, but now what would we do?

I guessed Stephen had succumbed to the pregnant Beagle's charms when he talked his son into dog-sitting while we were gone.

Four weeks later, we returned from China to six squirmy, gurgling bundles of joy. Mama Sunny looked at us proudly, as if to say, "See what I did while you two were off gallivanting?"

We saw what she did all right—with help from what looked like an Australian Shepherd or Blue Heeler.

Over the next few weeks, we fell in love with Oreo—named for the black "cookie" over her eye, Cleo—for her Cleopatra eyes, Big Jake—for his size, Blue—for his one blue eye, Muffin—for her golden color, and last-but-not-least, Scrappy, the runt of the litter.

Sunny was a protective and doting mother to her six pups. Though always watchful, she allowed our German Shepherd, Duke, to sniff and poke at the odd little creatures. We laughed as our big, black, ferocious-looking Duke would approach, sniff, and then leap back at the slightest movement from the curious puppies.

When the puppies were a month old, we'd grown a little weary of sleep interrupted by six yelping puppies, and we installed a dog pen in the backyard. We left the gate open, and built a "mini-gate," low enough for Sunny to jump over, but high enough to keep the puppies inside.

Not only did we sleep better, but it also allowed Sunny a break from her half-dozen rumbling, tumbling, suckling fur balls.

With Sunny and her litter tucked safely in the pen, we enjoyed peace and quiet as we crawled into bed. Gentle raindrops tapped on the roof, and the smell of wet earth wafted through open windows. I looked forward to my first undisturbed night's sleep in a long time.

But just as the peaceful weight of slumber settled over me, high-pitched cries drifted into our room from outside. It's okay, I thought. Just the puppies getting used to their new home. Go back to sleep. But the cries soon became frantic, frightened.

And it wasn't the puppies; it was Sunny.

Bright flashes of light flickered outside, followed by claps of thunder that shook the house. The patter of rain turned into a roaring, torrential downpour.

Snug and dry, I fought the call to go outside, but my conscience wouldn't let me ignore Sunny's cries. Climbing out of my warm bed, I pulled on my shoes and raincoat, grabbed a flashlight, and ventured into the cold downpour.

The scene was frightening. A torrent of water poured down the slope of the backyard and through the dog pen like a rushing river. In the strobe-like bursts of lightning, I discovered the puppies had been washed to the edge of the pen, where they huddled together, shivering and whimpering. A wild-eyed Sunny struggled to pull each of her babies over the mini-gate.

I ran to the pen, cold water splashing through my nightgown.

Shining my light on the wet mob, I counted. One, two, three, four, five. Only five? Who was missing? Scrappy! Visions of the littlest puppy being swept away by the water flashed through my mind.

I scanned the pen with my flashlight to see if she might have been swept to a different area by the flood waters.

Nothing.

I scooped up an armload of five soggy puppies and ran to the house. Sunny stayed by my side, jumping up constantly to check on her babies.

Inside, I called upstairs to my husband. "Stephen! Scrappy is gone."

His feet thudded on the upstairs floor. "What do you mean, gone?"

"I have five of the puppies, but Scrappy's missing. There's a river going through the backyard. I'm afraid she was washed away."

We searched the yard, calling for the little runt. Sunny scrambled around in a frenetic fit.

"Where's Scrappy?" I asked, wishing Sunny could comprehend.

She ran to the back deck. Did she understand? I followed, keeping my light on her white-tipped tail. Sunny stood at the edge of the deck, tail erect. I knelt to look beneath. There in the spotlight sat Scrappy, looking like a wide-eyed, shivering rat.

"We found her," I called, at once relieved and amazed.

Sunny had disregarded her fear of thunderstorms to save her puppies. Though Scrappy was the only one she'd been able to carry out of the pen, she'd tried mightily to rescue the others, even through thunder, lightning and rain.

As I held the shivering runt, impulse drove me to rock her back and forth, and I began to recall the times when my own instincts made me ignore my fears to protect my children.

Later, Sunny rested in her indoors pen, surrounded by her six puppies. She looked up at me with those big, brown eyes.

I smiled, realizing a mother's unconditional love is not exclusive to humans. And then I wondered. Maybe dogs are more like their humans than we know.

~Jan Morrill

# The Houdini Dog

*Dogs are miracles with paws.*
*~Attributed to Susan Ariel Rainbow Kennedy*

We found him at the Animal Shelter in Paradise, California. Of uncertain heritage, the three-month-old puppy had silky, white fur and six large spots on his body and rump. Adorable black patches encircling his eyes made him look like a masked bandit.

"Oh, Mom," my eight-year-old daughter, Kari, exclaimed, hopping up and down as she tugged on my arm. "He's just beautiful. Can't we take him home?"

"Hmm," I said through pursed lips as I observed the puppy's friendly but calm behavior. The shelter worker had said that the animal's small paws indicated that he'd probably be no more than twenty-five pounds when fully grown.

Friendly, calm, and not too big, I thought. "Okay, Kari, it looks like he's just the right puppy for you."

Kari picked up the little dog and held him tight. "We'll call him Dudley."

That evening I made a comfortable bed in the kitchen for our new puppy. My heart warmed at the sight of my little girl and Dudley cuddling on the floor. I could already picture Kari teaching Dudley cute tricks, romping together around our large, fenced backyard, taking walks in the neighborhood.

The first indication that Dudley was going to be trouble happened that very first night. We'd put up a baby gate to prevent the puppy from leaving the kitchen. There was another entry, into the living room, but that was blocked by a louvered door. And no dog could open that. Right? But it appeared that's how he was escaping. We spent a sleepless night, hiding around the dining room corner, trying to discover Dudley's exact method of escape. Finally we saw it. The little imp simply hooked one front claw into the space between two wooden slats in the louvered door and pulled. Click. The door popped open. Dudley ran out, joyfully wiggling his little black rump and, when he spied us, left a big, yellow stain on the carpet.

Months passed and Dudley grew into an affectionate and sweet-tempered pet. Neighbors admired his silky white coat and long, flowing tail. But his size was a surprise to everyone. Within a year's time, he'd grown into a powerful sixty-pound adult, making a mockery of the adoption papers claiming Jack Russell parentage.

Dudley continued to confound us with his escape maneuvers. Now he wasn't just getting out of the kitchen. Once he learned that he could climb our six-foot backyard fence, there was no stopping him. Freedom apparently just felt too good to our roving Rover. We nailed boards vertically to the top of the fence, but the dog just found ways to get under the fence. We installed chicken wire along the fence, burying it at least a foot underground. Then Dudley started demolishing the fence itself. I inspected the backyard each day, feeling like a rancher, riding fence, making sure my "cattle" didn't cross into our neighbor's property.

"That dog is just too smart for his own good," the man across the street complained, as I retrieved Dudley from his garden for the umpteenth time. "You'd better think about chaining him in your backyard."

"I'm sorry, Mr. Bolger. We're going to put in one of those invisible fences. That should keep him in his own backyard."

But it didn't.

"Take him for a long walk every day," Kari's young friend, Emily, instructed. "Then he'll be too tired to get away."

We were already doing that.

The funny thing was, none of us could figure out how Dudley was getting out. Not my husband, our two teenage sons, or Kari or me. The dog was a regular Houdini. I can't be sure—and my friends laughed when I expressed my suspicions—but I could have sworn that Dudley checked the windows to make sure no one was watching before he sidled over to his mysterious escape spot.

I felt downright mortification when one of our neighbors called Animal Control. "That's the last straw," I announced to the whole family one evening over dinner. "Dudley is going to be a house dog. He can still go for walks every day and we'll take him to the dog park. But that's the extent of his outside activities!"

And that was that. Kari played with Dudley inside the house, and when her friends came over, cavorted with them in the backyard. Dudley watched from the family room sliding glass door, his big brown eyes unbearably mournful. It broke my heart to see him like that. But I was not going to risk destroying good relationships with our neighbors.

One windy, summer evening, Kari played by herself in the backyard. I was in the kitchen, preparing dinner. The temperature had been in the triple digits for several days and I'd opened all the screened windows and doors for ventilation. Dudley, who was watching his girl from the family room, began to bark and whine. I yelled at him to stop making such a racket—that is, until I heard him growl. Paradise does have its occasional bear or cougar sighting. I hurried to the family room door to call Kari to come inside. That's when I noticed the long, vertical rip in the screen door, large enough for a sixty-pound dog to pass through.

My heart pounding, I shoved the screen door open and rushed out onto the back patio. I could just make out the reflective tape on Kari's sneakers, bobbing up and down in the darkness as she sprinted toward the house. Dudley was right behind her.

"Mom!" Kari exclaimed, her big, blue eyes dark with annoyance. "Dudley won't let me play."

Seconds later, I heard a loud, ominous crack, followed by several, sharp snaps. The ground rumbled and I thought it was the beginning of an earthquake. I flipped on the outside light just in time to see part of the large oak tree in the backyard suddenly crash to earth. There it lay, its huge branches spread out on the lawn, taking up half of our yard.

Kari and I stood there, in awe. Neither of us could speak as we both realized what had just taken place. Our Houdini dog had escaped the house and snatched my little girl from death under the crushing weight of a giant oak in the nick of time.

We hugged each other tight. Through tears, we praised Dudley, who simply wagged his fluffy tail and gazed up at us with adoring eyes. Then I wondered. "What if all of Dudley's exasperating escapes had been a glorious preparation for this single, critical event?" Could be. Atta boy, Houdini—er—Dudley.

~Dena Netherton

# Bargain

*The dog was created specially for children. He is the god of frolic.*
*~Henry Ward Beecher*

On a spring vacation, in the 1950s, my family went to South Dakota. The trip was a combination of sightseeing and visiting relatives. It was exciting to visit the Black Hills, Mount Rushmore, and other historic places. But the visiting relatives part wasn't all that much fun for me as an eight-year-old. I was definitely bored and quite shy as we stopped along the way to see various relatives I had never met. By the time we got to Great Aunt Kitty's house (my grandmother's sister), I stubbornly refused to get out of the car. Little did I know that Great Aunt Kitty's house would prove to be the best part of my vacation that summer, and provide the best medicine a shy and soon to be crippled eight-year-old would ever receive.

After several unsuccessful tries by my parents to convince me to be polite and come meet Aunt Kitty, she took matters into her own hands. She approached me and knelt down beside the car door and whispered, "Won't you please come help me? I have a litter of new puppies, and one is very shy and scared. He won't come to anyone. But maybe he will come to you as he knows you're shy too."

Well, shy or not, I figured I needed to try and help a poor puppy that was scared just like me, and off we went to the barn. There in one of the horse stalls was a momma dog and four pups. Three of them were running around and yipping and barking like any happy puppy does. But tucked away in a dark corner under some horse tack and saddles was one little male puppy that was hunkered down and trying not to be seen, just like I had been doing in the confines of the car.

I got on my knees and crawled into the tiny dark space and hunkered down with him. I decided maybe we could hide out together until everyone else went to the house. He and I could just hang out together, avoiding all the noise and people neither of us was interested in. After the adults left us, the pup slowly began to lick me and then began to play. He and I spent most of the visit running around inside the horse barn and exploring the world together. By supper time, I still refused to go inside, but Great Aunt Kitty said I could bring the puppy with me. No one could pry the pup away from me.

By the next morning, the relationship with the puppy had become concrete. No one could separate us and it became another ordeal for my parents to try and get me to leave with them. Again, Great Aunt Kitty came up with the solution. She offered me the pup to take home as my very own. It sounded great, but my mother wanted no part of the idea. After more tears and refusals from me to leave the pup, my dad said, "Well, that pup would probably fetch Great Aunt Kitty a good price at the auction barn, so we really couldn't possibly take her prize puppy." At which I promptly got my little purse and took out the rest of my allowance that I had saved to buy souvenirs on our trip. I had a whole dollar and some change, which to me was a lot of money. I offered it to Great Aunt Kitty, who of course accepted it as though it were a vast fortune.

By this time my parents decided the only way they were going to win was to give in to me and let me have the dog. By the time we got back home to our farm, spring break was over and I was back in school, but rushed home eagerly every afternoon to be with my new companion who I had named Chip. The once shy pup was the terror of the farm yard, chasing the chickens and the cattle and everything that moved, and leading my father to joke about my "bargain."

Shortly after returning to school, we were all vaccinated with the very first polio vaccine, which proved to be a disaster for me. Instead of just a mild reaction to the inoculation, I was one of a few thousand children across the country who actually got a full blown case of polio from the vaccine. The lab had inadvertently not killed the entire live polio virus in a few batches and it had disastrous results for the children who got the bad vaccine.

As spring turned into summer, I spent most of the time in the hospital, and when I came home, I was no longer just a shy child, but one who could no longer walk. Chip was again my sole comfort and interest in life. From the moment I came home, Chip never left my side.

Through all the painful therapy I had to undergo, Chip, was there and when I would refuse to try and walk, he would jump at me as though to say, "You can do it! Come play." He instinctively began to take things from me and hold them just out of my reach, so I would have to stretch and work my muscles to retrieve them. That was something no therapist could get me to do, but Chip made it worth the effort. He knew how to make work seem like play. By the time fall rolled around, I was able to stand and Chip was always there to encourage me to try harder and take another step.

Chip knew that deep inside all I needed was encouragement and that one day we would again chase the cows and chickens together. And so it was that I learned to try a little harder, stretch myself beyond what I thought I could do, and achieve the freedom to live and love and trust in a dog my father teased me about it... the best bargain I ever got, even though he would never be worth much as a farm dog. He proved himself a wise and wonderful friend.

~Christine Trollinger

# A Real, Living Lassie Come Home

*Perseverance is not a long race; it is many short races one after another.*
~Walter Elliott

When I was in grade school, I discovered *Lassie Come Home* in the school library. It told the story of a dog's loyalty and devotion to her people. I believed that the story was true, because I had known and loved my very own "Lassie."

He was a large red-sable Collie that had wandered onto the farm where I grew up. That was before I was born. He was full grown, and my parents did not recognize him as belonging to any of the neighbors. They had not intended to keep him, so they simply called him "Collie." However, he stayed, and I eventually adopted him as my dog.

The spring I was four, my older sister came home from our great aunt's with a Terrier-cross puppy. My parents said either the puppy or Collie had to go. We could not keep both dogs. I was outvoted. My mother called "Party Line," a local call-in radio show, and advertised Collie, free to whoever would come get him.

A man in a pickup with racks on it took Collie away. The next morning, there was Collie, under the blooming bridal wreath bushes, waiting for me. Later that morning, the man came and took him away again. The next morning, Collie was back! This was the pattern, and to me, it seemed that he came home for weeks. Then suddenly one morning, he wasn't there. My mother said that his new owners were tying him up to keep him at his new home.

When I started kindergarten, a boy in my class told me about his dog "Pup." Then, he said, "You know, my dad got him from your folks." His dog was my Collie, and his new home was only two miles straight west of mine. I often questioned the boy about him.

When we were in fourth grade, the boy made the announcement that his father was selling the farm and moving the family to town. The day after the auction, I asked him what they did with "Pup." I was hoping that they brought him into town. I knew the house they'd moved in to, and it wasn't too far from the school. I was hoping to have the chance to slip away from school to see him. But no, they had given the dog away to someone who said they would take an old farm dog and give him a good home. The man who took him lived over forty-five miles away.

When I got home from school two days later, my mother asked my sisters and me if we remembered "Collie." She told the story of how someone else had taken Collie from the auction to a new home. But the morning after the auction, the man went outside only to discover that his new dog was gone. He called "Party Line" and explained that the dog he'd brought home was missing. He was hoping that someone would call in saying that they had his dog. "This morning," my mother explained, "another caller to Party Line said that the dog had shown up in his yard just before sundown last night. They'd fed the dog, but this morning, he was gone."

It became a daily ritual. Each morning a new caller told the same story on Party Line—the dog wandered in the night before, they fed him, and then in the morning he was gone. As people followed the phone calls, it became evident that "Pup" was going home. He was traveling a straight line to the southwest, stopping each evening at a farmstead. With sunrise, he'd be gone, only to show up farther west that night. The last call came from a house located just a mile northeast of his home. The caller said the evening before the dog had come into their yard. After he'd eaten what they'd fed him, he had curled up on their doorstep to sleep. In the morning, the farmer found "Pup" still curled on the doorstep where he'd died sometime during the night.

Some said, "He was a very old dog." I knew that he'd stopped only because he was close enough. He was going home to those he'd loved and served, to his people.

~Maxine Leick

# The Dog that Couldn't Bark

*Love is, above all, the gift of oneself.*
~Jean Anouilh

Many years ago, in what appears to be a different lifetime now, I had a friend named Jonathan who lived only a few houses down the street. He was a cool kid and a real pal, and in retrospect I can see that he had all the usual qualities and hang-ups of a typical boy. He was fun to be with because of his innocent enthusiasm, and he knew all the best places to hang out in the neighbourhood, but he also had severe acne that made him self-conscious, and his round face often looked like a ripe honeydew melon that sprouted bright red raisins.

The best part about Jonathan, though, was his dog. This is not to say that my friend was any less memorable than his pet, but that dog had a very peculiar quality about him. A friendly Bulldog that never met anyone he didn't like, or immediately want to lick, Bowzer was born without any vocal chords. It was a freak of nature, and a congenital condition that had no plausible explanation, but here was a dog that simply couldn't bark. He would yap his mouth all day long like any canine, but no sound ever came out. Jonathan's parents affectionately used to refer to their pet as "the mute brute."

Even though he couldn't make any sounds, Bowzer sure made his presence known anyway. We couldn't play a pickup baseball game in the neighbourhood park without an extra infielder, outfielder, base runner, or ballboy running around on four paws like his life depended on bumping into every single player on the field, regardless of which team that player played on. For all of us, it became an accepted part of our playtime that Bowzer would somehow be involved in whatever activity we decided on.

Except for the local public swimming pool, of course. Jonathan never had a need to tie Bowzer to a leash and to wrap the leash around a tree or a post, because we all knew there was no way that Bowzer would run away. Oh no. If that dog had fingers and feet, I could swear that he would have climbed that chain-link fence to come frolic with us in the water.

Then, one day, something terrible happened to Jonathan, and we all had to grow up much too quickly. His parents were called away to the hospital because his grandmother was ill, and so Jonathan was left at home by himself. It was early in the evening and no one really thought anything bad could happen to him. But, as it turned out, two men had chosen that house for an unannounced visit.

Soon after his parents locked all the doors and left in their car, with Jonathan securely ensconced inside their home, the men broke into the house from the back door, with theft on their mind. Jonathan's family wasn't super rich, but even as a kid I could tell they had nice things in their house. I suppose the robbers thought so, too.

Jonathan was in his bedroom and heard the noise from the break-in, and maybe because he panicked, he didn't yell or scream for help. Bowzer was in the bedroom also, and heard the noise as well, but because of his birth defect, he couldn't make a sound. I bet, though, that his face was yapping like mad. Had the robbers heard a dog barking, maybe things would have turned out differently.

As Jonathan tells the story, the robbers made their way through the entire house and probably figured that no one was home. Maybe, just maybe, they would leave before they came to Jonathan's bedroom. But no such luck.

One of the robbers opened the door to Jonathan's bedroom, and was startled to find a boy huddled amongst the pillows of his bed.

The robber was even more startled though to discover a fifty-pound Bulldog charging at him. Maybe Bowzer couldn't bark, but that didn't mean he didn't have teeth. And, as Jonathan recalls, it certainly didn't mean that Bowzer was not intent on taking as big a bite out of that robber as he could.

With an angry dog chewing on his arm, the robber began yelling in pain. The second robber suddenly appeared, and that's when Jonathan saw the gun. The last thing he remembers is hearing one gunshot. And then it all went black.

Jonathan survived that horrific episode, luckily, without any physical scars, but he was never the same afterwards. He lost his youthful enthusiasm and innocence. He lost the desire to play and was seldom seen in our usual hang-out spots. He eventually lost his acne as well, and his awkwardness. But, even now as an adult in mid-life, he still mourns the greatest loss of all.

That gunshot had a target, and the target wasn't Jonathan. After that night of the break-in, the dog that couldn't bark never even yapped his face anymore. He didn't run around a baseball diamond like a demon. He didn't pretend he could bore a hole through a chain-link fence to play with us in the water of a swimming pool. The only thing Bowzer got for defending his territory and protecting his master was a nine millimeter bullet through the heart.

The robbers were arrested and jailed a few days after the break-in. Jonathan's parents never left him alone in the house again, and they never got another dog, either. How could you replace a dog like Bowzer?

Whenever Jonathan and I cross paths now, we reminisce about the many good times, and the one bad time. And it never fails to move us to tears to talk about Bowzer and his courage. The lesson has stayed with us always: some things are irreplaceable. It doesn't matter that we're both grown men now and that some people believe men aren't supposed to cry. The memory of Bowzer is worth every single tear of laughter and sadness.

By the way, if you're wondering what profession Jonathan chose, it should not come as a surprise. He's a veterinary doctor. Me? I became a lawyer, and I sit on the board of an animal shelter. Every once in a while a Bulldog comes through the shelter. I call Jonathan to see if he wants to volunteer that day. There's no need to tell him why, and he never asks. He just shows up, in memory of Bowzer.

~Joseph Civitella

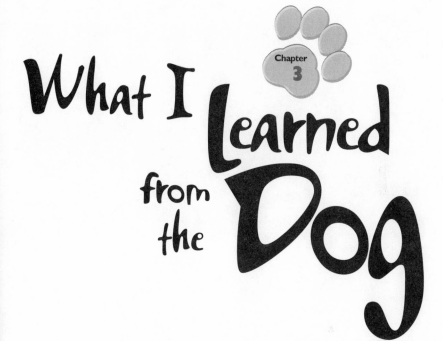

# What I Learned from the Dog

**Chapter 3**

## Learning to Listen

*The most important thing in communication
is to hear what isn't being said.*

~Peter F. Drucker

# Peanut

*In order to really enjoy a dog, one doesn't merely try to train him
to be semi-human. The point of it is to open oneself to the possibility
of becoming partly a dog.*
~Edward Hoagland

I never believed the old adage "take time to stop and smell the roses." I mean, who had that kind of time, especially in L.A., where it was commonplace to work sixty to eighty hours a week? But Peanut taught me to make the time.

Last November, I was laid off. The latest TV show I had been working on (as a writers' assistant) had been cancelled. I wasn't eligible to receive unemployment, so I didn't know what I was going to do. This last job had left me pretty burnt out, so I needed to re-evaluate my career goals. I had always wanted to write a book, and being that November is "National Novel Writing Month," I decided now would be as good a time as any to do so. NaNoWriMo encourages people to write a 50,000-word book in a month (1,667 words a day). Which sounded great, but I still had to find a way to get a paycheck, too.

Just as I was about to send out a mass e-mail to everyone I knew, and even people I didn't know, saying I would do almost anything for work, I got a phone call from a writer friend, Mike, asking if I could dog-sit. Now, I had cat-sat for him before, but, as we all know, cats and dogs are very different beings. Although I have no pets of my own—that's what happens when you are young and single, live in a small apartment that barely fits one (let alone an animal), and work in TV—I had pet-sat for many a cat, bird, fish... but never for any dogs.

Mike asked how I was with dogs. "Great," I said, though I had feared them as a child (I blame the German Shepherd with the big teeth that grew up next door to me), and had never watched one in my life. "Awesome," he said back. "My writing partner, Pam, needs you to watch her dog for a few weeks." A few weeks?! Why did I lie, again? But I did need a job. "Actually, probably for a month," Mike said. A month?!

I met with Pam the next day, as well as her dog, Peanut. He was a cute brown mutt of a dog, not too big, but not too small. He wagged his tail at me when we met and looked much less threatening than the German Shepherd I used to know. "Good, he likes you," Pam said. Really? She then told me Peanut would need three walks a day, and warned me, "He may be slow the first block, but he'll speed up for the remaining three." Pam said that Peanut was getting older and had arthritis. Aww, the poor guy. "No problem," I said. She handed me the keys, said Peanut would see me tomorrow, and that was that. "Oh, and would you mind sleeping here for the month? He likes someone here with him," Pam said. "Sure," I replied, wondering what I had just gotten myself into. I had gone from never-watching-a-dog to living with one?!

The next day, I returned with a suitcase and my laptop, fed Peanut, and got his leash ready. He seemed to be moving at a relatively normal pace going down the driveway, so I wondered what Pam had been talking about. But then we arrived at the sidewalk, where Peanut came to a standstill, smelling every flower in sight. Uh-oh.

Now, I am not the most patient person. I am used to a very fast-paced, never-stay-at-home kind of lifestyle, so walking Peanut took some (much) getting used to for me. I watched Peanut sniff this flower, then that one, looking at my watch, wondering how long this would go on. Can't we just get this over with, so to speak? Doesn't he just want to do his business and go home? I felt like a parent with a child, when the child keeps asking "Why?" to everything and the parent keeps patiently answering. I wondered if I could make phone calls or text people while Peanut did his thing, but then I thought that would be rude. Plus, how would I scoop and text at the same time? (I had even forgotten about the scooping part until our first walk, but that is a whole other story!) I decided to try making phone calls anyway—I was desperate—and would just hang up or have people hold while I scooped.

I tried to nudge Peanut along, but no such luck; that dandelion was far more persuasive than I was. Pam's voice kept repeating in my head, "He may be slow the first block, but he'll speed up for the remaining three." Hmm. Three more blocks?! I hoped she was right.

Day after day, walk after walk, I found something remarkable happening. While walking Peanut, I stopped putting people on hold, then stopped talking to people on my cell phone altogether. It also became difficult to talk to passersby while on my phone; since Peanut was so cute, everyone stopped us. I stopped bringing my phone altogether, making the walks all about Peanut, getting to know his neighbors, and a time for technology-free reflection (something everyone, especially in L.A., should try). I also started thinking about what kind of job I would next attempt to get. Peanut and I would have many discussions about this; he would look at me when he liked one of my career path ideas, or turn his head away from me when he didn't. Peanut and I agreed that my assistant days were over; I needed to reach higher. And I found myself working on my book—at least, ideas for it—during each of our walks. I would scribble them down as Peanut paused to talk to the dandelions.

Every night after our walks, I would work on my novel. In mid-November, I was supposed to be at the halfway mark, around 25,000 words. But I was barely at 15,000. How would I ever catch up? The same way Peanut walked—a little bit every day, dandelion by dandelion, word by word.

A writer I admire once wrote that every writer should get a dog, for it teaches discipline. I was skeptical... until Peanut. (Thank you, Jennifer Weiner.)

By the end of the month, I didn't want Peanut's owner to come back; I loved this dog. Peanut taught me patience. These days, with or without Peanut, I go on slow walks around the neighborhood, always stopping to smell a flower or two. The old cliché is true: "Take time to stop and smell the roses." Before, I never would have interrupted my fast-paced life to do so. But, post-Peanut, I agree. We should. And I always leave my cell phone at home.

To Peanut's credit, I completed my novel. He would also be proud to know that I stopped being an assistant in TV and just associate-produced a documentary for The History Channel. I owe that little dog a lot. Thank you, Peanut.

~Natalia K. Lusinski

# Traveler

*Courage is resistance to fear, mastery of fear—not the absence of fear.*
~Mark Twain

The dog charged across the field, nose sniffing the air, and headed straight for the tractor, where my husband, Jack, was mowing the wild grasses. He padded alongside the tractor until lunchtime when he followed Jack to the house. They shared a pizza. The dog was dirty and thin, and he ate, and ate, and ate, as if he hadn't had a good meal in days. After the food was gone, he lifted a paw to shake hands, then curled under the mesquite tree for a nap.

That hot summer afternoon, I knew we had a new dog, unless he had run away from home, and his owners were looking for him. On the chance that some heartbroken child was crying for his missing dog, I put the part-Australian Blue Heeler in the fenced backyard until I could run an ad in the newspaper and locate his family. He howled and scratched at the gate and let me know right away he was not a yard dog. So I let him out. He'd probably stick around anyway, since he seemed to like us. Or was it the pizza? I was wrong, however.

The dog lifted a paw for a handshake, his way of saying thanks for the food, I suppose, and then trotted down the road to the neighbor's house.

"Stop by anytime," I called to his retreating back. He kept on going.

"We'll never see him again," I told Jack.

Jack agreed.

I was wrong a second time. The dog showed up for breakfast the next morning, and since then he has visited us at least once a day to see what's on the menu. He loves his dry dog food soaked in milk. I buy the kind for older dogs, since I believe he is no young thing. Lately, however, Traveler (so named because he likes to wander) prefers people food like chicken and steak. Smart dog. He visits our son next door to see what they're eating. When the neighbors on the other side of us are outside, he bounces over there to see what's happening.

A few days after Traveler took up residence in the country, I put his picture in the local newspaper, asking anyone who knew this dog to please call. No one claimed him, and he's now our neighborhood pet, roaming at will, accepting hugs and handouts and love from all his families. Our son set up a small tent on his front porch where Traveler sleeps when it's cold or rainy. Traveler has learned that the country is a great place to live. He chases rabbits and snaps at dragonflies. He plays with armadillos until they escape into their burrows. Once, he tangled with a skunk. Big mistake. The skunk taught him which animals to leave alone. Traveler also figured out that a tilt of his head and a tail wag can earn him a pat on the head, a kiss, and perhaps an extra helping of dinner.

I'm learning from Traveler as well. Watching him enjoy his meals, play with the grandkids, take long walks with Jack and me, and snooze peacefully under the shade of the mesquite has helped me put things in perspective and accept my life as it is, the way he accepts his. When Jack's health problems threaten to overwhelm us, I look at Traveler, who faces each challenge—food, shelter, and fear—head on, and makes the best of his situation. Even when he is afraid of something, he stands tough. I try to do the same.

For example, one Sunday afternoon, Traveler saved Jack's life. Jack and the dog were in the driveway when Traveler started barking. It wasn't his normal "I am hungry, please feed me" or "Come out and play with me" bark, but a shrill, almost panicky yap, yap. I went outside to see what was causing the commotion. The dog's attention was focused at a spot beside the chain-link fence.

"What is it?" I asked.

Jack strolled over to the fence and looked around. "I don't see anything."

Then I heard a rattle, rattle, rattle, like maracas or a baby's rattle, a sound that is quite familiar in these parts. A diamondback rattlesnake issued its warning, telling us to beware.

Jack has trouble hearing certain pitches and wasn't aware of the danger. "It's a snake," I said, and cautioned him to stand still, until we could pinpoint the reptile's location.

The grass was fairly high along the fence row, and we couldn't spot the snake at first. Traveler kept barking, but kept his distance. Finally, I saw the diamondback, next to the chain-link fence. It was a big one, three to four feet long.

I pointed. "Over there."

Now knowing where the snake was, Jack circled the spot and went into the house for his gun. The rattler was no match for a double barrel shotgun. At the first blast, poor Traveler took off, more frightened by the boom of the gun than of the snake. Had he not alerted us to the diamondback's presence, however, Jack surely would have been bitten.

Later, Traveler returned. He had recognized the danger, and even though he feared the snake, he held his ground. We rewarded him with hugs, and ear scratches, and food, of course.

This little dog that belongs to no family in particular, but to every family in the neighborhood, helps me separate the important things in my life from the less important. His bravery helps me face whatever life hands me with courage, the way he faced the snake.

I still wonder where Traveler came from. Did he know we'd need his courage one day? I bet he has a story to tell. But he's not talking.

~Beverly McClure

# How You Play the Game

*I named my dog Stay so I can say, "Come here, Stay. Come here, Stay."*
~Steven Wright

"**S**end him out." The fun-match judge commanded.

"Hike!" My Husky, Hoss, obediently took off for the far fence.

Most obedience trial competitors use the more common terms, "Run," or "Go Out," to send a dog running across the ring. My "hike," a sled dog command, was sort of a joke. On the way up to the Utility Class level, a dog trainer either becomes obsessive compulsive, or develops a sense of humor. I indulged in both.

"Sit!" I called when Hoss reached the far fence. He obediently turned and sat.

"High-bar," the judge directed. The choice of jumps was up to the judge. Both the high-bar and the solid board jump were set at the same three-foot height. A competitor does not know which jump the judge will choose.

"Over!" I shouted and pointed to the high-bar.

Hoss dug into the grass, ran and leapt, hurling his sixty-five-pound body, easily clearing the three-foot jump. If only he would do that indoors.

Hoss was officially Aerie's Hossbarkerplayer CDX, a large gray and white, full-coated Siberian Husky. We earned two AKC obedience degrees together, a CD, the basic obedience degree, as well as the coveted intermediate CDX, Companion Dog Excellent. Elegant and devoted, Hoss was impressive. He displayed a quiet authority that other dogs did not challenge. He was a leader.

He was my best friend and ego builder. I was Hoss's breeder and trainer. I was prepping him for competing for the advanced AKC obedience degree, Utility Dog.

Huskies are not usually a first choice as obedience dogs; they are often too independent. Hoss was an extraordinary dog. He was a quick and willing learner even in advanced work. He learned to sniff out the one dumbbell I had handled and retrieve it. Hand signals were a cinch. Hoss was a fun dog to train. Hoss learned it all and was ready for evaluation.

Like most competitors, we started competing at fun matches, informal practice shows used to prepare dogs and handlers for the real thing. To earn an AKC obedience degree, a dog must pass three sanctioned trials; easier said than done. The exercises are tough, the judging unforgiving. No corrections are allowed. Only one command is permitted for each exercise. If the dog fails one exercise, he fails for the day.

Dog shows consist of controlled chaos. There are tons of distractions — lots of other dogs and handlers, noises, sights, smells, and often something unpredictable from the novice exhibitors. Fun matches help trainers gauge whether or not their dogs are ready for a sanctioned show.

My problems started when I started showing Hoss at indoor fun matches.

"High-bar," the judge commanded.

"Over!" I pointed to the high-bar.

Hoss looked toward the high-bar and then looked toward the solid jump. He ran for the solid and jumped it. We failed.

At other indoor fun matches, if the judge selected the solid jump, Hoss sailed over the jump. However, if the judge selected the high-bar, Hoss disobeyed my directed signal and jumped the solid jump instead. I was frustrated. He knew the difference between the command for the solid and high jumps. He worked well at practice. Why was he being disobedient?

At the peak of my frustration with Hoss, a somewhat famous dog trainer offered a suggestion.

"You know what you need to do with that dog?"

"I've tried everything. He only does this indoors."

"Go home and get a broom handle. If he doesn't jump that bar, beat the hell out of him."

I nodded.

The next day, I got a broom and went out in my yard to train. Siberian Huskies with Utility Dog degrees were very rare. I wanted recognition.

The first time Hoss incorrectly chose the solid jump, I grabbed his collar firmly. He sat submissively.

"No," I said sternly as I looked into his loyal brown eyes. Instantly my heart changed. I did not want a utility degree as much as I wanted the devoted love of my dog. If I had beaten him, he might have fearfully submitted. I did not want that kind of relationship. I wanted a clear conscience more than notoriety. I never touched the broom handle.

I sent Hoss over the jumps many more times and he never missed my command. We quit the day on a good note.

The next morning, Hoss tried to raise himself to his feet. He screamed. The scream of a hurting Siberian Husky is both ear-shattering and heart-wrenching. Several more times he screamed as he tried to stand. We were off to the vet.

Hoss had a bulging disc in his spine. The initial injury probably occurred a few months prior when Hoss hit the dashboard when we almost had an accident. He loved to ride in the passenger seat. Although I saw him hit hard, Hoss did not show any pain at that time. However, this was about the same time his jump troubles started. My guess is that each jump aggravated an originally minor injury. The obscure high-bar probably took more precision and effort to jump than the solid jump. Both probably hurt. Still, he obeyed my commands.

I also learned Hoss had progressive retinal atrophy, a degenerative eye condition that first shows up as limited night vision. At indoor fun matches, the light was dim. The high-bar was skinny and alternately striped black and white. Hoss probably could not see the bar. The solid white board jump stood out. In spite of limited vision and pain, Hoss gave me his heart. He jumped the only thing he could see. He obeyed me the best he could understand, even if it hurt.

That instant I looked into Hoss's eyes, my life changed for the better. One pause for compassion averted a lifetime of guilt. If I had followed the advice of that famous trainer and beaten Hoss, I would have forever believed that I caused his back injury. I was blessed choosing the success of compassion over the success of accomplishment. "How you play the game" was branded on my heart.

Hoss retired that day. With rest, his back pain subsided. He lived a long life as a beloved pet. I probably could have shown him at outdoor shows on sunny days when he could see both jumps. However, I did not want to ask him to jump. He would have given me his all even if it caused him pain. He had already given enough.

~Jane Marie Allen Farmer

# Chuckie?

*Dogs laugh, but they laugh with their tails.*
*~Max Eastman,* Enjoyment of Laughter

So many things were going through my mind that day. I was feeling blessed over my new part-time teaching job at the community college. Full-time work was what I really needed, but this was an exciting new start. My sister, niece and nephew had just moved here, to North Carolina, from Virginia and were trying to adjust. And, the function of the Holy Spirit in our day-to-day lives had been turning over in my brain for weeks, ever since we discussed it in our Wednesday Night Bible Study class.

The Holy Spirit was a concept I was having trouble completely understanding. I had had an innate sense of right and wrong all of my life. Was that simply it? Our Bible Study leader explained it as God's way of speaking to us. Did he mean a voice? I just wasn't sure what he meant. I had been praying for God to help me understand. But, so far, there was no answer.

To clear my thoughts, I went for a walk and then sat down on the back steps to reflect on this beautiful, cold January day. I was thanking God for my many blessings when a completely different thought interrupted my prayer. "Take your newspapers to the Humane Society." I answered out loud as if someone had actually spoken to me, "I could do that." I began to gather them. It was a good idea. One of my New Year's resolutions was to do that more often. The Humane Society uses the newspapers to line the animals' cages, so they need lots of them.

It only took two trips to the outside cabinet at the shelter to unload my papers. When I closed the cabinet door, I was startled by one of the ladies from inside standing behind it. She wanted to see if I needed help. I told her no, but I told her that I'd like to come in and take a look around. What was I saying?? I never did that! I had not been inside there in two and a half, maybe three years! It made me too sad. All those sweet faces whining and begging for me to take them home was too much. But, I felt as if I HAD to go inside.

I went to the puppy room first. There were three black and brown pups crying for attention. I stuck my fingers through the cage and they licked madly. I yanked my fingers out, laughing. I walked on through to the cat room. There was a beautiful calico sitting straight and tall, not making a move or a sound. I kept moving. No kittens. That's good.

I knew I was looking for something, but I couldn't imagine what it was. The thought occurred to me that maybe one of my dad's dogs had wandered off and was there. I decided to walk outside and take a look at the dogs.

There were only two dogs on the right side of the shelter. I asked the guy cleaning the pens if this was it. He pointed to the other side. I walked to the left side. No dogs at all. I thought the shelter was always full. Usually, I could hear lots of barking even when I was just dropping off newspapers... but not today. I thought I was being silly, and turned around and walked back towards the van. I was about a foot from it and stopped.

Go back. "Go back for what??" I mumbled to myself as I made an about-face.

"Do you have more dogs?" I asked as I reentered through the front door. The lady said, "Yeah, they're locked inside. It's almost time to go home."

My watch read 4:20. "Can I please go in a take a quick peek?" my voice said and my eyes begged. She looked resigned, as if she knew I was a woman on a mission.

The door opened. You never heard such barking, growling, yelping in your life! What was I doing? This was crazy. But, my feet kept going as if they were doing the leading. Halfway down the line, I fell to my knees. "Chuckie, is that you?"

Chuckie is the most adorable, loveable Jack Russell Terrier you ever saw. He belongs to my niece and nephew and they love him dearly. He had been a constant in their lives amidst tragedy and change. Their dad had died right in front of them and my sister on their farm in Virginia, after falling from the horse he was riding. He was such a great dad and his death had left a giant hole in all their lives, and ours. My sister had tried for two years to run the farm by herself. Now, she had given up all that was near and dear to them and moved here to be closer to the family. Chuckie was part of the old and new home and a loyal, eager companion.

Chuckie had been missing for about three weeks. I had forgotten about him in the hurry and bustle of my own life and the holidays. He disappeared about a week before Christmas. When my sister told me, I couldn't believe it. I prayed to God to bring him back. "Oh Lord," I cried, "Please don't let them lose Chuckie too." But, Christmas had come and gone and with the New Year and my new job, I had forgotten Chuckie.

But God had not! And He had not forgotten a little girl and boy far from home, in new territory, longing for their dad and getting to know a family they had only seen on occasion. He also hadn't forgotten their aunt, who was trying to understand the workings of the Holy Spirit. Tears streamed down my face as I looked through that fence at that happy little dog, standing on hind legs, front legs moving excitedly up and down as if playing with a tiny invisible yo-yo. He was dancing with joy and, quietly on my knees, so was I.

I rushed back to the front desk and called my sister. While we were waiting for her arrival, I told the lady my story—how I had been led there and didn't even know what I was looking for. I told her the dog had been missing for three weeks and that I had forgotten about him. I asked her how long he'd been there.

She said, "You won't believe it, but someone just brought him in today!"

She was wrong. I did believe it!

~Sharon Rice Maag

# Canine Counselor

*Who knew that dog saliva could mend a broken heart?*
*~Jennifer Neal*

Adam is my three-year-old Australian Shepherd. He is my constant companion. I joke that if Adam could have his way, he would be glued to my right leg and tag along with me every minute of every day.

I met Adam when he was just seven months old. He was an abused, abandoned puppy. I requested a "meet and greet" at his foster home after looking at Adam's profile and photo on the Austin, Texas-based Aussie Rescue organization's website. When I arrived for the visit, Adam's "foster mother" ticked off a list of do's and don'ts to keep me from scaring or arousing anger in Adam. Rolling my eyes, I simply sat on the floor and waited to see if Adam would come to me. He did. After circling me closer and closer, Adam finally nudged me with his nose to cautiously ask for a touch. Without looking at him, I gently stroked his head. Within five minutes, Adam surprised his caregiver by crawling onto my lap, showing me his belly, and begging for more attention.

Shortly after Adam chose me as his "momma," the coordinator of the rescue organization confided in me that she had been very concerned that Adam would never be adopted due to the bad treatment he received during the first several months of his life. Like a toddler's formative first three years, dogs have formative first months where lifelong impressions are made.

Now, more than two years after he came to live with me, Adam still has issues with strangers. I take him with me whenever I can, to expose Adam to other people and other environments. Some days he is calm, other days he either barks at or cowers from strangers. He is especially afraid of children.

One day recently, I took Adam with me to the Hill Country Children's Advocacy Center where I had a few meetings scheduled to help promote an upcoming fundraising event. The staff had met Adam before and liked him a lot. It was supposed to be a quiet afternoon at the center, but I left Adam's leash on him in case I needed to keep him out of trouble.

As I sat in the front office working on my laptop, three people entered the lobby. A police officer and an older woman escorted a teenage girl into the room. A member of the advocacy center welcomed them and asked the teen and her grandmother to have a seat on the couch so that she could meet with the officer. From my seat in the front office I watched the young girl crumple onto the sofa. She pulled the hood of her sweatshirt over her head and tugged at the long sleeves, tucking her hands into the cuffs. The girl looked very nervous and scared. Her grandmother looked worried and uncomfortable.

When the group first arrived, Adam had been laying at my feet. He quickly sat up to watch the activity. Adam moved in front of me, ready to snap into guard mode if anyone approached me. I patted his head and told him everything was okay.

Adam is usually not interested in other people if they do not seem threatening and keep their distance. But today, he sat and looked at the teen as she tried to lose herself in her oversized sweatshirt. Adam cocked his head from one side to the other as if he was trying to understand the situation. He watched as the girl waved away the staff member who wanted to take her photograph for her case record.

Suddenly, Adam stood up and walked over to the teen. I jumped up to grab his leash, but he had already made his way across the room and around the coffee table. He sat down next to the young girl and rested his head on her thigh, looking up at her with his big amber-colored eyes. I froze, stunned at Adam's sensitive actions.

As the teen bent down to hug Adam, I quickly walked around the coffee table, afraid that Adam would suddenly snap at the young girl. Instead, Adam let the girl squeeze his neck. He even put his paw on the teen's knee, asking to shake, and licked her hand.

"This is my dog Adam," I said as I quietly walked around the coffee table and touched Adam's head. "He was a badly abused and abandoned puppy before I gave him a good home. Good boy, Adam."

In just a few minutes, the teen seemed to shed her fear of being at the advocacy center to report her abuse. She pushed the hood off her head. Soon after, she removed the sweatshirt that had been used as a form of protection, but must have been oppressive on the hot summer day.

"I see that you have met Adam," said the advocacy center counselor as he walked into the lobby. The young counselor could have passed for a teen himself. "You know, he had a harsh life before Kelly adopted him and gave him a good home. His life is a success story. We're going to do everything we can to enable you to have a success story, too. First, I'd like to get your photo for my case file, then are you ready to come back and talk with me?"

The teen nodded, asking if she could have her photo taken with Adam.

"Of course!" I said.

After the photo was taken and the teen gave Adam one last hug, she walked down the hall and into the comfortable interview room to tell her awful secrets and start down the road to recovery from abuse.

After the teen left the lobby, I sat down on the couch and hugged Adam. I was shocked, yet joyful and proud at the same time.

Without saying a word, the teen's grandmother reached out and touched my arm. The tears glistening in her eyes and rolling down her cheeks signaled her unspoken gratitude for Adam's kind and caring actions.

The incident that afternoon at the advocacy center made me a true believer that animals have a sixth sense, a sensitive intuition about the world around them that enables them to understand and react to the moment much better than we humans. I am so proud of Adam!

~Kelly Carper Polden

# Our Royal Jet

*A daughter is a gift of love.*
~Author Unknown

My husband, Jim, and I were enjoying a quiet evening and planning a Caribbean cruise when our phone rang.

"Hi Mom. I've got a little problem."

Flattered that Kathy, our animal-loving elder daughter, still valued my advice I listened. "That dog I rescued several weeks ago is very loveable, but she's too hyper for our other dog. I've decided that with Dad traveling so much and us kids gone, you need a pet to keep you company. She'd love running around your huge fenced backyard."

Caught unprepared, I swallowed a sigh. How could I tell my elder daughter that I relished my quiet time without hurting her feelings? "Dad's right here. Why don't you talk to him?" Like any sensible wife, I passed the phone to her father.

While they chatted, I recalled how Kathy and her husband had gone to a Seattle restaurant several weeks earlier. While dining, they noticed a small dog shivering in the rain as it wandered outside in the parking lot. When Kathy mentioned it to the server, he said that someone abandoned the puppy a week earlier. Restaurant employees had been feeding her, but none could give her a home.

After dining, Kathy took a box of leftovers and fed them to the dog in the parking lot. By the time she reached her car, the dog had devoured the food and followed her. When Kathy opened her door, the dog jumped inside.

Rain continued to fall so Kathy talked her husband into stopping at the veterinary clinic on the way home. After Kathy explained the circumstances to the vet, he examined the dog and commented that the puppy was a rare Sheltie-Basenji mix and in good condition except for cigarette burns in several places on her body. Unable to let the abused dog go homeless any longer, Kathy adopted her.

She named the dog Jet because she soared like the jet airplanes Kathy flew regularly as a flight attendant. Now, it seemed that Jet was too flighty for Kathy's other dog. One of them had to go. So what did Kathy do? She did what every clever daughter does when she has a problem. She called her parents.

I should have known better than to let her talk to Jim. He always was a pushover for his daughter's requests. He agreed that we'd adopt Jet.

A few days later, Kathy called and advised us that she had followed her vet's suggestions and given Jet a sedative, put her in a traveling kennel and boarded her on a plane. Jet would be arriving in Denver in a few hours.

We drove to the airport and as soon as I saw the small orange puppy, with the white blaze on her forehead and white-socked feet, huddled in her travel kennel, I melted. Jet resembled a little fox and looked at me with frightened brown eyes when I opened the kennel door. Shivering, she staggered out and collapsed at my feet. When I picked her up and gently stroked her soft fur, she licked my fingers and snuggled in my arms.

For the first week, she avoided Jim whenever he had a cigarette in his hand. As days passed, she became more comfortable with us. My husband's gentle ways soon won her over. She greeted him at the door when he returned from work each day, "helped" him with yard work, and slept at his feet when he read the newspapers or watched TV.

I soon learned that Basenjis were often royal dogs of Egyptian pharaohs. They don't bark, but Jet's Sheltie genes did, so she was a great watchdog. In keeping with her royal status, we let her sleep on a bed in a spare bedroom, but otherwise, she wasn't allowed on any of our other furniture.

Some mornings, I awoke to find her asleep on the floor beside my side of the bed. She became my shadow and stayed close whether at home or on our daily walks. As days passed, she played out in our backyard, calmed down and became a very affectionate and disciplined dog. She kept off the furniture and responded when called. She even walked regally as we strolled our neighborhood, where curious people frequently asked if she was a pet fox.

One cold winter night, months later, while Jim was out of town on a business trip, Jet and I went to our respective beds while winds wailed and slapped snow against our windows in below-zero weather.

I fell into a deep sleep quickly. It was still dark when I heard Jet whine and felt her paw rub my shoulder.

"What are you doing on my bed?" I grumbled. Winds were still howling and I was in no mood to take her outside in that weather. When she continued to whine, I sat up and quickly realized the house was too hot. Something was wrong with the furnace!

With Jet at my heels, I raced to the furnace room. Fortunately, I remembered Jim's instructions on what to do if this very event happened. Had Jet not awoken me, the overheated boiler might have exploded and damaged our home. Jet had saved my life!

After that, Jet seemed to know that she had earned special privileges. She waited until we were asleep, crept up on our bed, curled against Jim and pressed her paws against my back. Sometimes she even pushed me out of bed.

What could I do? Royalty demanded royal treatment.

~Sally Kelly-Engeman

# Forever Friends

*The best kind of friend is the one you could sit on a porch with,*
*never saying a word, and walk away feeling completely understood.*
*~Author Unknown*

During a very difficult time in my life, comfort came from an unusual source—a Redbone Hound. Candy, my Pomeranian, was one of the most special pets I had ever had. She was smart, playful, friendly, and cuddly. Her favorite "activity" was curling up on my lap. However, if I said, "Let's go to town," she would beat me to the car. She could hardly contain her excitement when I pulled into the drive-in restaurant. She loved chewing on the ice from my soft drink. When I suggested going to the neighbor's house, she would run in circles. That meant she would get to see her best friend, Stormy.

Stormy, the Redbone Hound, returned her friendship. Although he looked like a giant next to her, his gentleness when they played together amazed everyone. We lived in the country with lots of room to roam, but Candy preferred to stay inside. She ventured outside alone only in times of necessity. Stormy would often watch for her, and they would spend some time running through the yard together. After a while, the big hound would flop down, and Candy would curl up as close to him as she could get. At times, Stormy would even come to my house and bark until I would take Candy out to play with him.

I took Candy on a weeklong trip to visit my family. Although she was well-behaved, she never seemed to want to play with anyone or even to enjoy her toys. She stayed curled up on my lap most of the time. When we returned home and pulled into our driveway, she got so excited I could hardly hold her still. As soon as I opened the door, she headed for the neighbor's yard. Stormy came bounding toward her. Their excitement was nearly uncontrollable. They jumped and rolled around together until they both collapsed on the porch. For days they stayed close to each other at every opportunity.

One morning while Candy was outside I heard a loud banging on my door. I couldn't imagine what was happening. When I opened the door, there was Stormy. He nearly knocked me over as he suddenly jumped up, put his paws on my shoulders, and barked.

Just as quickly, he jumped down and ran off the porch, barking furiously. He turned to see if I were following and, when he was sure I was, headed for the dirt road. My heart turned over. I couldn't make myself go in that direction.

I screamed and turned, running to the neighbor's house. Their boys came out, ran to the road, and soon verified my worst fears — my precious Candy had been killed. The boys kindly took care of the situation for me.

Sobbing, I sat down on the foundation of a garage being built. In just a few moments I felt a nudge on my arm as Stormy eased his head onto my lap. I held onto him tightly.

Every few minutes he would raise his head and lick my arm or cheek. My pal and I sat there for hours. Stormy refused to move, even to eat. Frequently, he would sigh deeply or make a low whine. His hurt seemed as deep as mine.

For a long time afterwards, Stormy would be waiting for me when I got home from work and would walk to the house with me. We often just sat quietly together on the porch. Good friends can communicate without talking.

~Joyce Anne Munn

# 30

# Figment of My Imagination

*I think the next best thing to solving a problem is finding some humor in it.*
~Frank A. Clark

We were forever reminding our teenage daughter to keep the patio gate closed.

One Friday morning as I was returning from my walk, my husband was waiting in front of our home with a worried look on his face. Figment, our dog, was missing! The gate was left open and Fig was now roaming freely.

My husband had to leave for work and although I also had to work that day I had some time to begin the search. Unfortunately we had never taken the time to order a name tag for Fig... we always took such good care of him... and he was always with us — on or off the leash!

Figment was a Springer Spaniel/Australian Shepherd mix. He was champagne in color with one blue eye and one brown eye. We taught him all the dog tricks that make a dog entertaining, respectful and obedient.

I exhausted my search and finally had to leave for work. My intention was to stop at the animal shelter on the way home, hoping that someone would have found him and taken him there for pickup. We live in a hillside community near a freeway. I prayed all day that he would avoid that direction!

I reached the animal shelter just as they were closing and was taken to the dog kennel—soooo many precious pets with no identification. No way to contact their owner to come and rescue them. As I walked the aisle I approached one of the kennels... there was Fig, I thought! He was soooo excited... they were all excited! I looked closely and saw that this dog had two brown eyes. It couldn't be Fig. Where was the blue eye? I still held out hope so I said "sit"... every dog sat!

I left the kennel depressed and worried. We were facing the weekend and the kennel was only open a few hours on Saturday and closed on Sunday. Where was my dog?

Saturday I had a prior commitment and was unable to get to the shelter, so my husband assured me he would leave work early and stop on his way home. He arrived at the shelter as the woman in charge closed the window and locked the doors. She told him to come back Monday! WOW!

After a very depressing weekend I stopped by the shelter on Monday. There was the same dog... my dog??? Two brown eyes!!!! Again, I said "sit." Again, everyone sat! I said, "speak" and I had a chorus going all at once! I left... leaving behind a dog that had to be thinking, "What more does she want, I did everything she asked!"

I went home and called a friend to go by on Tuesday and check for me. I needed a fresh opinion! My husband assured me that it could not be our dog if he did not have one blue eye and one brown eye. Our dog would soon be on death row!

Our friend did go by on Tuesday but I would not find out what he thought until I got home and could listen to my messages. On my way home from work I picked up our daughter from school and took her directly to the shelter. "I will wait in the car," I told her. "You go in and tell me what you think."

A few minutes later, our daughter came running out of the shelter yelling, "That's our dog!" I said, "What about the eye?" She said, "Forget the eye, that's Fig!"

We paid the fees, brought a very distraught and relieved dog outside into the sunlight... AND HIS EYE TURNED BLUE! Bless the sun!

At home I listened to my messages and there was one from our friend, "Nope, it isn't Fig; he has two brown eyes!"

Lessons learned... Always have an identification tag on your pet. Always keep your gates closed when pets are outside. And, never, never get me mad or I won't recognize you!

~Kristine Byron

"The genius over there calls me 'Spot'."

Reprinted by permission of
Ray Delgado ©2009

# 31

# Dog Sanctuary

*A dog is one of the remaining reasons why some people*
*can be persuaded to go for a walk.*
~O.A. Battista

There is a small, old-fashioned ice cream parlor in the pleasant little town of Urbana, Ohio. Decades of existence give Kerr's Sweet Shop a comfortable, well-worn atmosphere, like the feel of your favorite pair of jeans.

Urbana is such a tiny town that most everyone knows everyone else personally. As a matter of fact, they usually don't just know you, but your father and grandfather and perhaps they even knew your great-grandfather. There was once a young boy who visited this ice cream parlor quite often on his way around town with his Boxer dog, Gar. Gar was short for Gargantua, named after the famous giant because he grew to be such a big dog—"ninety-seven pounds of pure muscle!" the boy proclaimed proudly.

Whenever he visited the ice cream parlor, which was almost daily in the summer, the boy always ordered two ice cream cones—a chocolate one for himself, and a vanilla one for Gar. The boy was a self-proclaimed "chocoholic," and he felt bad that Gar always had to settle for vanilla, but he knew that chocolate is dangerous for dogs. Gar didn't seem to mind; he wagged his stubby tail gleefully when the boy held out the vanilla cone for him to lick as they sat together on the steps outside the ice cream parlor. The boy half-kiddingly said that if they could find a way to harness the energy of that tail to a generator, they would have enough power to light all of Urbana for weeks on end.

One time the boy was sick with the flu and wasn't able to leave the house to go to school, much less the ice cream parlor. After four days, or maybe a full week, when he was well again, the boy took Gar out for their routine walk around town. The dog trotted happily beside him, no leash required, only stopping a few times to sniff at bushes and hydrants and trees. When the pair came into view of Kerr's Sweet Shop, Gar suddenly left the boy's side and dashed across Main Street. Pausing at the far corner, he glanced back, as if imploring his owner to follow. So the boy did—he followed Gar right up through the door into the ice cream parlor.

The boy walked up to the counter, asked for "the usual," and sifted through change in his pocket to pay. But instead of "the usual" ten cents—a nickel for each cone—the man working as ice cream scooper said the boy owed a quarter.

The boy was confused. He ordered only two single-scoop cones: one vanilla, one chocolate, just as he always did—that should be a dime. The man smiled and said, "Well, your dog there's been comin' in the past few afternoons around this time, and he kept barkin' and barkin' and wouldn't stop. We figured since you always get a vanilla cone for 'im, and he likes 'em so well, that we'd just give 'im some ice cream even if you weren't with 'im. So we've sorta been keepin' a tab for 'im here. I hope that's okay."

The boy laughed and assured the man it certainly was. In fact, he told them to keep the tab running if Gar came in again by himself—which the dog occasionally did. Even years later, the boy still got a kick out of telling the story about his crazy dog with its very own charge account at the local ice cream parlor.

———

My grandpa—"Gramps" I affectionately call him—was that young boy and his story about Gar and the ice cream parlor is one of my favorites. Ever since I was a little girl, I have begged him to tell that story over and over again, wishing I had a Boxer dog just like his beloved Gar, a dog I would raise from a puppy and take for walks around town and get ice cream with, a dog who would sleep at the foot of my bed at night and be my best friend.

My dad grew up listening to the same stories, and while he was open to the idea of getting a Boxer, we lived in a small condominium—way too cramped for a big dog that loves to run around and play. Then, during the summer before I went into the third grade, we moved to a bigger house—with a backyard—and suddenly my dream of owning a Boxer seemed wonderfully within reach.

That year, as with previous years, a Boxer puppy was at the top of my birthday wish list. I never really expected to get one, at least when we lived in the condo, but when my first birthday arrived in our new house—I was ten years old—Gramps came over for dinner to celebrate. He gave me the last present himself: a book about caring for your Boxer puppy. I lifted the cover to find a note written inside: "The real thing will be coming in a few weeks." And sure enough, on a sunny spring day a short time later, I played fetch with my new puppy, Gar, for the first time.

Gar soon lived up to his namesake's reputation as quite a goofy character. He doesn't much care for ice cream, but he does love oatmeal cookies—not chocolate chip, though, because Gramps was quick to tell me that chocolate is bad for dogs. And Gar often "works on his tan" while napping on the porch in the afternoon sunshine. Gramps refers to Gar as my "brother" and spoils him like he is indeed another grandchild, and so it is no surprise that Gar absolutely adores his "grandfather."

Another thing Gar adores is going for walks around the neighborhood. If I even whisper the word "walk" he will immediately start jumping around frantically, scratching at the front door in excited anticipation. If I am later than usual in asking, he lets me know he's ready to go by whining at the cupboard drawer where his leash is kept.

Every evening, I take Gar out for a two-mile walk around our neighborhood, and though I tell him I am doing him a favor, the truth is it has become one of my favorite parts of the day, too. It is time all to myself, to escape from the hectic routines of the day and take a few minutes to think and reflect upon my life and my dreams. Gar and I walk on a path that runs alongside an orange grove, with a view of rows upon rows of green trees stretching towards the distant hills and shimmering Pacific Ocean. My favorite time of the day to take a walk is just before dusk, when the sun is beginning to set and the California sky is filled with warm, soothing pinks and reds and golds.

Some teenagers' special place is their room or a specific hide-out, but my sanctuary moves—it is anywhere beside my dog. Walks with Gar keep me grounded and sane and content, able to enjoy the quiet moments of life that make it so miraculous: a tiny yellow flower blooming through a crack in the sidewalk; the innocent, glee-ful laughter of children playing in the neighborhood cul-de-sac; the slobbery wet kiss of a dog as he looks at you with unconditional love and devotion. Especially when I am worried or stressed or sad, walk-ing along beside—or rather, being pulled along behind—my wacky, exuberant, eighty-six "pounds of pure muscle" somehow always makes me feel better. It is a place for me to reflect upon my many blessings and be thankful for all I have.

Sometimes it is easy to get sucked in by the nerve-wracking, unimportant minutiae of life while forgetting about what's really important: the love of family and friends, the freedom to be yourself, the quiet tranquility of evening walks with the best birthday pres-ent ever—and, yes, the occasional chocolate and vanilla ice cream cones.

~Dallas Woodburn

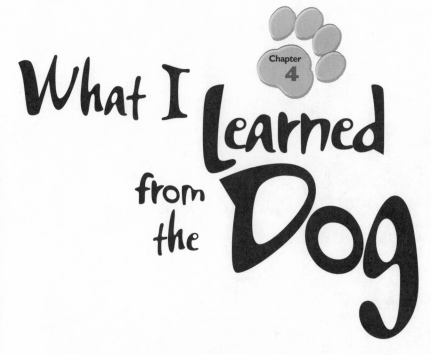

# What I Learned from the Dog

**Chapter 4**

## Learning to Overcome Adversity

*Adversity is like a strong wind. It tears away from us all but the things that cannot be torn, so that we see ourselves as we really are.*

*~Arthur Golden*

# Cold Goldie

*What we see depends mainly*
*on what we look for.*
*~John Lubbock*

It was a bitterly cold morning.

When I left the house, I had to think where I had parked the car. The usually empty parking spots in front of the house were taken when I came home the night before, so I parked on a side street half a block away. I tucked my chin low inside the collar of my coat, ineffectively trying to cover what I could of my face against the cheek-numbing air and walked to the car.

Mercifully, the car started.

As was my habit, I let it warm while I tied my tie, which I had draped around my neck under my coat. Then I just sat, listening to the radio, watching two thawed spots appear on the driver and passenger sides of the windshield. Slowly they grew, as heater and defroster overcame the biting cold.

At first the spots were small, and I could see little outside. Out of the small thawed spot in front of me, a bit of the world appeared — the top of the car in front of me, the second story of the apartment building at the end of the block, and a poster on the telephone pole next to the apartment building.

The hand-lettered poster had been there for more than a month. I had stopped to read it weeks ago.

Lost Golden Retriever
We miss him greatly
Reward. Call...

We lived in a busy part of the city with much traffic. Lost dogs and cats seldom fared well here.

As the windshield cleared, more of the outside world became visible. I noticed that at the base of the telephone pole where the sign was posted lay a Golden Retriever.

I squinted and looked harder. "Naaaa... give me a break, no way," I said out loud to myself.

The dog just lay there, curled up tightly against the cold.

The internal debate began.

"You have to go check out the dog," said my better half.

"What? Are you crazy? It is below zero. The sign has been there a month. No way could a dog last in this neighborhood, living outdoors for a month," said my colder and lesser half.

"But you have to check."

"But staying warm would be so much better."

"Go on, go check it out."

"Let's get to work. Remember, you were going in early to get some extra things done."

That was the clincher. Who wants to rush to work?

So I got out of the car and walked towards the dog. As I crossed the street, the dog raised its head and watched me warily. As I got within fifteen feet, it stood up and began to move away. I stopped, squatted and held out my hand, calling to the dog.

"Here boy, come on, here boy, here boy. It's okay...."

I stood up and took several steps towards the dog, holding out my hand, but it kept its distance. So I squatted again and called it, reaching my hand out as I did.

I kept calling, moving towards him, and he would back away, never letting me get within ten feet. The cold began to penetrate even my heavy coat and I imagined the conversation the police would have as they pondered my squatting, hand extended, frozen body.

The dog, having more common sense than I, would have been long gone to someplace warm.

The dog had no distinct markings—just a typical, overall golden color. Judging from the near gray on his muzzle, he was an older dog. He did have a collar, and a red rabies tag, but I could not get close enough to see the engraved numbers on it. It looked like there was a shred of blue cloth hanging from the hook that attached the tag to the collar. I wondered if he had once had a bandana around his neck, and had caught it on something, ripping it off in the process.

So I rose, and returned to the car, grabbing the sign from the pole on the way. Fortunately, the car was wonderfully warm at this point.

I decided to call the number on the sign later that morning. "Did you lose a dog a month ago," I asked the woman who answered.

"Why yes, we did. It was six weeks ago when we were visiting friends in the city," she said. "Why do you ask?"

I told her my "Golden Retriever under the 'Lost Golden Retriever' sign" story. She sounded dubious, especially given the length of time that her dog had been gone. I told her what little there was to tell about the dog—the collar, the red rabies tag, and the shred of blue cloth.

"Oh my God!" she said. "Our dog was wearing a blue bandana around its neck when we lost him." She said she would drive down and look in the neighborhood.

She called back later that afternoon, and indeed, had found her dog, thinner, but in amazingly good shape for living six weeks outside.

I have often wondered how they taught that dog to read.

~Daniel James

# The Beast

*When the world says, "Give up,"*
*Hope whispers, "Try it one more time."*
*~Author Unknown*

A morning rarely dawned so perfect.

I inhaled the brisk air and felt my heart sprint into an enthusiastic rhythm. Though cool, the Colorado sun warmed my back as it rose over the horse farm not far from my house. The slightest breeze danced on my skin. Just enough to keep a runner from overheating, I mused. My ever-faithful jogging partner, a sleek black Labrador named Nika, pranced and pulled, mirroring my eagerness to start our run and embrace the day.

Paws and peds covered the first several blocks with tangible enthusiasm. We raced forward with determination, like Superwoman and Wonder Dog, ready to leap tall buildings and race speeding trains. Convinced of our invincibility, we pushed harder, ran faster, demonstrating our skill and impressing passing motorists and gawking neighbors with our unmatched prowess.

Until we hit "The Beast," my less-than-affectionate name for a massive, nearly two-mile long steep climb.

It's funny how soon I forget the burning pain in my legs and vice-like grip on my chest between running days. Only a few paces into the Beast's incline and it all came back with sudden clarity. I gasped for air, my vision narrowing to tiny pinpoints of light. Far short of superhero status, my enthusiasm and springy steps evaporated, abandoned somewhere at the base of the hill along with my bruised ego. A vision of the newspaper and cup of coffee waiting on my kitchen counter appeared as a glorious beacon, tempting me to relinquish cape and tights and turn back toward home.

With a glance I noticed Wonder Dog wasn't doing any better. Her thick, pink tongue had grown five or six inches. It hung limp out the side of her mouth, leaving a wet trail of drool for the paramedics to follow. She continued to faithfully follow me, putting one paw in front of the other, but without her former eagerness and conviction.

Her weariness touched me. And in that moment, I felt a sudden—though small—spark of renewed determination to press on. I couldn't allow this seemingly insurmountable mountain to get the better of us. In an attempt to boost both our spirits, I managed to squeak out a quick accolade: "Good girl, Nika! Keep going... you can do it!"

I didn't think about what I was saying. It was automatic... a human-to-canine pep talk as we struggled to scale an impossible peak. Of course, I was talking to a dog. She didn't have a clue as to what I was saying, Wonder Dog or not. Still, at the sound of my voice and the warmth of my optimism, her ears perked and shoulders pulled back. Sluggish paws picked up their pace and the wagging tongue found its way back into her mouth. In a fraction of a second, she glanced my way and almost smiled.

"I'm cheerleading a dog, for heaven's sakes!" I needed to pull myself together. Still, I couldn't ignore the profundity of the moment. With a few simple words, I changed our course. One moment we were on the verge of quitting. The next, our feet picked up the pace and we pressed on. Though weary and discouraged myself, with a few kind words I impacted a dog's ability to go further. I'm sure I could've accomplished the opposite with ill-chosen comments and a harsh tone. Instead, the Beast was brought down and Superwoman and Wonder Dog flew like heroes the rest of the way home.

Life is full of beasts to conquer. For some, it is the seemingly impossible climb of cancer and chemo. For others, their beast takes the shape of parenting a toddler. Or teenager. Uphill climbs come in all shapes and sizes, common only in their ability to defeat, discourage and tempt tired travelers to quit. Sometimes all that's needed is a few aptly spoken, well-timed words of encouragement from a fellow runner. Someone who sees the struggle, dares to jog alongside, and cares enough to say: "Keep going! You can do it! You're not alone—I believe in you!"

Nothing brings down a beast like a little dose of hope.

~Michele Cushatt

# Beyond the Fear

*To conquer fear is the beginning of wisdom.*
*~Bertrand Russell*

"A guide dog could be your eyes," a well-intentioned friend said to me. Was he joking? Over several years, family and friends watched while a retina disease robbed me of my sight. My blindness added to the problem of not wanting a dog near me. "Dogs scare me," I told my friend. Sudden movements startled me. My hands turned to ice if a dog ran over to greet me.

Having control brought a sense of comfort to my world. Four-legged creatures seemed too unpredictable. They moved quickly and I couldn't see them coming. If I heard the jingle of collar tags, I curled my hands into tight fists. Panting sounds which moved closer and closer triggered an inner alarm. A visit to the dentist seemed more desirable than a dog's lick.

The anxiety was bad enough, but dealing with neighbors who had pets brought more stress. "My dog won't hurt you," they'd say, but it didn't calm me. Americans love to love their dogs. People treat their canines like family members. Their attitude puzzled me. Secretly I wished friends would put their dogs in a room far away from me. Fortunately, few of my friends and family had dogs.

But I did feel like prey walking in my neighborhood with my white cane. Terror melted my self-esteem. Taking a daily walk wasn't fun anymore. As my world shrank, I sought a solution. Staying active ranked high on my list. So that suggestion from my friend seeped into my soul. If getting a dog worked, great. The bonus might be more independence and that would be priceless. If I found that having a guide dog wasn't for me, I could close this chapter forever. I applied to the guide dog school.

One day, a letter in our bundle of mail caught my husband's eye. Nervous with anticipation, Don fumbled with his glasses. He read the letter addressed to me, "You are accepted at the Seeing Eye Guide Dog School." Now, my denial lost its luster. Until this moment, the application process was merely filling and sending out forms. I grimaced and asked, "When does class begin?" February seemed a long way off, but time snuck up on me.

When we arrived at the school, I put my hand on the doorknob and I muttered to myself, "Here I am at Dog Camp USA." Don and I were greeted by several staff members. One of them was the dog trainer. He would coach five other students and me and select a dog for each of us. My hearing is good, but I was so distracted that I couldn't remember his name. "Call me Mr. O," he said. Then, Don gave me a hug before leaving. Tears pricked at the back of my eyes. The door slammed behind Don. I listened while his footsteps faded down the hall. Our home was hours away, so I wouldn't see him any time soon. Being a quitter never appealed to me, yet I felt stuck, like a person who hates spiders being told to bond with one. Surely, being a student for twenty-seven days would seal my fate.

Sitting across the table from Mr. O, I blurted out, "I'm afraid of dogs." He was silent for a moment, but then found a way to work with my problem. "You don't have to bond with every dog you meet, just one," he advised. Going back to my room, the phrase he used stuck in my brain. "One dog at a time," played over and over like a favorite line in a song and calmed me a little.

Day two of the training, I met my "spider." The trainer called me from my room. I joined him at a student lounge where he pushed a leather leash into my hand. "Meet Misty. She's a fifty-pound female German Shepherd." My weak knees betrayed my smile. Her large size probably guaranteed that she had large teeth to match. "Don't you want to look her over?" All I knew was that I didn't want to touch her mouth. Misty panted and sniffed me, so she surely picked up on my fear. Then, Mr. O suggested, "Go back to your room and get to know her."

As she hauled me, my feet seemed to slide over the floor. She found my room easily. How did Misty know where I was staying? But still, I wasn't impressed enough. Shivers ran up my arms and the expression "cold feet" had more meaning. I forced my fingers to trace her head. Her rubbery nose and rough tongue were odd sensations for my fingertips. Misty had a tapered snout and ears that stood up. "Is she a wolf or a dog?" Misty, eager for attention, nuzzled me as I collapsed on the edge of the bed. "Please sit over there," I said, waving her away. She padded to her rug. Finally, I heard her paw the rug and settle down. Meanwhile, I had a chance to breathe, but not for long.

"Oh no, here she comes again." Misty's determination surpassed mine. Once again, the sound of her clinking tags moved toward me and she licked me like I was a piece of meat. Her plea for attention kept up for hours, so I held her leash. That way, there were no surprises and I always knew where she was. Misty acted like a determined lover and I was on my first date.

I shared a room with another blind woman, who played on the floor with her dog. She said, "Come touch him. He's so soft." "Maybe later," I said, thinking, "probably not." Misty started to pull me toward the door. She sensed Mr. O's arrival even before he knocked on our door. My dog's wagging tail slapped my legs. Her erect ears brushed my hand. These were signs of happiness, I knew. Learning to read Misty's behavior was one of many firsts. Opening the door, I said, "She's devoted to you." He chuckled, "She will be as loyal to you, if you let her. Right now, come to a lecture on grooming your dog." This instruction would be one of many — planting the seeds of responsible dog ownership.

The first night Misty slept in my room, I had a small victory but not the way I'd hoped. The instructions were to put her on a short chain near the head of my bed. I was so exhausted that I stretched out on the bed, fully dressed. Rolling over on my left side, I felt Misty's warm breath on my face. She must have looked like a sentry, standing guard over me. To escape my discomfort, I rolled to the other side of the bed. Now, my roommate's pup stood and breathed on me. "Lie down," I said to any dog who might obey. Covering my head with a pillow, I made a barricade. My blindness kept me from seeing those sharp, pointed teeth.

The next morning, Mr. O called my name. As I stepped out of the van, I just wanted this ordeal to be over. "Carol, good luck." I heard each student shout from the van as I waited for Mr. O's instructions. Irritation crept into my voice. "Luck?" I snapped. "I need courage." It was my turn to take that first walk. Could I remember what we learned at the lectures? Usually, my nimble fingers never failed me, but today they were clumsy. "Check the leash and harness," I heard Mr. O say. To my relief, all the buckles and snaps were fastened correctly.

I took a deep breath, squared my shoulders, and gave the command, "forward." The energy in my voice surprised me, but not as much as the power of Misty's pull. We lurched forward. Dropping the handle, I let out a big breath before beginning again. We moved ahead with more poise, and then fell into step like dancers. Her paws and my sneakers patted on the concrete. Misty led, setting a rhythmic pace. The movement of her body pulsed down the harness. I gripped the leather bar, hoping to read more of this language between us. Shocked at this new communication with her, I couldn't ignore the chink in my fear. Little did I know that Misty was learning to read me, too. Mr. O, following a couple of paces behind, said, "That's good." A spontaneous smile lit up my face. Yet, learning to trust Misty's pull would still take some time.

Sun streamed on my face. I pictured us bathed in a new light; maybe Misty felt it, too. I smiled when I realized that I, who was so skeptical, was thinking about the dog's feelings. The wind tossed my hair as our walk became more brisk. The feeling of independence boosted my confidence and reinforced my determination to go on. "One dog at a time" turned into "one day at a time."

Then, as weeks became months, I tallied all we had done together. Going to the corner store seemed easy with Misty by my side. Crossing busy streets to meet friends at a local restaurant became routine. Since I wasn't alone, I didn't feel vulnerable. I learned from my new best friend, Misty, that with her by my side, I had the courage to walk on — through the fear. Misty's loyalty allowed me to find a trust like I had never known.

~Carol Fleischman

# Canine Angel

*Angels have no philosophy but love.*
~Adeline Cullen Ray

I called and whistled for Kishka until the neighbors glared me into apologetic silence. They were understandably weary of hearing my desperate voice disrupt the peace of another lazy summer's afternoon. Yet I had to try. My seven-year-old Malamute-mix had been missing for several days. She'd never before strayed far from home. I feared something terrible had happened to her. Kishka was far too intelligent to leave voluntarily. Why should she? At my house a dog's life meant an existence that hovered between splendid and spoiled beyond belief. So I scoured the neighborhood again for my lost pet.

The photo I carried showed her Malamute heritage plainly. The mix part however, had always been a mystery, even at the shelter where I adopted her six years earlier. Damp Missouri heat wilted me as I walked from house to house. I'd hold up Kishka's picture and hear the same response.

"Sorry. I haven't seen your dog."

Lack of success didn't stop me from asking. At first people clucked in sympathy. Soon they shifted to tolerance and then closer toward exasperation.

I decided it would be wise to expand my search. The newspaper contained a few lost and found ads that revealed nothing more significant than the ill-timed discovery of someone's empty leather wallet.

Next I drove to animal control. Inside were rows of cold steel cages crowded full of furry faces. Each one had hopeful eyes that made me swallow hard. It seemed every shade, shape, and size was represented except the one I sought... thirty-five pounds of gray and black fur that framed a tan mask, with a bushy tail curled over like a question mark. My search had dead-ended again.

I didn't want to believe that anything dire could have happened to Kishka, so I revamped my attitude. With no facts to the contrary, I reasoned someone must have taken advantage of her merry, unsuspicious nature and claimed her for their own. I could almost see her playing fetch with happy children, eating a beefy meal, and drowsing on a fluffy pillow.

However, even my overactive imagination couldn't convince me to put away the food and water dishes just yet. It would make her absence seem too permanent. I wasn't ready for that. I sat down to ponder my next move when a sharp jangle from the phone jolted me. I hurried over to pick up the call before my already tattered nerves could fray even more. On the other end of the line, I heard my mother's voice ask a strange question.

"Is Kishka at home?"

"No." I blinked away the sting of truth. "I haven't seen her in days. Why?"

"Well, there's a dog at my house that looks a lot like her."

Could it be possible? But good sense quickly ruled out hope. Mom lived more than six miles away. True, I'd taken Kishka to her house before, but never in any other way than by car and via a convoluted combination of highway and side streets.

"I don't think so, Mom. It must be a stray."

"This dog's skinny. And really dirty. But she's friendly. Just like Kishka."

Her voice sounded decidedly less certain.

"Lots of dogs are friendly. Especially when they're hungry. I'll bring over some food and see what we can do for the poor thing."

I lugged Kishka's bag of kibble out to my car and lifted it inside. The dog deserved one good meal before I took her to animal control.

Then I remembered the rows of steel cages and shuddered. Or maybe I'd bring her home with me instead. It couldn't be very hard to find a family for a nice dog. That idea sounded much better. I relaxed into the seat and began to make a mental list of possible candidates.

Mom's name went right to the top. She'd been through a rough and lonely time since Dad passed away unexpectedly the previous year. She kept to herself more than I liked and didn't show much interest in things she used to enjoy. A loyal canine friend could be the perfect medicine for her. Then I wondered why I hadn't thought of suggesting a pet long before now.

A few minutes later, I arrived at Mom's house. I saw her in the front yard feeding something that looked like ham to a thin dog that nibbled politely from her hand. Its fur was brown, spiked with dry mud. Both Mom and the dog noticed my car at the same time. She raised her hand to me while the dog pranced around the lawn, bushy tail waving like a victory flag. My jaw dropped. It was Kishka.

I jumped from the car. Kishka ran over and greeted me as she always did... with great slobbery kisses. I hugged her and smoothed a hand over her coat. A few particles of clotted dirt fell to the ground and familiar gray fur peeked through. Wide-eyed, I looked up at Mom.

"I can't believe it. How in the world did she get here?"

Mom offered a theory.

"Could she have followed some kids?"

"I don't know any reason kids would cross roads and zigzag through millions of subdivisions straight from my house to yours. There has to be another explanation."

Mom shrugged and directed her attention back to the dog. She handed over another piece of ham and laughed out loud.

"Kishka, you're really something, traveling all this way to see me. You can come back and visit anytime you want."

Kishka's tail swept back and forth even faster.

Then it struck me. Mom's surprise guest had lifted her spirits far more than anyone else had been able to do. I hadn't seen such genuine delight on her face since before Dad died. A plan began to form. Without another thought, words tumbled from my mouth.

"I'm going to take this gypsy home for a bath and dinner. Then we'll both be back. I've got an idea to discuss with you."

I drove home with Kishka pressed close against my side. I looked at her and couldn't suppress a grin of my own.

"Good girl, Kishka. How did you know what Mom needed? And how did you ever find your way to see her?"

Kishka's ears perked up as I spoke. She yawned and a pink tongue lolled out. Her mouth seemed to curve unmistakably into a mystical dog smile.

There are some things we'll never know. Dogs have a close connection to people. Could Kishka somehow have sensed Mom's plight and set off to help her? Or did some heavenly intervention take place that day? It's a mystery we've never solved. Strangely, Kishka never wandered away from home again. I suppose she didn't see the need, for I took her on regular trips to see Mom until the day she got a dog of her own... a Cocker Spaniel pup that kept her happily occupied and helped reopen the door to her heart.

And although we never figured out the secret of Kishka's pilgrimage, there was one thing I finally realized. The mysterious mix in my little Malamute could be only one thing. Pure canine angel.

~Pat Wahler

# Cold Crime

*The greatest crimes are caused by surfeit, not by want.*

*~Aristotle*

For months we put up with our dog's raids upon the refrigerator. With no one at home during the day, Tubbs would help himself to whatever he fancied: hot dogs, sticks of butter, lamb chops. He managed to wedge his nose between the refrigerator door and the rubber gasket. After prying it open and looting the shelves, he left the door ajar, a telltale sign.

Not that we needed any clues. All we had to do was follow the trail of greasy wrappers and Styrofoam containers. They usually led to Tubbs, hiding under the kitchen table, a guilty look on his face—or was it indigestion?

A shelter puppy, he was of dubious ancestry. They claimed he was part Husky, part Lab. I believe he was a descendent of The Great Houdini's dog, except instead of getting out of tight situations, he gets into them.

The local handyman who came to fix the refrigerator door scratched his head upon hearing my story. "One of my customers had a cat who turned on the TV," he said. "He'd lie on top to keep warm." Nonetheless, he'd never heard of a dog breaking into a refrigerator.

After examining the door, he said we had structural damage from Tubbs's repeated attacks. And as the model was fourteen years old, he advised me to junk it. "The new models have heavier doors," he said. "He'll never get in."

Thus my husband and I found ourselves in a gigantic appliance center with aisles of gleaming refrigerators in designer colors. Some were so big they had walk-in freezers. One had a TV screen built into the door. When the salesman asked what we had in mind, I said we wanted a refrigerator door so heavy it required two hands to open. Then I told him about Tubbs's amazing ability.

"That's a new one to me," he said.

"It's a rare talent," I said, and one we could live without.

After testing dozens of refrigerators, we found an appropriate model. The door was so tight it would discourage an orangutan.

Back home we set about emptying the contents of the old refrigerator. Some items were so ancient, we classified them as UFOs: unidentified frozen objects.

Still, it was a sad moment when the delivery men hauled the old fridge to the curb, putting a gleaming new model in its place. Soon we were ooh-ing and aah-ing over the new appliance. It offered everything: ice on demand, spacious no-defrost freezer and best of all, a door that closed with a thunk.

I'd love to say we lived happily ever after, but I'd be lying. The following morning we left the house, secure in the knowledge that our groceries were safe. Upon arriving home, however, we found chaos. The dog had managed to break into the refrigerator, stealing a pound of thinly-sliced Virginia ham and a half pound of provolone. A mangled and punctured canister of Parmesan cheese lay under the kitchen table. Tubbs had done it again!

There's a saying: "The best solutions are the simplest." Before outfitting the fridge with a combination lock, I got another idea. It happened while my brother and his family were visiting. The day they left, I watched him secure the suitcases atop their station wagon. He used long bungee cords. The proverbial light bulb went off in my head.

Now before we leave the house we have a checklist: coffee pot unplugged, answering machine on, industrial strength bungee cords circling the refrigerator.

It's a small price to pay compared to the spoiled food and ruined meal plans of the past. In the meantime, I'm waiting for Tubbs to discover he can gnaw through the bungee cords. Until then, what's for dinner?

~Sharon Love Cook

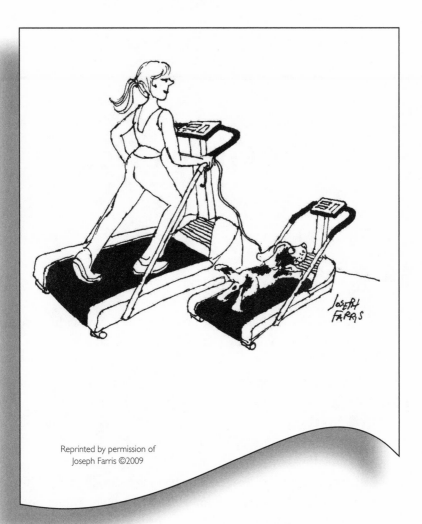

# The Giving Dog

*Movement is a medicine for creating change in a person's physical,
emotional, and mental states.*
~Carol Welch

"Mommy, will you read this book to me?" my little girl
called.

After a glance at the green cover with a tree on
the front, I replied, "Not that book sweetie; ask Daddy to read it."

"Why won't you read this book, Mommy?" she asked.

"I get sad when I read that book, but Daddy will read it to you," I
said turning back toward the washing machine I was loading.

As I emptied pants pockets I couldn't help but think about my
own giving tree — a four-legged companion who played nurse while
I was confined with a chronic illness.

Dropping from 139 pounds down to eighty-eight, every joint in
my body hurt. My frightened family watched helplessly as I became
confined to bed, unable to tolerate light or noise. In an effort to find
a companion to stay with me in the dark, quiet bedroom, my mother
bought a pug-nosed Shih Tzu puppy.

"Hey girl," I would whisper as she was put on my bed each day.

With her big, chocolate eyes Chloe seemed to say "hello" back.
Her slate-colored fur would rub against my cheek and neck as she
found a comfortable spot on a pillow next to my head. She had puppy
energy to burn, but she chose to deny her desires in order to spend
hours on the bed comforting me.

I would empathetically look at the tiny creature next to me. "You need to be outside where you can dig, bark at the birds, and chase squirrels."

Tears would roll down my cheeks occasionally as I realized my ill health was stealing Chloe's enjoyment of life. Months of playing guinea pig to medical tests and prescriptions led to an exasperated, last ditch effort of seeing a nutritionist.

"She's withering away to nothing," my mother cried to the nutritionist.

The nutritionist spoke to me as I barely held my eyes open, "You've got to find a way to exercise."

"How can I exercise when I can't even walk on my own?" I asked breathlessly. "My mother had to double park, help me out of the car, and hold me up to get me in here."

"Maybe you can't walk now, but one day you will. Tomorrow if you can only make it to the front door, just do that. Then in a few days try to go to the end of your porch, then to your mailbox." Her point hit home.

A few days later I looked at Chloe's dutiful form, curled up in small ball barely big enough to fit inside my hand. "Come on girl, I'm going to take you for a walk."

The word walk was foreign to Chloe, so it didn't disappoint her when we never made it outside the house. But with several months of nutritional therapy, and a new resolve to get Chloe outside, we finally made it to the backyard.

"Ah-choo!" I looked down at the delicate puppy. Spring had come in full force and Chloe was so low to the ground that she was covered with pollen. Shih Tzu puppies are adorable when they take their tiny paws and rub their eyes!

"Come on, girl, let's get you back inside." Her flat face was bright yellow and I couldn't help but laugh.

The old adage proved true as laughter became my best medicine. Days of grimacing pain turned into days of joy as Chloe changed the whole atmosphere of the once morbid house.

"Woof!" she barked one day as she discovered her own reflection in the mirror.

"Have you seen my underwear?" my mother would call. The culprit would quickly be found running through the kitchen with underwear wrapped around her head.

"Chloe, come back here with that," would echo from down the hall as Chloe leapt through the house, streaming trails of toilet paper behind her.

Chloe's tiny eight-week-old frame grew, her tail uncurled into a beautifully flowing one, and her curiosity provided all the humor I needed. Soon she was big enough to wear a tiny blue collar and leash as we began to explore the beautiful world outside. Short trips to the mailbox turned into a mile-long trek.

"Look at the big dog," I would say as Chloe would stand erect for ten minutes at a time, mesmerized by an aged horse walking slowly in its pasture.

Now both Chloe and I have grown up since then. My walks with Chloe turned into 5K races with a handsome young man. Getting married and moving down the street from my companion, Chloe, was difficult.

For the first two years, when I would visit Chloe she would turn her back on me and walk away. Chloe didn't understand why the person she cared for the most was no longer there. But Chloe had a new person to take care of—my empty nester mother.

I'm so grateful that I had the season of learning unconditional love from Chloe. I'll never be able to repay her for her years of caring. But I hope I can live a life that is giving and selfless in return.

"Daddy finished reading *The Giving Tree*. Now, will you read me a book?" a small voice called. My thoughts drifted back from the laundry to my little girl.

"Absolutely," I replied. "Let's read a story about dogs."

~Erin Fuentes

# My Chemo Hero

*Better to lose count while naming your blessings
than to lose your blessings when counting your troubles.*
~Maltbie D. Babcock

My friend Terri, who worked as a volunteer at our county animal shelter, told me about the white pup with brindled markings that included a patch around one eye and who reminded her of Petey, the dog that appeared on *The Little Rascals* show. I can still recall the sadness in her voice as she relayed how a policeman had found the eight-week-old puppy, sealed in a cardboard box that had been tossed into a snow bank. The puppy was trapped, alone and shivering in below-freezing temperatures. The box had been abandoned late on a Saturday night in the parking lot of a large mall, one that would not open again until Monday. If that policeman had been less observant, the dog could not have survived those thirty hours. He took the pup to the animal shelter where she was checked over, warmed up, fed, and placed in a cage for the night.

When Terri reported for duty on Sunday morning she immediately fell in love with the tiny pup. Her markings identified her as an American Staffordshire Terrier, a breed that fell under the Pit Bull classification. At the time, shelter regulations prohibited families with no prior shelter relationship from adopting Pit Bulls, because those breeds were under attack by anti-"vicious dog" activists and this was the shelter's way of preventing their adoption by unsavory characters.

"If someone we know doesn't take her, she'll have to be put down," Terri sobbed.

I had heard Terri's refrain about other animals she had tried to place, but this time was the right time. My husband and I had recently purchased our first home, and were anxious to adopt a dog. Terri pulled some strings, we signed affidavits and waivers of liability, agreed to participate in obedience training, and the puppy was ours. The paperwork stated she was an American Staffordshire Terrier and would grow to approximately forty pounds as a medium-sized, adult dog.

That small bundle of love immediately brought joy to our new home and, after several days during which she remained nameless, we eventually settled on the name Bimbo, because she resembled an animated character from Betty Boop cartoons with that same name. Her antics never failed to entertain us, and over the years she grew into a gentle ninety-pound giant. Bimbo was the first dog I'd ever owned, and she turned me into a dog person almost overnight. She taught me all the usual things that dogs teach their owners: unconditional love, go for the gusto, and live each moment to the fullest, but those lessons are not what this story is about.

After more than ten years during which Bimbo continually proved that you can't judge a "Pit Bull" according to the stereotype, our beloved Bimbo was diagnosed with lymphoma, a cancer that attacks the lymphatic system. While still reeling from the shock of her diagnosis, we faced an overwhelming decision—either put her down or try a few rounds of chemotherapy to see if she would go into remission. I researched the potential side effects of the foreign-sounding drugs, and became adept at navigating the world of veterinary oncology as Bimbo's advocate. We opted for chemo and Bimbo was the perfect patient. She enjoyed the weekly car ride to the animal hospital, wagged her tail with enthusiasm as we entered the clinic, and spread her good nature and love to all members of the veterinary staff the entire time we were there. I realized that Bimbo remained fearless and optimistic because she had no preconceived notions about the meaning of the word cancer. She accepted whatever each new day brought to the table. If she felt tired or ill, she rested. If she felt good, she played with her toys and lived that day to its fullest.

Mere months after we learned of Bimbo's illness, I discovered a small lump in my breast that turned out to be an aggressive form of breast cancer. I sat in the office of my new oncologist, listening to him rattle off the names of the chemotherapy drugs I was certain I'd be blasted with in the upcoming months. I became almost giddy, because my drugs were some of the same drugs that were being given to Bimbo. Suddenly I was navigating familiar terrain, because I had witnessed how Bimbo had tolerated the side effects that are so common with these toxic but necessary treatments. And if Bimbo could do it, so would I!

Bimbo and I journeyed through our chemotherapy side by side. By following her example, I learned to rest when I was tired, eat when I was hungry, and take advantage of every energetic moment I was granted. When my compromised immune system caused chills and fever, Bimbo crawled under my blankets to provide additional warmth. And after Bimbo's third remission failed, I was there to comfort her with my love as she rested her head in my lap and took her last breath.

During the remainder of my treatments and recovery, I was inspired to share what I learned from my chemo hero. If chemo is so hard for me, I thought, how do little kids do it? Many young children do not understand the word cancer. When confronted with cancer, children may sense the fears of their siblings, parents, or grandparents. They may feel guilty for causing their families to be upset. I wanted to share Bimbo with those littlest cancer patients, who must fight a huge daily battle with this grown-up disease. I wrote a story called *Dogs Get Cancer Too*, in which Bimbo teaches children to discuss their fears while enabling them to realize that cancer sometimes can have a positive side. It invites children to identify with Bimbo while encouraging them to express their feelings and reassuring them that they are not alone.

I then formed an organization called Bimbo's Buddies so I could communicate her message of hope and courage to all pediatric cancer patients. *Dogs Get Cancer Too* has evolved into an illustrated picture book, and our mission is to provide these kids with free copies of the book and a companion plush toy created in Bimbo's likeness. In this way, Bimbo will live on and continue to be the model she was for my own journey with cancer, by teaching children how to navigate their illness.

I have often wondered whether that dedicated policeman knew what a special pup he found on that snowy night, and how, by saving Bimbo, he played a role in her being able to help so many others.

~Ann M. Sheridan

# It Takes a Village

*We cannot live only for ourselves.*
*A thousand fibers connect us with our fellow men.*
~Herman Melville

When we drove our son to college in Virginia, we left our dog Dillon at a horse farm in Monroe, Connecticut, about fifty miles away from our place in Old Greenwich. She'd stayed at the farm before and it was doggie heaven—no leashes, no crates, just the freedom to roam and play. Her second morning there, however, Dillon pursued some critter into the woods and wound up in unfamiliar surroundings a very long way from home.

"Dogs are very here and now," says Dr. Risë VanFleet a Pennsylvania-based child psychologist with a background in canine behavior. When a dog leaves its home something else has caught its attention. "What led the dog astray is a doggie kind of thing."

The mommy kind of thing, of course, was to try and figure out how to get her back from four hundred miles away.

From a computer center in Front Royal, Virginia, I put together a flyer I could e-mail to the police and animal control officers, as well as family and friends back home. We asked everyone to forward the e-mail, hoping to generate interest beyond our own circle and increase the number of people on the lookout for our lost dog, a variation on the African adage that "It takes a village."

Without realizing it, we'd stumbled on the method most likely to be successful, according to Dr. Linda Lord, a professor at The

Ohio State University College of Veterinary Medicine who studies how people recover lost pets. "Lost dog signs were associated with recovery but they seemed to be more effective seven days or more after the animal went missing," she said.

She was right. It was three days before we had our first sighting and the news was not good. A Shelton veterinarian had seen a Springer Spaniel get hit by two cars on a busy state road and then miraculously leap up and run into the woods.

We were heartened, however, that the calls continued. Dillon, apparently uninjured, was seen by a Shelton firefighter, a tree warden, a grandmother and some teenagers, but no one could get near her, and every call came days too late.

We returned to Connecticut and went straight to Shelton. Armed with a map of the area, we marked each spot where Dillon had been seen. A route seemed to be forming though she was not on a course that would have taken her home. Dr. Nicholas Dodman, a professor of animal behavior and the author of *The Well Adjusted Dog*, explains dogs aren't really like the Collie that crosses Great Britain to find his family in the 1943 movie, *Lassie Come Home*.

"While dogs have extraordinary terrain observation skills and an ability to map in their heads, a dog dropped a long distance from its home is not likely to find its way back."

When the map suggested Dillon was headed south, I drove to Stratford to post flyers and hopefully shorten the lag between when people saw her and learned she was being sought.

The plan worked. My search was about to end with a stunning swiftness. Shopping at a store one half mile from her home, Peggy Gottfried saw the flyer. Dillon had been in her Stratford neighborhood that very morning. In fifteen minutes I was on her street where, across a wide expanse of yard, I saw Dillon.

I'd been warned a lost dog sometimes goes into "survival mode" failing to recognize its owner.

"Try to look at it from the dog's point of view," Dr. VanFleet said. "The dog is still out of its element and still trying to figure out what's what, is the danger over?"

Dillon did not come to me right away so I sat down on the sidewalk and waited. Finally she got curious. She took a few hesitant steps and stopped, a few more and stopped again. Then her expression changed. She started to run with a slow motion, forward momentum that accentuated every flap of the ear and lolling of the tongue. Into my lap she flung herself, a whining, panting, writhing bundle of foul-smelling, burr-encrusted fur. I cried noisily as her ragged claws scratched my legs and her drool dribbled down my neck. Never have I wished so hard that an animal could talk.

While I can only imagine what our pampered house pet must have experienced during her two weeks in the wild, it's no mystery according to Dr. Marc Bekoff, author of *The Emotional Lives of Animals.* "Dogs have a really strong sense of place and what happens to dogs is that they feel lost just like you and I would."

In her analysis of how people find their lost pets, Dr. Lord noted, "Nothing takes the place of having a visual ID tag. A microchip is a good backup system." No doubt she is correct. But in our case, no one could get near our dog, let alone read her collar.

Our challenge was mobilizing an army of eyes by sending out e-mails, posting signs and even plastering Dillon's photo and our phone number on the family minivan. Dillon's remarkable story has taught me that when it comes to happy endings, the tools can be both low and high tech, but ultimately, it takes a village.

~Christine Negroni

# Tale of the Tail

*He has told me a thousand times over that I am his reason for being: by the way he rests against my leg; by the way he thumps his tail at my smallest smile.*
~Gene Hill

I had always believed that, with enough motivation and encouragement, every dog's tail wagged. I thought it came naturally, indicating excitement or happiness. Until I met Romer.

After our fourteen-year-old Shepherd mix, Ebby, died, we decided to adopt two dogs from a rescue society. We spoke with a rescue volunteer over several weeks, but none of the dogs available for adoption seemed right for us.

Then one day, the phone call came without warning. "They have to be removed from their home today. Can you come for them this evening?"

"They" were two adult Boxers. Lacy, six years old, and Romer, four years old, were not brother and sister, although they came from the same home. They had to be moved immediately, but the rescue volunteers had no place to keep them.

We rushed out and purchased new dog food, treats, leashes, and dog beds. We had never adopted adult dogs before. I wondered how the dogs would adjust. Would they try to run away? Would they fight over the beds or would they each lay claim to their own?

Lacy and Romer appeared confused but friendly when we picked them up. It was late evening, and they had been removed from the only home they had ever known, caged in a strange backyard, and then taken by us in an unfamiliar vehicle to yet another strange house. We prepared ourselves for fearful or even aggressive behavior.

We pulled into our garage, and led the dogs into the house. Their beds sat invitingly on the floor in the living room. I grabbed a couple of dog treats with the idea of beckoning them to the large cushions, but it wasn't necessary. They headed straight to their new beds. Each chose a cushion, curled up, and promptly fell sleep.

Lacy immediately made herself at home. Cute and cuddly (for a fifty-pound Boxer!), she was, and still is, every bit the lady. Her greetings were soft and gentle, and when she licked us it felt more like licks from a cat than from a dog. The best part of leaving the house for us is being welcomed home by her. Whether we've been gone a few minutes or several hours, she covers us with her dainty "kisses," her little stump of a tail wagging with the energy of the Energizer Bunny.

Romer was a different story. He had been attacked by another dog on a continual basis in his former home and didn't trust anyone, not humans, and especially not other dogs other than Lacy. Gangly, clumsy, and seventy-five pounds, Romer reminded me of an awkward teenage boy. He was never quite "at home." His entire life had been spent in an abusive environment, and he was not about to let down his guard now.

He would also greet us, but without Lacy's exuberance. In fact, his tail never moved, and I do mean *never*. It appeared to be frozen in place. He broke my heart. I didn't think it possible for a dog to never wag his tail. We wondered if his tail muscle had been paralyzed from a previous injury.

For the first few weeks, we believed it was just a matter of Romer becoming accustomed to his new family and environment. He and Lacy established a routine and he appeared content. Eventually, Romer felt safe enough occasionally to roll onto his back to have his chest and belly scratched. Even then, he did not completely relax. It seemed like he was always doing the doggie equivalent of looking over his shoulder, forever on the alert, as if waiting for something bad to happen. Two months later, he was still on edge and I had run out of ideas.

I've always been impatient and task-oriented, even in my relationships. When I spent time with friends, it was usually for a specific activity. I'm not the type to chat idly over a cup of coffee or lounge on the front porch with a friend. Even so, I knew that the best relationships grow when you invest time in the other person, and Romer was no different. He required patience and time, both of which I had to make an effort to give.

How do you communicate to a dog that he's safe and secure? That no one will attack him anymore? That he is home for good, and we would never let harm come to him again? We sat on the floor with him, playing with him and petting him. We continually reassured him, "It's okay. You can relax. You're safe now." I knew the words meant nothing to him, but I prayed he would sense our hearts.

Lacy and Romer settled into our home and trained us well. We learned which foods were their favorites, which treats they liked best, and what toys they enjoyed the most. We also learned what time they woke up in the morning to be fed and let out, and what time they preferred to eat dinner and go out for their final nighttime walk.

Both dogs were hungry for affection, constantly wanting to be touched or petted. They would sit or lie near us, a part of their body usually brushing up against our legs. At the very least, they had to be in the same room we were. If we left the room for any reason, they followed close behind, almost bumping our heels as we walked.

Lacy continued to greet us with abundant joy, tail continuously wagging, whenever we were apart for more than a few minutes. Romer's greetings consisted of jumping on us and covering us with drenching licks, but still without a hint of tail movement.

I finally accepted the fact that, after the previous four years of combined neglect and abuse, he might never wag his tail again. Still, we continued to pour our love on them both. We showered them with the gift of time and affection, caring for their needs, and giving them the stability of a safe routine. During this interval, I also learned to relax in my human relationships. I began meeting friends for coffee or lunch, with no agenda other than to enjoy a developing friendship by spending time with that person.

Several months after we adopted Romer and Lacy, we walked into the house after having been out for the afternoon. As usual, Lacy ran to greet us, her tail wagging enthusiastically and non-stop.

Romer was right behind her. My eyes welled up, but even through the tears, I could see Romer's wagging tail.

~Ava Pennington

"Are you here, Alfred?"

# Shih Tzu Lifeguards

*My goal in life is to be as good of a person my dog already thinks I am.*
~Author Unknown

Heroic dog stories usually involve big dogs. Everyone has heard about Labs saving swimmers from drowning, or German Shepherds finding people under rubble after earthquakes. This story, however, is about how two tiny dogs saved my life. Chubby and Munchie, who together don't weigh twenty pounds, pulled me from the river and kept me from drowning.

I lived alone in a little yellow house in Gladstone, Oregon, near the Clackamas River eight years ago. My furniture, truck, household utensils, and clothes were mostly gifts up to that point in my life. I didn't own the house or have a cent saved after college and four years of teaching. All my earnings, and about nineteen grand in student loans, went toward alcohol. I dove into the drink at seventeen and slowly drowned out life. I hit rock bottom and almost shot someone. The near death of a fellow human scared me enough to dry out. Now dry, I suddenly had money. I didn't think to buy a new truck, nice clothes, or fancy TV. I bought Munchie, a black and white Shih Tzu puppy who fit in the palm of my hand.

Now Munchie and I lived in the little yellow house in Gladstone near the Clackamas River. Before long she became more than a handful. Shih Tzus demand a lot of attention. I didn't notice this growing up with her namesake, Munchie number one, who split her affection among six family members. I decided Munchie II needed to share her abundant love and so I bred her with my sister's dog, Gizmo. When the puppies were born my sister picked up the biggest one, a virtual copy of Munchie II, and said, "Look at this little chub chub." Chub Chub, a.k.a. Chubby, became a wonderful outlet for Munchie's overflowing energy, and the two girls would spend hours every day playing and wrestling together.

Now it was Munchie, Chubby, and me living in the little yellow house in Gladstone near the Clackamas River. Forgetting how scary drowning was, I soon dove back into the mind numbing cold and floundered again. I stopped fighting the current and sank to its depths. Three years flowed by, and I ended up in the hospital. Another near death, this time mine, made me quit drinking. This only lasted two months until I was pulled under again. Three more years washed by in a blur. I drank my way out of the teaching profession and started a landscaping business. I drank my way out of that business, my house, and everything I owned.

It was now Munchie, Chubby, and me living in a little yellow tent in Gladstone on the Clackamas River. I remember sitting in camp with my friend and the kindred spirit I had met on the river. He was homeless, my age, a drunk, and loved my small dogs, because he used to have a little Lhasa Apso, "Have you ever seen dogs fight and wag their tails at the same time?" I asked. We were watching the dogs wrestle and were laughing at their antics. Munchie will wag her tail even when she's growling at squirrels or strange dogs. She's happy even when she seems mad.

"They don't even know they're homeless," my friend said as he lovingly petted Munchie.

They gladly entertained us and were good at keeping us out of the law's eyes. People didn't think, "There are a couple of vagrants to run out of town," when they saw us playing with merrily romping Shih Tzus in the park.

Even the people who knew we were living on the river didn't want to run us out of town. My friend and I talked to over a hundred people who walked through our camp to go to the fishing hole or play in the river. Everyone loved my dogs. They started conversations. "Are these your dogs?" People would ask and laugh as outgoing Munchie wagged her tail so gleefully it spun like a helicopter.

"Yes they're mine," I replied as antisocial Chubby hid behind me viciously growling, which people also found amusing, because there is nothing vicious about a seven-pound dog. "I lost my house, so they stayed in my van when I worked, but it got towed. I had to quit. I couldn't keep them tied to a tree when I worked," I said.

"How awful," they'd reply and stay to chat a while. I guarantee they wouldn't chat or even look directly at the homeless people in Portland. They saw two guys with clean clothes, a clean camp, and purebred well-loved dogs. Since we seemed temporarily down on our luck, no one called the police to report vagrants in the eleven months we were on the river.

The winter of 2007 was cold, and I drank away the chill. I drank away all motivation to do anything. I didn't want to work. I didn't socialize since people weren't visiting the river in the cold. I drank away the sadness of having no Christmas tree and missing my family during the holidays. I got 190 proof moonshine, drank, went under, and didn't surface until March.

I remember lying bundled up, with Munchie sleeping at my side and Chubby at my feet that cold March morning. I was wondering how I would get some booze that day. "I need money or a job," I thought. Then, "It would be easier to jump in the river," popped into my mind. I immediately pictured Munchie frantically running up and down the trail looking for me. I saw Chubby sitting faithfully by the tent waiting for me. The heart-wrenching thought of abandoning them pulled me fully to consciousness. Now the lives of my dogs were at stake. The near loss of someone else's life and my own near death never before got me to say what I said that day. "God help me," I said.

Three days later I ran into the wife of my old A.A. sponsor whom I hadn't seen in years. I told her my situation. "How can I help?" she asked.

"I need someone to watch my dogs so I can get a job," I said.

"I'll take care of them," she said without hesitation.

I was in a clean and sober Oxford House within the month, because two small Shih Tzus kept me from drowning. I had a job the day after I moved into my new home. Today, ten months later, I have more money than I've ever had in my adult life. I gladly go to church, and I pray unceasingly. I am building my landscaping business again and will own all the equipment, debt-free, before summer starts, because two tiny dogs rescued me from the river.

I learned that little dogs can be lifesavers like their large breed cousins. These diminutive dogs pulled me from the river and back into society. Seven-pound Chub Chub and twelve-pound Munchie kept me from drowning, just like Labs four times their combined size. As I write this, I mourn my camp partner, who died a week ago. I know he would still be alive today if he had his little Lhasa Apso to save him.

~Jeff Mainard

# The Stray

*There is no education like adversity.*
~Disraeli

That Friday I woke up just as our car pulled into our new driveway. Dad called out, "Louis, we're at our new home here in Memphis, Texas!"

"Our house is at the very edge of town," Mom said, "but your school is just several blocks straight down this sidewalk. On Monday your dad and I will drive you there to get you enrolled and you'll walk home after school." At eight and going into the third grade I wasn't too excited.

I'd been in four schools already! Never long enough to make any friends. The frequent moves were necessary because my daddy was a Reserve Lieutenant who was put in charge of one CCC (Civilian Conservation Corps) camp after another during the Great Depression. My parents said we were lucky; Daddy had work when most people didn't. I wished I could feel lucky like they did. But I just felt lonely—always the new kid in class, never having a friend. I begged my folks to let us adopt a dog from an animal shelter but Daddy said we moved too much and some rentals wouldn't allow animals. So I could only dream of having my very own dog to walk me to school, play fetch with, and be my friend. You'd think that after I was bitten by a Bulldog I'd cool a little toward that dream, but the bite just made me want a dog more... for protection now.

The next day—Saturday—I was out in the front yard, while we

were moving in, when I felt eyes watching me. I looked up into the big friendly brown eyes of a huge tan dog with floppy ears that were soft to pet. He had the friendliest wagging tail I'd ever seen. The dog really seemed to like me. Could it be that, because I couldn't adopt a dog, that this dog was adopting me? Daddy saw him and came over. "Nice and clean for a stray," Daddy said, hunkering down on his heels, to look the dog over. "He's an older, intelligent mixed breed and you can play with him. But just remember—don't name him because we can't take him with us." My heart sank at Daddy's words, though I enjoyed playing with the dog all day. But come Sunday and Monday he was gone. I figured he'd "moved on" as Daddy said it was the nature of strays to do.

Monday went like every new kid's first day at a new school until I was on the way home. I was walking on the sidewalk halfway home when a huge Boxer roared out at me from between the yellow house and the blue one. He barked and growled ferociously. Scared to death, I ran! But the Boxer ran faster! Lucky for me a woman came running out of the yellow house and stopped him just in time. She had a hard time dragging him into the house. I couldn't help thinking, "Am I gonna be this scared every day for the whole school year? I can't stand it!"

Dad and Mom tried to calm me down and tell me what to do—but I was so scared I couldn't even hear them. I didn't eat much supper and hardly slept all night.

On Tuesday's walk to school, my heart hammered when I neared the yellow house. Suddenly the stray dog showed up, right in front of me on the sidewalk. I felt better with the stray beside me. But as he and I were right in front of the yellow house, I heard the Boxer start growling and I turned to run home. The stray headed me off. He nudged me to face forward and walk, so I did. Suddenly the Boxer raced out from between the yellow and blue houses, growling and barking, teeth barred. The stray growled back, fur standing in a ridge on his back, and jumped between me and that terror bearing down on us. Again, I wanted to run but the stray gave me the strangest look that seemed to say, "Stay calm and look him right in the eye."

So I did. Strangely that ferocious dog skidded to a halt and stood there blustering hatefully while we walked calmly on down the street toward home.

I thought it was all over but that wise old stray didn't. The third time that Boxer roared out at us, instead of our walking off, the stray stood our ground while the Boxer blustered. I stood with the stray but my heart was pounding. Nonetheless we stood together until the Boxer stopped blustering and walked off between the two houses. The Boxer never bothered me again.

When Dad and I talked about all this he asked me what the stray had taught me. I said, "When you're so scared that you've just got to run, don't! Dad, that's what the Boxer wanted me to do because it was fun for him and he knew he could outrun me. Instead, walk like you're not afraid. When you get close, stay calm and look what you're afraid of in the eye. Then stand your ground until you're not scared anymore."

Dad responded, "Son, that stray is way too valuable to leave behind. You've just got yourself a dog of your very own!"

~Louis A. Hill, Jr.

"Are you MY pet, or am I YOURS?"

# Dare to Move On

*A dog is the only thing that can mend a crack in your broken heart.*
~Judy Desmond

Many of us have thought about the horror of dying in a Nazi concentration camp, but what about the challenge involved in resuming life beyond the experience? How did it feel to survive this horror when family members, friends, and neighbors did not? Did the memory of torture, starvation, deprivation, and death ever fade to the background of their lives?

Those questions ran through my mind after a new neighbor moved into the house next door to me. I lived in a close-knit community of loving and caring people in a quiet neighborhood in Indiana. Although no one knew much about Mr. C, we did know that he was an Auschwitz survivor.

I used to sit on my front stoop and watch as he pulled into his driveway after work each evening. He would bolt for his front door with eyes trained on the ground and shoulders curled forward as if to make himself less visible. Even as a child, I recognized the fear in his body language. I wanted so much to reach out to him in kindness but had no idea how to do it.

Mr. C was temporarily forgotten after my parents presented me with a Golden Retriever puppy for my eighth birthday. I have never loved anything so instantly and so completely in my life. Molly was smart and playful and very mischievous but her antics filled me with delight.

As the free days of summer were drawing to their sad and inevitable end, I was tossing a tennis ball with Molly in the front yard. When Mr. C pulled into his drive, she abandoned our game and bolted toward him — ignoring my calls for her to return to our yard. She was sitting in front of him as he climbed out of his car, with her pink tongue dangling and her eyes bright with friendly curiosity. He dropped his lunch pail and pressed himself against his car. I looked at Molly but couldn't see anything scary about the little blond bundle of fur. As a matter of fact, I could have sworn she was smiling.

I apologized for my free-spirited puppy, assured him that she'd never hurt him and took the opportunity to introduce myself and welcome him to the neighborhood. Molly had given me the chance I'd been waiting for to say hello. I didn't know it then, but Molly would be the catalyst for the unlikely friendship that would develop between us. She made such a point of greeting him each evening upon his return from work that he always had a dog biscuit in his pocket for her.

One Sunday I looked out the window in horror when I saw Mr. C jogging from his mailbox with Molly nipping at his shoestrings. I was just about to rescue him when I saw him laugh, scoop her into his arms and plant a kiss on the baby-fine hair on her forehead. It was the first time I'd ever seen him laugh. There's nothing like a puppy to make the world seem a little brighter.

Mr. C and I ended up sitting on his front porch with a glass of tea while we watched Molly play in his yard. It was a routine we would observe every Sunday afternoon for years to come. On one occasion, Molly had been hopping in the grass, trying to catch a small frog and we laughed when we noticed blades of grass clinging to her whiskers.

"My dad says she has a bit of the devil in her," I quipped.

"No," he said solemnly. "I have met him and he is not in one so filled with love."

Molly would sit on the ground at his side with her head resting on his thigh while Mr. C told me stories about his experience at Auschwitz. I could see the blue lines and numbers of the tattoo spread across his forearm as he ran his hand over her fur. He spoke about the living conditions, the inhumane treatment, and the friends he had lost. This masterful storyteller reminisced about the heroes who had emerged and the great acts of courage he had witnessed. Those stories soon gave way to tales of his life in Germany—funny stories about his family and his experiences growing up. He told me how he met his wife, the love of his life, and how he convinced her to marry him despite her parents' disapproval. Sadly, she had not been one of the survivors. How, I asked him, had he able to move beyond those terrible times when so many had not?

"I welcome each and every day," he said in broken English. "I remember to greet the sun and give thanks for my food and I tell you stories about my loved ones so that they know I have not forgotten."

Mr. C joined my parents and me for dinner on many occasions. When we went on vacation, he kept Molly for us. When Molly had puppies, we offered him the pick of the litter. He chose the smallest male and named him Frank Sinatra.

Many years later I got a call from my parents at college warning that Molly was sick and not expected to survive. I made it home in time to say goodbye to my beloved childhood pet. Mr. C and Frank were there to say farewell, as well.

"She saved me, you know," he said with tears in his eyes. "She saved me."

Mr. C. lived well into old age with Frank Sinatra by his side. If you had asked him how he made his way back from the darkness of a concentration camp, he would have told you a lively tale about a blond puppy named Molly who led him back into the sunshine.

~Vicki Kitchner

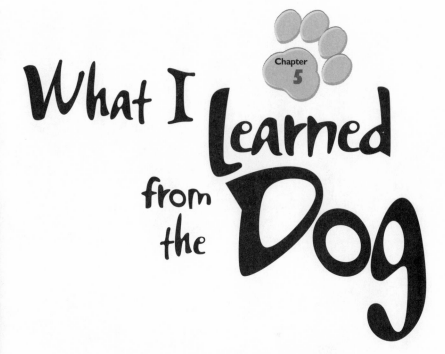

# What I Learned from the Dog

Chapter 5

## Learning to Heal

*Oh, my friend, it's not what they take away from you that counts.*
*It's what you do with what you have left.*

*~Hubert Humphrey*

# Heaven Sent

*There is no psychiatrist in the world like a puppy licking your face.*
~Ben Williams

When my friend Louise showed up at my door, her hands firmly planted on her ample hips, she let me know in no uncertain terms that my hermit days were over, at least for a weekend.

In a tone that left no room for objection, she said she would be picking me up next Saturday morning, nine o'clock sharp, and informed me I would be joining her in house-sitting for her boss, making it quite clear that she'd take care of the house and the dog, a Dalmatian named Lucy. All I would be required to do was accompany her and swim, relax, and enjoy the beautiful scenery as I saw fit.

I wanted to refuse Louise's generous offer, desperately. I felt safe in my seclusion, and didn't want to put myself at risk yet. I still felt too fragile after what I'd been through the past eighteen months. My husband had left me and my two elementary school-aged daughters to fend for ourselves, and I had been raped which left me pregnant. The resulting baby had to be given up for adoption because of my poverty. My grief seemed to have no end.

Yet the following Saturday morning, there was Louise, true to her word, ready to pick me up and take me away. We drove northward through the city until we were finally winding among trees, creeks, and curvy roads. We stopped in front of a rambling ranch house on a graciously landscaped, slightly sloped lot. Walking through the front door, we stepped into a large entryway, down a few stairs, and into a great room. I don't remember much else about the house after that, because we'd reached the backyard, and I was enthralled by the beautiful quiet lagoon that had been created around the swimming pool. Outlined with natural rock formations, fresh, clean water from the hidden filtration system softly cascaded back into the pool. Shrubbery and flowers poked out of the rocks with palms and large ferns behind them. A tall wall in back of the foliage gave the pool privacy, and I easily imagined myself being alone on a deserted island. I wanted to cry; I felt that I didn't deserve to be in such beauty.

Suddenly, I felt a wet, persistent, sponge-like sensation in my hand. Looking to see what it was, I was startled to see a very young Dalmatian peering up at me; her paws were much too big for her to be full grown, and her left eye was framed by one of the many black spots that punctuated her white coat. "This must be Lucy," I thought anxiously, and I stepped back, my reaction sparked by my fear of dogs I didn't know. Laughing at me politely, Louise showed me upstairs where I could put my luggage, and much to my astonishment, Lucy padded close behind. For some reason she was keen on knowing me, but I tried to ignore her. I wasn't interested in expending any energy on cheerfulness.

After Louise prepared an early dinner, we donned our bathing suits and headed for the pool. Lucy stayed at the edge until we got out, and as I lowered my body onto the towel to dry off, she immediately started nuzzling my hair. "What do you want, you silly dog?" I said, petting her. Lucy's wagging tail moved faster and she stooped to her elbows and barked, jumping up as she continued to shake her tail. I realized, to my surprise, that I was enjoying her fun sweet nature.

The rest of the weekend, Lucy would not leave me alone. She ran circles around me, seeming to sense my sadness, determined to make me smile with her silly antics. Finally, late Sunday, I couldn't take it anymore, and as Lucy pushed my hair off my back to nuzzle my neck, I started giggling; first a little hiccup, then gradually building up to a good guffaw. Rolling over, grabbing my belly, I tried to stifle the side-splitting hoorahs. Lucy, apparently delighted at the effect she'd had on me, started barking to my laughter. Sitting up, I pulled Lucy into my arms and just hugged her. Licking my face, she took the embrace as long as I wanted to give it.

It was the first time I'd been happy—truly happy—since my losses. I looked heavenward and thanked God for this beautiful animal and her ability to bring me out of the dark squalor of my sadness.

Twenty years later, I can still picture every one of Lucy's spots, her blue eyes, and the one black ear which was always angled backward. I'm pretty sure Lucy is no longer here with us, but I'm certain that among all the relatives and friends that will greet me someday in Heaven, Lucy will be right there, once more barking along with my laughter.

~Kathleen Lumbert

# Therapy

*We long for an affection that is altogether ignorant of our faults. Heaven has accorded this to us in the form of canine attachment.*

~George Eliot

In the mental hospital where I was confined for bipolar disorder, demons hid reality. There was no more gentleness, no more goodness, no more peacefulness. I lay tethered to a bed by my wrists and ankles to prevent me from harming others or myself. Sleep evaded me. Every naked nerve lay exposed, while the softest of sounds pummeled my brain like a locomotive crashing full speed into a brick building.

I was in seclusion, locked behind cold, impersonal steel doors. It was just me in my little world of horror. I cried. I screamed. I begged for mercy. I prayed for death.

And yet I lived. Day after endless day I existed. I breathed in and out, but joy was far removed from me, a thing of the past, and I lived without the slightest inkling of hope that things could get better. Slowly the psychosis cleared, and I was transferred to a ward with others who were sick in their minds and weary of soul. But I remained in my small, depressed world where little made sense. I lived in a state of chronic mental confusion, delusional and downcast.

Day after day I wandered aimlessly through the patient lounge, seeking solace but finding none until, quite unexpectedly, something caught my eye—something I recognized as Beauty. Two tiny, adorable dogs dressed in bibs which read "Pet Therapy," snuggled in a wicker basket, and patients had begun to gather round. With a force I can only describe as instinct, I arose and went to the little canines. I noticed that a smile had crept across my face. How foreign it felt. I touched the dear little creatures that held out their petite paws in warm welcome to me, and there I remained for several minutes, still smiling in the knowledge that the world, indeed, still held something precious and sweet and innocent. As I smoothed their curly, flocculent fur and received their wet kisses and gazed into their soulful, gentle eyes, I wept. But they were not the tears of the depressed. This time my tears contained droplets of hope. Hope that life existed apart from mental torment, hope that I could smile again, and hope that I could experience joy again.

Two fluffy, miniature dogs were more potent than the drug companies' medications and more powerful than the most frightening delusions. For the first time in my weeks of confinement, my nerves were at rest, and it was then that I began the slow but positive process of healing.

It has been eight years since that mixed bipolar episode and, during the interim, my illness has waxed and waned, par for the course for this illness. But always, when I'm on the brink of despair, I remember the gentleness of two pet therapy dogs that showed me that, no matter how dark things get, there is always an element of hope.

~Marjee K. Berry

# Canine Cupid

*Love makes your soul crawl out from its hiding place.*
*~Zora Neale Hurston*

I was aimlessly punching buttons on the remote, trying to find something on TV that would occupy my mind for a while. The sky outside was as dark as my mood. A thunderstorm rolled in just before dusk. The heavy rain and blowing wind intensified my gloomy disposition, and soon I was engulfed in self-pity.

After three years, you'd think I would have adjusted to being a widower. Though I coped fairly well during the day I had a tough time getting through the nights. My friends and family urged me to get out more, but I didn't seem to know how to socialize without Marie at my side. I was lonely. I was ready. I just didn't know how.

Boredom had taken me to the edge of sleep when the soft rap came at my door. For a moment I thought it was the TV, but when I glanced at the screen there were cowboys riding across the desert. Blinking the sleep from my eyes, I turned and looked at the door. Had I been dreaming? Who would come visiting in this weather? Then the rapping came again, soft, hesitant.

I jumped up and hastened to the door to let whoever was on the other side come in out of the rain. I had no porch so they must be getting soaked. When I pulled the door open I was surprised to see a small, attractive woman peering back at me, her face full of question marks. In the few seconds she had stood at my door, she had gotten a good soaking. In her arms she carried an equally wet small black puppy.

She opened her mouth to speak, but before she could utter a word, I pulled the door open wider. "Come in out of the rain, miss. No need to get any wetter than you already are." I figured she needed directions or was looking for a neighbor and had ended up at the wrong house.

Giving me a grateful nod, she stepped inside, apologizing at the same time for dripping water on my carpet. Even with wet strands of hair in her face, I noticed how pretty she was.

I was about to comment on her puppy, when she thrust him toward me. "I almost hit your puppy. It was raining so hard and he is so small that I almost didn't see him in time to stop. When I slammed on the brakes he ran into your yard, so I thought he must be yours."

She must have noticed an odd expression on my face, because she blushed and blurted out, "He is yours, isn't he?"

I took the puppy from her. "Thank you. This is very kind of you. Not many people would stop in this kind of weather to bring a dog home."

She grinned. "Well, he sort of brought himself home. I just wanted to make sure he was safe." She reached over and scratched behind his ears. "I love dogs. I would have been devastated if I had hit him."

"Look," I said, surprising myself at my boldness. "You must be miserable. Why don't you take your coat off and let me make us some coffee. The least I can do is let you dry out a little before you go."

She hesitated, biting her lower lip and sizing me up. "A cup of coffee would be nice," she said, apparently deciding that I didn't look like a serial killer or a crackpot.

She took the puppy from my arms. "If you'll get me a towel, I'll dry him for you while you make the coffee."

When I carried the coffee into the living room, the pup was curled up in her lap fast asleep. "He sure likes you," I said, grinning at the warm sight. She had pulled her legs beneath her, and in the soft light she looked almost like a little girl.

"Animals know when someone likes them," she said. "He knows he is safe with me."

She was easy to talk to, and her warm laugh seemed to awaken my heavy heart. Her presence made me realize why my house had seemed so empty for so long. It needed the hundreds of little things that a woman does to breathe life into a house and make it a home.

When she stood to leave, my heart leaped inside my chest in a surge of panic. I had to keep her longer. Her voice, her laughter, her mannerisms were a soothing balm to my loneliness and pain. "Let me take you to dinner," I said.

She shook her head. "You don't have to do that."

I stood up and faced her squarely. "I want to," I said.

"Okay," she said, gently sitting the yawning puppy down on the floor. "If you're sure you're not just being kind."

When we walked to the door, the puppy trotted after her, whining. I laughed. "He wants to go home with you."

"I'm sorry," she said, bending over to pet the pup. "I didn't mean to get him so attached to me."

"I don't blame him," I said. I fought down the urge to tell her that I wanted to run after her too.

Ronda and I became a couple soon after that. Whenever she came over to my house, the puppy would run to her eagerly, clearly preferring her to me. On one such occasion, when he rushed over to give her kisses, whimpering with joy at seeing her, I blurted out, "You may as well marry me, Ronda. Cupid is miserable when you aren't around." I took her in my arms. "So am I."

With tears in her eyes, she nodded happily. "You never did tell me why you named him Cupid," she said.

"There's a story behind it," I said. "Someday I'll tell you."

Some day, when the time is right, perhaps on our first anniversary, I'll tell her why my dog is named Cupid. I'll tell her that I had never seen the dog before in my life until she showed up on my doorstep with him in her arms. I called him Cupid because he brought us together.

I figured the three of us were destined to be together because I had tried in vain to find his real owners when she first left him with me. But from the very beginning, Cupid obviously wanted her. I'm glad that they both tolerate me.

~Joe Atwater as told to Elizabeth Atwater

# The Perfect Reflection of God

*Let God's promises shine on your grief.*
~Corrie Ten Boom

"Look at that adoration!" the woman with the enormous cat said about the dog, who was wandering around sniffing at things while trailing his leash. She had been asking me questions while fawning over him. I was standing at the reception desk in the veterinarian's office getting my latest dose of dog-owner encouragement from the vet tech.

"What kind of dog is he?"

"I don't really know—I think part Lhasa Apso."

"How old is he?"

"We're not sure, he was adopted."

"What's his name?"

"Benji. He's my mom's dog. Was..."

I answered distractedly. I was trying to keep everything the vet tech said straight while keeping a poker face over the amount of the check I was writing for the exam, vaccinations, specialty food, and medicine. I had inherited a dog with special needs.

I never knew I wanted a dog. As a single mom, I had three young children already. And now I felt like I had a new baby; he woke me up at night, sometimes more than once. For what, I didn't know.

He wouldn't eat food out of his dish; it had to be on the floor.

And he didn't seem to be able to eliminate unless he was attached to one end of a leash. He was used to going out in the morning, mid-afternoon, and at night. But that didn't work all that well with my telecommuting and childcare schedule. So, I was often impatient with him, frequently muttering, "Tick, tick, tick, dog; I've got a 3:30 conference call!" as he stopped to sniff, root, and "scroot," as my grandmother used to call the doggie-dirt-kicking thing which always sent ground matter flying in a perfect trajectory towards the other end of the leash to which I was attached. Grrrrrrrrrrrrr!

I tried putting him out into the side yard and would sing in a falsetto voice through gritted teeth, "Go potty, doggie! G'wan, go potty!" But apparently he did not go potty on command like my mom's former dog. He would bark and bark and bark at the side door, which was distracting during my conference calls, and no doubt annoying to the neighbors. The kids were too young to a) walk the dog and b) stay alone while I walked him at night, and as a result, I often found a puddle somewhere the next morning.

And, even though I gave him a bath once a week or so, I didn't really like how he smelled. "Stinky little beast," I thought to myself, no doubt scowling, as I cleaned up the aftermath of the bath—wet floors, wet walls, and enough wet towels to trigger just one more load of laundry. I didn't want him on the furniture and I certainly didn't want him in my room. That was the cat's domain. My sons didn't mind him in their room, though, and often fought over whose bed he'd sleep on.

"God help me," I frequently said aloud, and would then add, "Right," because I could hear my mom's voice in my head reminding me, "He will."

One day, I had been brought to my knees yet again to clean up a mess on the kitchen floor. "This is it!" I grumbled loudly. "I just can't take it! Anymore!" I resolved to ask the vet about finding a new home for the dog at our next appointment. Surely he deserved someone who was more enthusiastic about dog ownership.

The vet was understanding and compassionate, telling me she could imagine I'd be overwhelmed. That's an understatement, I scoffed inwardly, and tears threatened to spill over anew as I remembered the time when I had flung myself face down on my bed, sobbing, lamenting that I felt completely alone and resentful that I was in charge of "everything." I could no longer call my mom to ask, "How do you cook leftover lasagna without drying it out?" Or "Can you take so-and-so to soccer practice?" Or "Do these shoes work with this skirt?" Or "Do you want to come over for dinner and 'Family Movie Night?'"

But I couldn't indulge in self-pity for too long; I know I'm not really in charge anyway. That much was perfectly clear when my mom, who was healthy and vibrant just the weekend before she was hospitalized, became sick overnight, slipped into a coma the next day, and passed away less than two days after that. People asked me, "How?" "Why?" "Had she been sick?" "I don't know," "I don't know," and "No," were all I could answer. Doctors couldn't explain it either. Only God knew.

The vet assured me it would be easy to find a new home for the dog. What a relief! But after the comment from the cat-woman, I cried all the way home. I knew I couldn't go through with it. It would break my kids' hearts.

The vet pointed out that there might be some housebreaking "regression," likely because I couldn't indulge the dog the same way my mother could. Might be? But then I imagined how Benji must have felt going from being an "only child" to one of four (five if you count the cat)—and an orphaned one, at that—needing my love and attention. Thus I made up my mind to begin actively loving him: greeting him, petting him, smiling at him, and singing to him, as I did my children (and the cat).

Indeed, having a dog prevented me from hibernating that winter and becoming isolated in my grief over the sudden and unexpected loss of my mother. A friend at church had asked me if I had been away because I looked like I had "some color." I told him, "No, but I am outside with my dog every day for at least half an hour." If I hadn't been out one day in February, I wouldn't have seen the buds growing on a tree that had been felled and left for dead during a December ice storm. As I stood in the cold drizzle, waiting for Benji to finish sniffing a pile of leaves at the base of the tree, I was grateful to have a reason to get out, and grateful for one more reason to go on.

The day Benji and I walked to the town hall to get a new license for him, the town clerk asked me, "What kind of dog is he?"

I knelt down on the floor and rearranged his overgrown puppy cut. "He's mostly Lhasa Apso."

"How old is he?"

"Probably eight to ten, but I'm not sure; he was adopted."

"What's his name?"

"Benji," I said, distractedly, admiring how his long silky tail curled over his back.

"Look at how he can't take his eyes off you! What adoration!"

My dog wanted to love me all along—I was the one who needed to open my heart. I came to understand what my mom meant when she said that a dog is a perfect reflection of God.

~Caroline Poser

# Dog of the Month

*Nature teaches beasts to know their friends.*
*~William Shakespeare*

Frantic barking mingled with the thud-and-jangle of bodies hitting kennel doors, as we walked the aisles of our third animal shelter of the day. My husband Dave studied each dog, taking his time. I withdrew inside myself, sobs just a breath away.

Normally, these eager faces would've moved me, but my heart had turned to stone. Today, I could only think... Brandy is dead. All these dogs, and her sweet face nowhere among them.

Brandy had entered our lives at nine months, and we were her third owners. A small Collie mix with infinite good-natured energy, she'd just been much too much of an exuberant dog for their smaller homes, but we'd loved her on sight.

Just the night before this, as I'd baked Christmas cookies for a Children's Hospital bake sale, Brandy had asked to be let out. It was twenty below zero, and I'd hurried back inside to check my cookies. When she didn't bark right away to come back in, as cold as it was, I went out anyway. I called and called, but saw no sign of her—until we found her lying in the road. She'd jumped the fence and been killed, probably by the snow plow, one of the few vehicles that had passed on our quiet back road.

Grieving, I didn't want another dog, but after a horrible night, Dave knew he needed one. He could hardly wait for the next morning so we could make the rounds of the shelters. I trailed after him, numbed by all the barking, looking for Brandy, and hating every moment.

Finally, Dave stopped. "How about this one?"

I stared at the shaggy, medium-sized brown dog. He kept flinging himself at the mesh and yelping, but I couldn't even hear him over all the others. "This one?" My heart sank. I'd never before seen a dog who actually seemed to be scowling. My Brandy had had such an open, happy grin.

They said they'd just found him tied to the front door one morning, and he'd been there for nine long months. In fact, he'd had the distinction of being "Dog of the Month" and his photo had run in the *Pittsburgh Press*. It was an honor hardly in the same category as Prom Queen, but rather bestowed on the longest, hardest-to-place residents of this no-kill shelter.

"This one," Dave repeated, and minutes later, we left the shelter with Newton. He dropped the tailgate of our station wagon, but unlike Brandy, who normally jumped right in, Newton just stood there, no matter how much Dave coaxed. Finally, he just picked up our new dog and put him in.

I'd expected Newton to be excited to finally get out of the shelter, but he rode along almost dejectedly, head drooping. Much older than Brandy—probably between six and eight, our vet later told us—his eyes already showed some clouding and his muzzle had some white on it. What on earth had we done?

Newton's face wore a perpetual frown—as if he was either irritated or worried all the time. Actually, he was just plain weird looking—something like a little Collie mix, but with the face of an Afghan Hound in a bad mood.

When we got him home, we had to lift him down again. "I'll take him for a walk," I said. After all that time in a city kennel, surely, that would wake him up. All the woods and fields and little critters should smell like heaven to him.

But we didn't get very far. Newton plodded one step at a time, head down, running his nose endlessly over each dry leaf and twig.

In fact, his nose itself was running endlessly. Not only had we brought home a strange-looking, listless old dog, but one with a disgusting nasal drip.

Newton showed no more interest in the inside of the house than he had the outside. He just flopped down with his drippy snout on his paws and sighed. We had a dog again, and Dave was happy, but I wondered if the dog would ever be really ours.

Actually, it took close to a year. Our plodding walks became a daily routine, and when I took him to the barn, he hardly even glanced at the horses. The rest of the time, Newton just lay and stared ahead, wearing the same worried expression he'd had the first day we met him. His nose kept running, too—the vet said it was a kennel infection. He sure wasn't Brandy, but I felt so sorry for him. Often, I just lay next to him and petted him, and told him he was home now.

One day, things changed. Dave was listening to a radio program about a scientist who studied babies' communications. The researcher would play a snippet of a baby's crying and then interpret it: hunger, colic, serious illness. What was most dramatic, though, was Newton's reaction. At the first recorded baby cry, our depressed old dog sat up with a jolt, growled and barked. Suddenly animated, he avidly scoured the house as if looking for the baby. But as soon as the cry stopped, so did Newton, looking confused.

Once, Dave and I got into an argument, and our raised voices had the same electrifying effect. Newton growled and scooted for cover. "It's almost like he's been somewhere there was child abuse," Dave said. "Maybe dog abuse, too. If only he could talk...."

In time, the runny nose stopped running. Newton started lighting up when he saw us and walking with a spring in his step. In fact, he and I got in the habit of long, rambling walks—three, four, even six miles. I'd loved Brandy so much—for her goofy exuberance and sloppy affection—but Newton and I actually spent much more quiet time together, and it bonded us forever.

We'd thought we were bringing home a dog on his last legs, but we had him for fourteen years. If the vets were right about his age when we got him, Newton lived to be somewhere between twenty and twenty-two years old, and when we adopted three children, he became a big brother. In my favorite picture, he is sitting, looking alert, head up and grinning, his eyes focused on my face as his picture was being snapped. When I see it, I realize the infinite potential for love and companionship—and a long, happy life—that there is in even the unlikeliest, unwanted shelter mutt.

~Susan Kimmel Wright

# The Rescuer

*One reason a dog can be such a comfort when you're feeling blue is that he doesn't try to find out why.*
*~Author Unknown*

"I'm afraid you've miscarried," my doctor told me.

Miscarried? Wait a minute, I thought. My husband and I had barely had time to celebrate the fact that we were expecting our first child. Now the baby was gone?

The doctor told me that physically, I should be fine. Dealing with the emotions of losing a baby would be another story. He recommended I take it easy, rest, and give myself time to grieve.

I called my office and told my boss that I would be taking the rest of the week off. The work world would go on without me, I was assured. Condolences were passed on to me, although I was certain no one could possibly understand what I was going through.

Convinced that nothing would make me feel better, I curled up on the couch, armed with the remote control, a bag of chips, and my favorite blanket. My sick days had begun.

My dog, Gus, is what I consider a soulful dog. My husband had found him two years earlier, roaming the streets, dodging traffic and death. When my husband stopped the car to try to rescue the dog, Gus trotted over, jumped in the car, and said, "Let's go home." Since then, Gus had amazed us with his almost human-like expressions and emotions. Another one of our dogs is an incessant trash raider, and when we discover the mess, Gus will shake, tremble, and look at us like, "I'm so sorry. I tried to stop her."

As I wallowed on the couch, Gus started whining and pacing in front of the couch.

"Gus," I said, exasperated. "Please go away. I'm not in the mood to play right now."

Undeterred, Gus brought me his favorite toy from the toy basket.

"I don't want to play, Gus," I groaned. "Go play with someone else."

To my surprise, Gus jumped onto the couch, got as close as possible to me, looked up and sighed. I started sobbing uncontrollably, the emotions of our loss flooding me. I sobbed for the lost baby, for what could have been, for the baby we would never hold.

I heard this low humming noise, which jolted me momentarily from my sobbing jag. It was Gus, crying right along with me. I started laughing and crying at the same time, moved by this little red dog who both annoyed me and entertained me. The little dog whom we rescued was now rescuing me.

I gave Gus a big hug, threw his favorite toy, and got up off the couch. I turned on some music, sang at the top of my lungs, and at that point, I discovered Gus had another talent: he could sing, too.

Three years later, it is no surprise to me that our baby daughter Paige's favorite "person" in the whole world is Gus.

~Kristen Campbell Bush

# The Magic of Colleen

*Dogs are not our whole life, but they make our lives whole.*
~Roger Caras

In 1981, I went to work in a nursing home as a Nurse's Aide. My duties included waking the residents in the morning, bathing and dressing them, and getting them to the dining room in time for breakfast.

My first day on the job, I met Anna. She was a petite, beautiful woman with a sweet disposition and silver-gray hair. As I brushed her hair, she would sit with eyes closed, enjoying the attention I gave her.

There was only one thing that bothered me about Anna. No matter how much I coaxed her, she wouldn't say a word. Upon inquiring about her lack of speech, I was told that Anna hadn't spoken since she'd come to the nursing home. No one seemed to know why — Anna had always been a very social person with lots of friends.

The only time that Anna left her room was for meals. As soon as she had finished eating, one of the staff would push her wheelchair back to her room. She sat all day, gazing out the window, which faced a farm and pasture.

One day I walked into Anna's room. The sight that met my eyes stopped me dead! Anna was standing, clutching the windowsill. A chortle of laughter escaped her lips. I craned my neck to see what she was looking at. She was watching a Border Collie round up the cows and head them back toward the barn. Silently, I backed out of the room and went directly to the administrator's office. Ruth was a wonderful woman with an open-door policy. She wanted the best for the residents.

After I explained to Ruth what I'd seen and heard she told me that Anna had spent her entire life on a farm. Ruth explained that she had been thinking for weeks about starting an animal therapy program here at the nursing home. The theory that animals could help people heal was fairly new at this time but she felt that there might be a lot to be gained by allowing animals to visit the residents. Of course it would take some time to implement such a program; the animals would all have to be carefully screened.

It took six months before the program was initiated. The animals were to visit three times a week for two hours. Their owners would accompany them and the residents who wished to be a part of the program would gather in the Recreation Room.

The first day, only three animals visited—a Husky, a Poodle and a Persian cat. Ruth wanted to introduce the animals slowly so the residents could get used to their visits.

From the first day, the staff knew the program would be a success. The residents loved the pets. There were only two exceptions—Mr. Mannen, who was a crotchety old soul, and Anna. Neither of them paid any attention to the creatures that moved freely around the room.

Within a few weeks, the residents looked forward to Pet Day with much enthusiasm—all except Anna and Mr. Mannen. Hours before the pets were to arrive, the Recreation Room would be filled to capacity. I continued to ensure that there was always a place for Anna and Mr. Mannen.

At this time, Ruth decided to allow three more animals to visit. A total of sixty residents were taking part in the program and three animals were not sufficient to meet the demand. The newcomers were all canines; a Husky, a blond Labrador Retriever and a Border Collie named Colleen.

Colleen was a gentle, loving animal and a hit with all the residents. The first time she visited, Anna was in bed with the flu.

However, Colleen proceeded to work her magic on crotchety Mr. Mannen. She continued to return to his chair time after time, laying her head on his knee. Instead of brushing her away, as I expected, he sat and stared at her.

As Colleen was saying farewell to all of the residents, she ventured to Mr. Mannen one last time and laid her head on his knee. To my astonishment, he patted her head and spoke to her in a soft, gentle voice. This was a step forward, as Mr. Mannen never had spoken a kind word to anyone.

The following week, Anna was feeling much better and her doctor gave his permission for her to take part in the program. A half-hour before the pets were to arrive, I pushed Anna to the Recreation Room. She sat, staring into space, ignoring everyone around her. That is until Colleen walked into the room. As soon as Anna spied this lovely black and white creature, she laughed with delight and clapped her hands. Colleen immediately trotted to Anna's side, wagged her tail excitedly and danced on her hind legs. As Anna bent to touch her, Colleen began to lick her, her pink tongue lapping in and out rapidly. Anna hugged her close, tears coursing down her cheeks. As fast as they fell, Colleen lapped them up.

"Oh my dear Laddy, I've missed you so much," Anna cried. By this time there wasn't a dry eye in the room. Even old Mr. Mannen's eyes sparkled mysteriously. Everyone was surprised to hear Anna speak so plainly after two years of silence.

The next time Anna's sister, Mildred, came to visit, we told her that Anna was talking. She could hardly believe it. Ruth explained what had happened. Mildred told Ruth that when Anna had come to the home she had left behind a Border Collie named Laddy. The farm had been sold and a neighbor had adopted Laddy. He had been a direct descendent of a Border Collie that had been given to Anna by her father when she was a child. In fact, until she had come to the nursing home, Anna had never been without at least one, and more often two, Border Collies in her life.

Over the next few months, Anna and Colleen bonded in a special way. Anna began to talk to the other residents and walk with a cane. Every staff member of the nursing home knew that if Colleen hadn't come into Anna's life, the healing process would never have taken place.

Two years later, at the age of eighty-seven, Anna passed away peacefully in her sleep. As I stood at the cemetery and listened to the eulogy, I looked across the lawn. What I saw brought tears to my eyes and a smile to my face. There on the outskirts of the mourners lay Colleen, her nose on her paws, sad eyes gazing at the coffin. I was sure that Anna knew Colleen was there and I whispered a prayer of thanks for the magic that the wonderful Border Collie had brought into Anna's final years—the magic of Colleen.

Colleen taught me much about the human response to animal companions. I have never looked at a dog in the same light since Colleen brought the miracle of love to Anna.

~Mary M. Alward

# The Crooner

*Those who wish to sing, always find a song.*
*~Swedish Proverb*

Our little canary Petey stopped singing. I noticed tiny feathers at the bottom of the cage. Hurriedly, I reached for the bird book. Petey was molting, the process of replacing feathers that had worn out. The book explained that canaries usually will not sing during a molt. It went on to suggest feeding a nutritious diet and playing a CD of canary songs to keep our golden boy happy.

The next morning I was cleaning Petey's cage when I noticed our little Rat Terrier, Frankie, tilting his head to one side as he studied Petey silently perched on the bar of his cage. Our girls had named our little dog after Frank Sinatra. The name suited him, as he loved to "sing for his supper," as well as let us know when he needed to go outdoors. As I cleaned the canary's cage that morning, I couldn't help noticing Frankie's look of concern as he observed the sullen bird.

"Petey's not himself today. He's losing a few feathers and doesn't feel up to singing," I explained, feeling rather ridiculous attempting to explain molting to a dog. "Maybe if you sing a few bars Frankie, it will cheer Petey up!" I chuckled to myself at such a ridiculous notion.

I turned to retrieve fresh newspaper from the table. Just then, Frankie began barking softly.

He continued to gaze thoughtfully at Petey's cage as if he expected an immediate response. That's when it happened. Our golden boy began to accompany Frankie in song.

"I don't believe this!" I couldn't help shouting for my husband to come and witness the performance himself.

Frankie taught us an important lesson that morning. If you lose the song in your heart, it doesn't hurt to ask someone to help you get it back. Whenever it gets a little too quiet around our house, we know who to call. We call on the "crooner." He's always happy to accommodate anyone in need... feathers or not.

~Mary Z. Smith

# Being a True Buddy

*The true gift of friendship is the gift of yourself.*
~Author Unknown

He'd make a great farm dog, the worker at the animal shelter promised.

He was a large dog of indiscriminate origin, something like a white Labrador, with an intelligent look in his warm eyes. Mom and Dad had stopped by the shelter to find a replacement for a gentle Husky who had been the farm dog for years.

Buddy seemed an acceptable choice, so he rode home in the back of the car that very day.

I was already in college when Buddy came on the scene. As the youngest of eight, I was the last to leave the nest. Mom had been an only child and hated being alone, so she raised a big brood of us. Maybe with all of us out of the house, she missed some of the commotion and companionship.

Buddy turned out to be appropriately named and taught me what it means to give the gift of friendship. He brought no skills and fell short of his duty as a farm dog. For one thing, he was afraid of cows. He didn't bark when strangers pulled in the driveway, but greeted them with a friendly wave of his tail.

Buddy had nothing to offer but himself, which he gave completely and unselfishly.

He immediately laid his heart at my mom's feet and became her loyal subject. She couldn't go anywhere without a white dog trailing at her heels. When she mowed the yard, Buddy traipsed back and forth across the yard behind her. Mom loved to garden and the soil between the vegetable rows bore the tracks of a pair of Keds tennis shoes followed by four paw prints.

When I escaped the dorms on the weekends to visit the farm, Buddy eagerly trekked with me across the fields, but he always kept an eye toward the house and usually abandoned me to return to his true loyalty. Then, one cold day in March, Mom had a heart attack and was gone.

The farm, which had been a place of nourishment and growth, seemed so lifeless without her there. Buddy was as lost as any of us. When the back door opened, Buddy would jump up from his sleeping spot near the garage and run to the door. When he saw it was just me, he'd glare as though I was responsible for taking Mom away, then go lie down again. When Dad came home from town, Buddy waited by the passenger side of the car waiting for Mom to get out.

I have to confess to being so caught up in my own grief I didn't have much consolation to offer the dog. I also had to learn to do all those things that Mom had done so effortlessly.

As spring thawed, I was working in her flowerbed, trying to figure out which plants were flowers and which were weeds. Buddy lay in the grass a few feet away, watching my clumsy efforts. No doubt he was well aware that I had no idea what I was doing and that Mom would have done a much better job.

The grief caught up with me and I stood with my foot on the spade, tears streaming down my face. Buddy looked at me, then with a patient dog sigh, stood up and walked over to press his body against my legs. He looked up at me with warm brown eyes, then wagged his tail, as if to say we could help each other get through this.

He was right; he was a smart dog that way.

That summer, Buddy and I took long walks together across the rolling green hills, Buddy's crisscrossing path making him walk four miles to my one. When I held my hand at my side, it would rest perfectly on top of his silky head. Whenever the loneliness started to close in, I could wiggle my fingers and Buddy would slide underneath my hand without missing a step.

Buddy's joy for life inspired me through the years that followed. He sailed over fences like he was trying out for an Alpo commercial. He swam in the pond and entertained himself with a squeaky toy. He never did trust me alone in the garden and inspected the tomatoes and onions along with me. He lay at my feet under the ash tree while we snapped green beans.

When I came home on weekends, he would literally run circles around my car while I pulled in the driveway. No one else has ever been that glad to see me. He was scared of thunderstorms and electric fences, which only made him seem more human, somehow.

Buddy loved to ride in the back of the pickup and feel the breeze ruffling through his hair. We were driving across the hayfield one day when Dad hollered to stop. I hit the brakes a little too hard and cringed as four paws' worth of toenails slid across the metal pickup bed, followed by a soft thump when his body hit the cab.

With an apologetic smile, I looked over my shoulder to find Buddy's nose pressed against the glass. His annoyed expression seemed to say, "Next time, could you at least warn me?"

Time doesn't skip over any of us, farm dogs included. Buddy learned to use the gate instead of jumping fences and waited for the tailgate to be let down before he got in the truck.

It was Christmas Eve, ten years after Mom had passed away, that I came home to the farm and for once, Buddy didn't greet me. I found him huddled under the ash tree and it was evident his time with us was almost done.

I stroked his fur and thanked him as best I could for all that he had done for me. He seemed to understand; he was a smart dog that way. After Dad and I got home from church services, Buddy had crawled over to the edge of the field to die.

Once again, I sobbed at the loss that tore at my heart. Why did this have to happen at Christmas? Then I realized that Buddy had given me a gift. He knew I would be coming home that weekend, just as I had every weekend. He had waited for me, so that I could say goodbye.

Even in dying, Buddy gave himself, completely and unselfishly. And he taught me to live the same way.

~Susan Mires

# 53

## Chicken Soup for the Soul

# Billy Bob

*Blessed is the person who has earned the love of an old dog.*
*~Sydney Jeanne Seward*

t was obvious from the moment he showed up at the front door of the alcohol and drug recovery center that he was sick. He was painfully thin and wet from his travels on foot to the front door. His eyes had a "help me" look. Nobody expected him. He was totally unannounced and alone but his need was obvious and he was quickly accepted and warmly welcomed.

He made himself at home immediately, accepting the treatment and the kind words that were offered, though it was probably the food that he liked best, at least at the beginning. He gained weight in a hurry and looked and felt better, quickly showing what seemed like a limitless amount of energy and spirit.

It was impossible to figure his exact age just by looking at him. He had a deceptive quality—probably from his time spent on the streets—that swayed his appearance back and forth from looking young to looking mature, often depending on whether he was alone or with people. It was plain to see that he was streetwise and had been on his own for quite some time. We all knew he was lucky to have found the center and easily expressed his gratitude often to everyone.

By the time I arrived, about a week after he did, even I could tell that he had already fallen into the program and the schedule. He was up before the first man in the center and—like the rest of us—while he snuck a few winks whenever he could, he was often the last one awake at lights out.

I started walking every day as part of my own recovery, a few laps around the eight-acre property. The walk was hard at first since I was so out of shape, but it got easier each day. When he finally joined me in the daily walk, it got much easier. His simple presence and the idea that he wanted to spend time with me bought joy to my exercise. He was the best listener at the center and I trust he will never tell about the sappy emotions I revealed to him during our walks.

He walked alongside me, keeping pace step by step. Sometimes, something along our route caught his interest, making it obvious there were things in the semi-rural environment he had never seen before. When he discovered those strange things, he explored on his own while I continued my pace. But then, seeing I had gained ground on him, he would run at full gallop to catch up. Often, he ran so hard that he actually passed me; then he'd have to stop and wait for me to reach him, always with mischief in his eyes.

He did wander away from the center more than once and we worried about him, but he always came back. I suspected he returned because he had already seen enough of the streets and knew the security that the center offered him meant more than just a healthy meal, a safe place to sleep, and people who appreciated him.

I'm sure he was a major contributor to my own start to recovery, maybe more than the counselors, the doctors, and the other residents I saw in those first days and weeks. He gave me gladness and happiness and was a true friend when I truly needed one.

But as much fun as he was to be around and to walk with, the very best thing about him was his unequivocal acceptance. Alcoholic or drug addict, young or old, everybody got his complete attention and care. Maybe he shared himself selfishly (an old Alcoholics Anonymous saying: "You can't keep it unless you give it away."). All I know is that most of the men who were going through rehab were happy to repay him gratefully. He deserved it. He asked no questions and accepted everyone as a true equal, showing no favoritism. A man's background, age, or disease didn't bother him. Everyone was special to him and he gave them his total attention and spread his complete happiness evenly, honestly, and without self-consciousness.

There were some residents, of course, who didn't want anything to do with him, but I suppose that's normal. Most leery of all was the center's long-time resident cat, who'd seen it all, never trusted him and always looked at him suspiciously. But maybe that's just what cats do.

Tongue in cheek and not out of disrespect, the residents started calling him "Billy Bob" after the two founders of A.A.

I hope every recovery center can find a dog as sweet and friendly and happy and as loyal as Billy Bob. He was good treatment.

~Aaron M.

# 54

# Brandy

*You think dogs will not be in heaven?*
*I tell you, they will be there long before any of us.*
~Robert Louis Stevenson

The phone rang at precisely 9:00 P.M. as a drought buster of a storm raged angrily outside our bedroom windows. Instinctively, my wife and I both knew who it was and I answered the call with a dull numbness.

"Mr. Smith, this is John at the veterinary hospital," the voice flatly reported with a grave monotone. "I'm afraid things have taken a turn for the worse." My heart sunk and tears spilled from my wife's eyes behind me. She could tell from my wooden expression that the news wasn't good.

"I'd like your permission to do some emergency exploratory surgery, see if there's anything I can do to save Brandy. It's a long shot, but our only hope."

I paused, knowing there was more.

"But if I can't do anything, I'll need to put her down," he added with a solemn whisper. "It's the humane thing to do. She's very sick, and she's suffering."

I felt like someone sucker-punched me in the gut. I couldn't breathe.

"I need to discuss this with my wife, please, John," I managed, my voice shaky. "I'll call you right back."

I hung up and discussed the matter with my wife. We both

agreed that we wanted to be there for our friend, for our child, to provide a comforting and familiar presence. For years we had tried to start a family, with no success. Everything was tried during those tedious months, every imaginable process and method and old wives' tale and suggestion, not to mention countless prayers. But it was not meant to be; some things just aren't. Each effort fell short, and our marriage, though strengthened by the experiences, remained childless.

This dog was more than a pet to us; she was a precious jewel in our daily lives, a member of our family. She was a faithful companion, lovable, loyal, and humorous. We made the hard decision while wiping away tears, the humane decision, to bypass the surgery and go over in the evening rainstorm. We would hold our dear pet, Brandy, as she was given the needles that would help her to pass over to the eternal side of existence.

I called back to inform the doctor of our decision. Strangely, it took John five rings to answer his cell phone, despite knowing I was calling right back. He told me he'd have the phone by his side. Finally, the call was accepted with an echoing click.

"Mr. Smith," the voice hesitated with great emotion, "your dog just collapsed into my arms. Oh God, I think she's dying...." He fumbled with his stethoscope on the other end while I listened to the surrealistic nightmare in my ear, wishing I would wake up. "Oh God, I'm so sorry... she just took her last breath. She's gone." The man was in tears. I soon joined him, sobbing like a newborn.

Our drive over to the vet's office was a silent one until my wife suggested we relive special memories. There were many, and we found ourselves laughing, and then crying all over again. The dog had impacted our lives more than we realized.

Inside the doctor's office, abandoned and quiet on a Sunday night, we thanked John for being there to hold our friend as she passed away. It was more than sheer coincidence that he happened to be there. Moments later, our hearts were warmed when we saw her still, furry body. She was clearly at peace, as if she were merely sleeping.

After wrapping Brandy in cotton blankets, we laid her gently on the backseat of our car. Wet and still in shock, we slowly backed out and exited the parking lot with a reverent spirit.

About a mile or two later, my wife broke the solitude with a loud, startled scream. "Brandy just licked me! On the back of my neck! Honestly, I felt it!" My wife was ecstatic, thrilled beyond words.

I peered into the backseat, half expecting a modern day Lazarus miracle, but, of course, the dog was still and wrapped in blankets.

"Maybe you just felt something, honey, a wisp of air or something," I offered, confused yet intrigued.

"No, it was her; I know it was her," she insisted, assured of what occurred. "That dog has given me so many kisses over the years; it was exactly the same. I know it was her."

For several long moments silence returned to the compartment of our vehicle. Only the rhythmic reverberation of wipers working to clear raindrops from the windshield was audible.

"Brandy wanted to let us know she's okay," my wife explained, breaking the quiet. "I bet that's why she licked me. To let us know that she's fine, that she's moved on, and waiting for us." The event comforted our mourning hearts, and softened our sorrow.

The next morning we buried our precious daughter as it lightly misted from the dreary, carbonized skies. We read liturgy from the Episcopal prayer book and offered prayers for her soul. We gave thanks for her thirteen years with us, each one good, happy and healthy. I placed a University of Tennessee Volunteers baseball cap on her furry head, one I often wore on cold mornings as we walked together in the woods, before closing the box for the final time. My wife also added several of the dog's favorite treats, and all of her play balls. There were many. Even during her last days the dog played with those balls with the energy of a puppy.

The next evening our kindly church priest called to check in, having heard the news of our loss. We discussed animals and souls and heaven mostly. He assured me that the perfection of God's holy landscape would be dotted with all kinds of creatures, especially pets. If God cared enough to make it, He would surely care enough to desire it in His heavenly kingdom. But this I already knew. For on the rainy, dark night our dog left us, she also left a sign that she was still very much alive, a wet lick across my wife's neck, a canine kiss, from a Golden Retriever we knew as Brandy.

~David Michael Smith

# 55

# Tink's Wonder Therapy

*It is difficult to say what is impossible for the dream of yesterday is the hope of today and the reality of tomorrow.*
~Robert H. Goddard

After an early morning play date at the dog park had worn us out, we just wanted to stay home and be couch potatoes that Saturday. But then I remembered how blessed we were and knew patients were expecting Tink at the hospital. For such a little Wiener dog, she possessed tons of loving therapy to share with those in ICU.

"Come on Tink, ready for a bath?" I said. "Arf!" she barked, wagging her tail.

"It's time for your weekly doggie spa of bathing, brushing and clipping. Delta Therapy dogs have to be squeaky clean to work in a hospital," I reminded her as she hopped into the tub.

Later that afternoon, I dressed Tink in her official green vest, which signaled it was time to go to work. Tink always got a little jittery because she never knew what patient ailments awaited her at bedside visits.

"You'll do great today," I whispered in her ear as she was loaded into her carrier.

After arriving at the hospital, we stopped by the ICU nurses' station. This first stop always helped reassure Tink that therapy work makes a difference in the lives of patients.

"Oh Tink, I'm sooo glad you're here! I've had a tough morning, buddy, and I need a hug and kisses!" exclaimed Nurse Stacey. Tink loved the hugs and kisses too, wagging her long feathery tail as belly rubs were administered by a crowd of nurses and the usual contraband cookie was smuggled to her. Finally we began our "rounds" with the patient visitation list in hand.

Our first patient was Mugsy, a little girl who, after brain surgery, had been in the hospital for fifty-three days. A white turban of gauze sat atop her head. Blue and green wires poked out from beneath the turban tower. Mugsy could only flutter her eyes occasionally because she was so weak. Tink lay quietly next to her and I placed Mugsy's hand on Tink's soft fur. It was so soothing for both of them that they fell asleep.

"Wake up Tink," I said tapping her gently, "we need to go; your next patient is waiting."

Mr. Crabbitts had been in ICU for over a month recuperating from a heart operation.

He was crabby and sad and his rapid heart rate was making his recovery time extra long. As we entered his room, Mr. C propped himself up on one elbow, peered over the top of his glasses and grumbled, "Who's this at the foot of my bed?"

"Hi Mr. Crabbitts, my name is Martha and this is Tink." When he saw Tink in my arms with her big smile and wagging tail, he invited her up onto his bed.

"Tink, you remind me of my dog Whuffie. I used to read the comics to him every morning. Okay if I read the comics to you?" Mr. C asked.

Tink cuddled up next to him under his arm and with her head cocked, listened as he recited the adventures of Snoopy and Woodstock. This shared closeness created an instant bond felt by both and by the end of our visit, Mr. C's heart rate had dropped to within a normal range. Tink's wonder therapy was at work!

"Thanks for coming to visit me Tink. I'm going to tell Whuffie you loved the comics too!"

Our last bedside visit was with a young man named Jake. I could tell from the photos suspended above his bed that he loved skateboarding and had lots of friends. Jake was paralyzed from his shoulders to his toes, the result of a car accident. Lying flat on his back, the ceiling was his only view. He was unable to speak because of a tube down his throat. Jake's mom sat vigilantly at his bedside, quietly weeping and praying the rosary over him. As much as Jake tried, he was incapable of moving or feeling anything so I communicated with Jake through his dark brown eyes.

After introducing ourselves, I placed Tink on Jake's chest so both were at eye level. They gazed into each other's eyes for the entire visit. Twenty minutes had passed when I whispered "Tink, it's time to go." As I picked her up, Jake reached out his hand and moved his fingers for the first time! When I saw his fingers move, I put Tink's paw into Jake's hand and scratched her rough nails on his skin. Jake blinked and I knew from that blink that some feeling had returned in his hand. Jake's mom burst into tears and shrieked "It's a miracle! Thank you God! Thank you God! Thank you Tink!" The nurses came running over and shouted, "You're ready for rehab Jake! All thanks to Tink!" Tink joined in the excitement throwing back her head and barking a loud "arf!"

Later that day, as we walked to the elevator, we saw Jake being wheeled into the Rehab Unit to begin his physical therapy. I gave him a "thumbs up" and he returned a faint smile back to us. I knew that faint smile would be the beginning of many big smiles to come.

I was happy that we got off the couch that Saturday and remembered once again how blessed we were.

~Martha Penhall

56

# Spirit Run

*If you're alone, I'll be your shadow. If you want to cry, I'll be your shoulder. If you want a hug, I'll be your pillow. If you need to be happy, I'll be your smile. But anytime you need a friend, I'll just be me.*

~Author Unknown

We rarely see a streak of red now, in the distant hills, when we scan the surrounding countryside from our home. There was a time when we could count on it. We would look up and point excitedly, "There she is! Do you see her!?" It was a beautiful sight, exhilarating. We can still count on the beauty of that red creature now, but usually she's lying in a big lump at our feet or just running ahead of the truck to the barn and back. She's content now just to be. She's our dog, Ginger.

She adopted us several years ago when I learned that her owners had moved from a nearby home and abandoned her. She had been hanging out with our neighbors' dogs, scavenging for scraps of food and affection.

Well, I knew my husband, Lowell, felt we already had enough pets, with a Jack Russell Terrier, my son Chase's cat, and a goat. But when this timid, Irish Setter-type dog showed up one afternoon, I knew there was something special about her. In my head, I heard my husband warning me, "If you feed her, she'll never leave!"

So I fed her.

When my husband returned from the barn with my son, he stopped dead in his tracks when he saw us on the porch. I had one hand laid protectively on Ginger's head. Lowell just said, "Uh-uh. No way. If it were up to you, we'd have a dozen strays around here!"

He and my son began to pet her, and I started pleading her case. I didn't think I would be able to convince Lowell, but Ginger came to her own defense. When my son took off through the field toward the barn, Ginger went with him, staying right by his side, literally touching him the whole way. My husband immediately changed his mind and Ginger changed her fate and prevented a major battle in my household with that one loving gesture.

Before long, we observed behaviors in Ginger that revealed a disturbing past. Not only was she extremely timid and submissive, but she would flinch or cower at any sudden movement around her. She was so easily frightened that we all learned to move more slowly and deliberately around her.

She also hoarded food. She would hide or bury food and animal carcasses everywhere around our home. Although she was being fed well, even leaving food in her dish, she would often show up with scraps of food or food wrappers, and frantically search for a place to hide them. Once, I looked out the back window to see her with half a loaf of bread, the slices still intact, crammed in her mouth. She was madly pacing back and forth along the bank behind our house, looking for just the right spot to conceal her bounty.

Even her requests for attention were timid, although she incessantly craved love and affection. She would just gently place her snout against our leg or hand and stand there patiently. Sometimes we might feel a gentle nudge. Occasionally, if we were lucky, we would feel the delicate, fleeting touch of the tip of her tongue on our hand.

Most people couldn't resist petting Ginger, so she received a lot of love. But if Ginger wasn't able to get affection from us or from visitors, she would insist that Fred, our other dog, give her affection. Ginger would inch closer and closer to him, then nudge him with her snout until he would lick her face over and over again.

Fred—the ultimate "Alpha"—assumed the role of caretaker and guardian for Ginger, just as he had for our whole family, including our son, our cat, our goat, and our baby goats. Fred could literally walk under Ginger, but he watched over her as if she were his queen. He would groom her, clean her bed, and even boss her around a little bit. And, because Fred is a born hunter, he would catch poor little critters for Ginger to proudly carry back home. She would add those carcasses, and other found treasures such as bones and discarded deer hides to what we came to refer to as "the boneyard."

Over time, Ginger became less timid. She flinched less and less. She had found a home where she was loved, nurtured, and safe.

Then, one day, she began to run.

Previously, she would run with Fred on the hunt, or run to the barn and back with the truck, but she just started running in the hills on her own. It was thrilling, yet puzzling, to see her sprinting across one of the distant rolling hills around our home. She wasn't chasing anything or going anywhere in particular; she was just running. She looked so free.

It was during that time that I was struggling with some emotional and spiritual problems of my own. I had gone into the woods one day, with Fred and Ginger, to pray. For so many years, I had been burdened with a deep shame and regrets about my past that had darkened my whole outlook on life. I couldn't seem to forgive myself, and I didn't feel worthy of God's forgiveness, either. I sat down on a log and prayed for forgiveness yet again; I prayed for a release from that intolerable weight that plagued me. I desperately wanted to feel God's forgiveness, to feel renewal. Then, I began to cry.

Fred, our protector, had kept his position several yards away, standing guard. But when I began to cry, Ginger came to me, and tenderly raised her front legs, placing a large paw on each of my shoulders, with her face resting against my face.

She hugged me.

I reached out and hugged her back, as I sobbed even harder. At that moment, the sunlight burst through the canopy of the trees overhead, and I felt such a release, a lightness. I truly felt God's love and forgiveness and healing in Ginger's "embrace."

I have been able to let go of the burden of my past now. I can find beauty in this life, and I feel the freedom to live and love more freely. Since then, my spirit has continued to heal in countless ways.

Ginger doesn't run in the hills like she used to, unless she's assisting Fred in a hunt. But I know why she did run. Anyone whose suffering spirit has been healed by acceptance and unconditional love knows why Ginger ran—why her spirit had to run.

The scars from her former life may never completely fade away. Thankfully, she hardly ever flinches anymore. But we still have a "boneyard." We still see her anxiously searching to hide morsels of food, or proudly toting around some ghastly animal carcass. And we still treasure those few, delicate flickers of her tongue on our hand.

But now, Ginger's free to be.

And so am I.

~Veronica S. Hutton

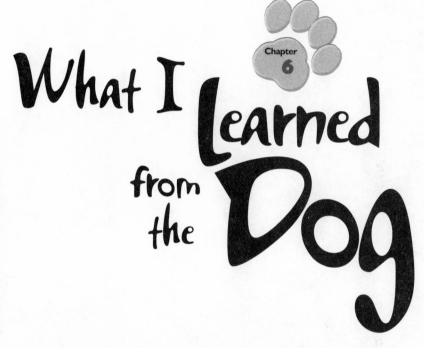

# What I Learned from the Dog

## Chapter 6

## Learning to Say Goodbye

*When you are sorrowful look again in your heart, and you shall see that in truth you are weeping for that which has been your delight.*

*~Kahlil Gibran*

# When It's Time to Say Goodbye

*There are things that we don't want to happen but have to accept,*
*things we don't want to know but have to learn,*
*and those we can't live without but have to let go.*
*~Author Unknown*

People with old or ailing animals often ask, "How do you know when it's time to let them go?" I once heard a veterinarian answer, "You just know."

The other morning our dog, Czar, let me know it was time. There was no mistaking the look in those big, brown eyes. Eyes that said, "I'm old and there is no longer any quality or dignity to my life. It's time."

After a long walk on the beach, trying to prolong the decision, I came home knowing there was no choice.

To make it easier for Czar, our veterinarian agreed to come on his lunch hour. I spent the morning sitting next to the old dog as he lay on his blanket, his head in my lap.

My thoughts drifted back to the day Czar came into my life. He was owned by people who perhaps shouldn't have had a dog as big as a Russian Wolfhound—or Borzoi—which is the official name of this breed.

Czar was never allowed in the house and I was told he spent much of the time standing outside, looking mournfully at the humans through the window. One day, the family maid said, "I'm sick and tired of washing nose prints off the glass. Either that dog goes or I do." Apparently good maids are harder to find than a good dog, and Czar was soon on his way to the animal shelter.

It was love at first sight when this tall hound and I discovered each other. He stood up on his hind legs, planted his front paws on my shoulders and greeted me with a big kiss.

When I was a little girl, we always had dogs, but usually of the small mixed-breed sort. I distinctly remember a series of vodka advertisements showing a pair of tall, elegant, snow-white Russian Wolfhounds. I dreamed of someday owning one, but honestly believed only the wealthy could afford such a beautiful animal. Finding a dog like Czar at the shelter was indeed a dream come true for me.

After several months of adjusting to each other, I put Czar through a ten-week dog obedience course. When you spend a great deal of time training an animal, you seem to bond with him ever more closely. On "Commencement Night" several friends came to watch, bringing "doggy" gifts for the new graduate. Czar gave the exercises his enthusiastic all and received the first place trophy.

Not long after that, my brother, Daniel, came for a visit, and after unpacking sat down in the living room. Five minutes later Czar carefully carried in a sweater from the guest room, depositing it in my brother's lap. Daniel is still wondering if perhaps Czar was trying to say, "You look cold, here's your sweater," or maybe, "I think you've stayed long enough. You can go home now."

I took Czar everywhere with me. One day while sitting on a grassy bank watching a tennis tournament, a small boy circled, and then finally approached. He stared at Czar for quite some time, then finally asked, "What do you s'pose a dog like that costs anyhow?"

"Oh," I answered absently, "probably about $500."

"Well," said the boy, "you certainly got your money's worth!"

While spending the final hours with Czar, I thought of this thing called grief and remembered the time when I stopped by the vet's office to pick up some medicine for a sick cat. The only others in the waiting room were an elderly man and woman, who were standing by some plastic plants in the corner, their backs to me. I sat there, watching, with curiosity. Just then the vet came out and said to them, "I'm very sorry. I was hoping surgery would help, but your Laddie was just too old. He didn't make it."

I will never forget the sight of that elderly couple, walking slowly toward their car, shoulders bent in grief.

In the old man's hand was a frayed, red dog collar.

When I started thinking about all my long walks on the beach with Czar — and how there would be no more — my tears fell down onto his muzzle, his tail wagged feebly, and he looked up at me as if to say, "Please don't cry. Just remember all the good years we've had together."

I sat with Czar, thinking about what animals bring to us. Some are trouble, especially in the early days of training them to fit into our lifestyles. But eventually they almost always give back total loyalty and love.

The last hours with this grand old dog went by too fast. Soon Dr. Brown arrived and moments later it was done... with the exception of tears and a deep gratitude for the quiet dignity of euthanasia.

There are people who avoid having pets because it hurts too much to lose them. But unless we expose ourselves to the painful lows in life, how can we ever experience the happy highs?

Before the day was over, friends dropped by. Some came just to hug. Some brought bunches of flowers. And today another note arrived from the local animal shelter saying a donation had been made in Czar's name so that other animals might live. (If you care about someone who has lost a pet, this is a wonderful idea.)

Czar had a long, good life and gave so much. The least I could give to him was a kind and gentle death.

~Bobbie Jensen Lippman

# A Mother's Love

*When you are a mother, you are never really alone in your thoughts.*
*A mother always has to think twice, once for herself and once for her child.*
~Sophia Loren

Mama shook her head. "This one didn't make it either." She held the tiny, black puppy for me to see before she wrapped it in a clean dishtowel and quietly removed it. Bonnie, our Scottish Terrier, didn't notice. She was too busy struggling to produce another pup.

Mama had awakened me shortly after midnight when Bonnie went into labor. I slipped from bed without waking my two younger sisters to sit beside our pet and watch God's miracle of birth take place. So far Bonnie had delivered two identical bundles onto the towels lining her box in the corner, but neither possessed the spark of life. At eight, I was learning that sometimes we have to accept death as a part of living.

A few minutes later, Bonnie strained and another pup plopped out, still wrapped in its translucent amniotic sac. Bonnie turned and with a mother's instincts, began to pull the restraining membrane from her baby.

"This one's moving!" I shouted.

"Shh. Don't wake your sisters," Mama reminded me.

We watched as the new life squirmed and whimpered and Bonnie licked her baby clean and dry. Soon another black puppy lay beside his brother, and the two wriggled their way to their mama's side where they latched on to nurse. Bonnie rested, finished with her job.

"They're beautiful," I said, yawning.

"Yes, and it's time for you to go to sleep." Mama guided me by the shoulders to my room and tucked me back into bed.

The next morning I awoke remembering the events of the night before and ran into Mama's bedroom where the newborns guzzled their breakfast. Mama had disposed of the two dead puppies during the night, and Bonnie seemed content caring for her surviving babies. She faithfully remained in her box except for short excursions outside and to her food bowl.

Later that day, I sat next to Bonnie, petting her and the pups, when Mama walked in carrying a basket of towels fresh from the dryer. Bonnie sat up, suddenly alert. She jumped from her box, rushed to Mama's side, and began to bark.

Mama looked down, puzzled. "What's wrong, girl?"

Bonnie continued to bark. Without warning, she jumped onto the bed, something we'd never allowed her to do, and pawed at the clothes basket.

"What on earth...?" Mama started to say. Then, all at once, she understood. Mama dumped the basket onto the bed where Bonnie pushed her nose through the linens, sniffing each towel.

I looked questioningly at Mama.

With tears in her eyes, she said, "Bonnie must have seen me wrap the dead puppies in the dishtowels before I took them away. She's looking for her babies."

When Bonnie satisfied herself that her pups weren't there, she jumped from the bed and returned to her family. Mama and I looked at each other in amazement.

For ten years, this scenario repeated itself every time someone brought in a load of clean clothes. We developed a routine of putting the basket on the floor first to let Bonnie sniff through it before attempting to fold the laundry. Whenever we forgot, she reminded us. Long after her pups grew up and left our family, Bonnie continued to look for the babies she had lost.

Even in the animal world, a mother's love never dies.

~Tracy Crump

# Sadie: Dog from Above

*God's gifts put man's best dreams to shame.*
*~Elizabeth Barrett Browning*

Our dog Sam had died. It was nine days before Christmas, and we were told that my terminally ill father, who lived with us, might also die before the holiday. As my husband, daughters and I hugged each other, it felt like a dress rehearsal in grief.

"In the summer we'll look for a dog," I said, but secretly hoped a dog would arrive as serendipitously as Sam had thirteen summers before. For now all I could do was pray for the strength to endure the anticipated loss of my father. And we did have a joyous Christmas with "Pa," as everyone called my dad.

In the winter days of January, we discussed the possibility of a new pet. "I want a fluffy dog," said Elizabeth, our eight-year-old.

"I want a big dog," said my husband Rick. I, on the other hand, have always wanted a "Scotty" dog. Sam had been a stray who found us.

"Mom, I saw a dog on campus that was big, fluffy, and had a Scotty dog mustache. We should get that breed—whatever it is," laughed Jenny, our twenty-year-old peacemaker daughter.

Pa had his opinions, too. "You can't go wrong with a herding dog," said Dad, as we drank our morning tea together. He had been a cattle farmer for most of his life. When Pa came to live with us in the fall, we had been told that his cancer was beyond treatment. But Dad had a positive attitude and was a joy to live with. He and his younger granddaughter watched the winter dog shows on television every Saturday morning.

Only our son Aaron, twenty-four and living in his own home, didn't have an opinion. "Sam was one of a kind, Mom; we'll never replace him." He just felt we should be open to a dog different from Sam. I wondered where he got his wisdom, as I recalled the night the sky must have opened up and a white dog appeared on our lawn.

"He's the dog God gave us," I always said.

"Yeah, but the devil makes him shed," my husband always added about our white Shepherd and Husky mixed breed.

At my friend Marilyn's suggestion that a dog's presence could be healing for us and a comfort to my father, we made a list of our needs and spread the word. The right dog had to be about three or four years old (not a puppy, but not so old that we would soon face another loss) housetrained, must love kids, tolerate a cat, and be trained to walk on a leash. It was a lot to ask.

I gave the list to God, and confessed to praying friends my latest prayer: "Oh, Lord, couldn't you drop another dog from the sky? And, if it's not too much trouble, could it be one that doesn't shed?"

No miracle dog came along, but a far greater miracle occurred as the season changed to spring. Little by little, my father seemed to get better. Hospice nurses and surgeons alike were in awe with the results of a June CT scan. My father's aggressive bladder cancer had not spread in nine months. Without the help of chemotherapy or radiation, his tumor had shrunk. It was a joyous time as we prepared for my dad to have a surgery in July that might give him years to live with us.

Then school was out, and it was summer. Jennifer and Elizabeth reminded me of my promise. On the first day of summer vacation we visited Animal Friends Caryl Gates Gluck Resource Center, a brand new, no-kill shelter in a wooded setting that had opened near our home. The Center also had a copy of our list that we sent after it opened on March 18th.

In the spacious facility that held forty dogs to adopt, the first dog in the first window caught our eyes. A black, fluffy-haired "pony" named Sadie was a dog so big that I shook my head from side to side to say "no."

"Bouvier des Flandres," Jennifer read out loud on the poster.

"Four months old," I read. "We can't handle a puppy...." I started to say.

"Couldn't we play with her while you get more information?" Elizabeth pleaded. I tried to explain that it wouldn't make any difference, but I inquired anyway.

"There's been a mistake," the rescue counselor said, as he read Sadie's report. "Sadie is three and a half years old, professionally trained, and would do well in a home with both children and cats," he read out loud. I couldn't believe my ears.

"Stand up straight, Jennifer, so your dad can't tell how big she is," I said to our older daughter, as I used her cell phone to take a picture of this ninety-five-pound dog that resembled a Poodle on steroids.

At home we learned that Sadie was a rare and noble cow herding breed from Belgium that nearly became extinct from serving Allied Forces as message dogs in World War I and II. It is the dog written about in *The Dog of Flanders*, the first modern dog story, a book I had fallen in love with when my fifth-grade teacher read it to our class. And to top it off, Bouviers are non-shedding.

But, my husband had to give his approval, too. "There is no way we can have a dog that big," he said to the girls as they got in the car. But he placed Sam's old leash in the trunk.

"I like her, but are we crazy?" he asked me by cell phone from the shelter. I thought of Marilyn's advice: "Listen to your head, but follow your heart." Sadie's story was one of sadness. Later, we learned that her first owner was a soldier who served in Iraq.

It was Father's Day, June 18th, when Sadie became our dog. Our three godchildren visited that afternoon, and Sadie planted herself at the edge of a blanket where the baby was trying to crawl off the edge. That night she settled herself at the foot of my father's bed.

"You're a nuisance," Dad said, but a smiled lingered on his lips, as Sadie sat by his elbow at the card table in his room where we ate all of our meals. Sadie was everything I'd prayed for—although my husband felt we had traded shedding for drooling. Just as nobody is perfect, Sadie did have one bad trait. She barked like crazy when someone arrived at our door.

My dad looked forward to his surgery, although he had a distant look in his eyes, and I wondered if the operation would be too much for him. Nine days before the surgery, life threw us another jolt. On a Sunday morning just before breakfast, Pa had a massive stroke that left him unable to respond.

One late night, Sadie stood by Dad's bed just looking as my husband and I sat on the sofa beside him. "Oh, Sadie-Girl, you don't understand," my husband said. Sadie turned, slowly walked to Rick and sunk her head deep into his hands as her eyes met his.

"Oh, Girl, you do understand!" he said, and hugged her as if they were Timmy and Lassie.

It was July 18th, exactly a month after Sadie had arrived, when my father departed. As we group-hugged beside my father's bed where he lay, Sadie was in our midst. It was a peaceful setting, with the girls on the porch swing and Sadie at their feet, when our son helped the undertaker carry Pa on his final trip down our stairs. As they emerged from the house, Sadie scrambled to her feet and stood at military attention. She never barked once.

~Jane Miller

# The Dog Nobody Wanted

*An animal's eyes have the power to speak a great language.*
~Martin Buber

Nobody wanted Little Bit.

The animal shelter Chihuahua with the tiny black body and oversized ears had been my widowed mother's constant companion for the past fifteen years. But she was one of the few possessions Mother failed to list in her who-gets-what-upon-my-death notebook. My brother Rusty got the fishing boat. My sister Mandy got the Christmas china. I got the antique dining room table.

But nobody wanted Little Bit.

"I can't take her," Rusty said. "My dogs would eat her for an appetizer." He was right. Little Bit would never survive in a family that owned a German Shepherd and a Doberman Pinscher.

"I can't take her," Mandy said. "Nobody's home at my house during the day. She'd be too lonely. Not to mention what she'd do to the carpet."

My siblings looked at me expectantly.

"I can't take her," I said. "I don't want her."

The words were scarcely out of my mouth before pictures of my mother flashed, unbidden, through my mind. She was standing at the stove frying chicken, with Little Bit waiting patiently at her feet for the first bite. She was climbing a stepladder to fill the bird-feeder, with Little Bit standing guard at the bottom. She was sitting in her worn recliner, watching *Wheel of Fortune* on TV, with Little Bit snuggled on her lap.

And the last, still-too-vivid pictures of Mother curled up in a hospital bed, cancer consuming her frail body. "Hand me my notebook and my pencil," she'd say. "I need to write some things down."

First were the funeral plans. Family and friends to be notified of her death. Details to be included in the obituary. Bible verses to be read. Hymns to be sung. Then it was on to who-gets-what. Methodically and deliberately, Mother listed from memory all the items of value in every room in her house and to whom they should be given. She left out nothing, from screwdrivers to shrimp forks.

Except for Little Bit.

It wasn't as though she could have forgotten about her. In complete violation of hospital rules, my siblings and I had smuggled the six-pound dog into her room—and her bed—several times. The reunions were always joyful and tear-filled. So why was Mother reluctant to say who would inherit her best friend once she was gone?

Perhaps because she already knew where Little Bit would end up. Rusty had a Doberman and a German Shepherd. Mandy had a full-time job. By default, Little Bit would come to live at my house after Mother died. Even though I didn't want her.

That's exactly what happened. And you know what? Everything I dreaded about taking on a house dog came to pass. Little Bit jumped on the furniture. She tormented my cats. She slept all day and yapped all night. She piddled—and worse—on the living room rug. She behaved like a spoiled princess.

"I don't know how much more I can take," I told a friend after two angst-filled weeks. "As much as I hate to do it, I'm going to try to find her someplace else to live."

But finding a new home for Little Bit was easier said than done. When inquirers called in response to the want ad I'd placed in the newspaper, I was honest about her shortcomings. Perhaps too honest. I soon discovered that an elderly dog who jumped on furniture, tormented cats, yapped all night, and piddled—and worse—on the rug was a hard sell.

Nobody wanted Little Bit. What was to become of her?

Late one afternoon, in total despair, I threw myself into my worn recliner and began to sob. Life wasn't fair. Not only had I lost my mother, I was stuck with her dog. The more I thought about the injustice of it all, the harder I cried. Until something plopped into my lap. A six-pound something with oversized ears, a graying muzzle, and big brown eyes that locked onto mine and wouldn't let go. Half-heartedly, I scratched the top of Little Bit's head. And then she began to cry. Not tears, of course, but the most pitiful whimpering I'd ever heard.

That's when it hit me. Little Bit hadn't been behaving like a spoiled princess. She'd been behaving like someone eaten up with grief. A living creature who'd had the human being she loved more than anyone in the world snatched away from her.

Just like me.

"You miss your mother, don't you, old girl?" I scratched the top of her head, wholeheartedly this time. "So do I. But you know what? We'll make it through this thing together. You and me." I blew my nose and reached for the remote control on the table beside my chair. "How about if we turn on *Wheel of Fortune* and see if that makes us feel better?"

But Little Bit didn't answer. She was snuggled down in my lap, snoring contentedly.

~Jennie Ivey

# Scruffy's Story

*Maybe part of loving is learning to let go.*
*~From the television show* The Wonder Years

"It's not my dog!" My husband threw up his hands in exasperation and disappeared down the hall.

"It's not my dog, either," I muttered, but I was the one who let the tangled mass of muddy fur into the house. The ungrateful newcomer had just marked his territory by baptizing my living room drapes.

It all started on the day before Thanksgiving when I pulled my Ford Tempo into our driveway after a challenging day of teaching. As I retrieved my book bag from the backseat, I had the uneasy feeling I was being watched. Cautiously I turned and stared into the piercing brown eyes of the most pitiful dog I had ever seen. His shaggy coat was covered with fresh mud and his head was scabbed with dried blood. His road-weary, gut-hungry, giving-up-on-life appearance pulled at my heart strings.

"Where did that dog come from?" I closed the front door behind me.

"Just leave him alone and he'll go home." Jim's pastor's heart did not extend to four-legged strays. "And whatever you do, don't feed him."

Our daughter's pre-adolescent nose pressed tightly against the living room window as she kept tabs on the long-haired stranger in the driveway. Her bone conduction hearing aid screeched against the glass. Bethany was born with bilateral aural atresia—no ear canals, no ear drums, and malformed middle ear bones. She was entering those years when it is vitally important to be just like everyone else, but she wasn't. And she wanted a dog of her very own.

Morning light revealed the bedraggled dog—still outside under the car. He looked weaker and hungrier... and sadder—if that was even possible.

I spent the morning in the kitchen—roasting, basting, mixing, and baking the traditional Thanksgiving dishes required for our family celebration, which included our son who was home from college. Our family joined hands around the table. Each person managed to voice an expression of gratitude without mentioning the hungry dog in the driveway. After the blessing and a finger-squeezing amen, the meal I spent hours preparing disappeared... and so did Bethany. She was back at the window, nose flattened and fingers splayed. I washed the Thanksgiving dishes and she watched her Thanksgiving dog.

Jim was deep into his holiday nap when I tiptoed into the laundry room to gather a couple of plastic bowls and a partial bag of the dog kibble that we kept around for our son's dog when he visited. Flashing a "shhhh" sign toward Bethany, I slipped out the front door to finish serving Thanksgiving dinner. Intense brown eyes followed my every move from the safety zone beneath Jim's car. I placed the bowls brimming with food and water strategically by the window on the front porch and I crept back inside. No sooner had I closed the door than a mass of fur streaked toward the window and began gobbling and gulping. The dog retreated to the driveway while I dished up second helpings; then he returned to the porch to dine more slowly. That was enough for Bethany. She was out the door, and started hugging the neck of the wayward pooch. Open door translated into open invitation and the tangled-coated stranger darted into the house. The ensuing commotion meant naptime was over. My husband emerged from the family room just in time to witness the wet curtain crisis.

The dog was in the house. That was nine-tenths of the battle as far as Bethany was concerned. She christened him Scruffy because of his rough appearance, but after rigorous bathing and brushing, his long black and white coat was quite presentable. I fixed a bed for him in the family room, but he soon abandoned it for Bethany's bed.

Who would dump such a pretty dog? He had no collar and no microchip, so we advertised in the newspaper, posted "found dog" signs, and contacted local animal shelters. No one seemed to be looking for a small black and white dog.

Jim and I had our reservations about a street dog of unknown origin taking up residence in our daughter's room. We promised Bethany a new puppy in the spring—one she could raise herself—but she had already fallen in love with the dog in the driveway. The dog that wasn't perfect in every way. The dog that needed her as much as she needed him.

Scruffy became Bethany's constant companion. She dressed him in doll clothes. She tried her bone conduction hearing aid on his head. Bethany wanted to be a doctor, so Scruffy became her first living patient. She examined him with her plastic medical kit—taking his blood pressure, checking his heart, peering into the ear canals she didn't have. She matted his black and white coat with tears of frustration when classmates called her "robot-head" because of her hearing aid, or when she missed an activity because she didn't hear the invitation, or when she was just plain adolescent angry at her parents. Scruffy was privy to the secrets of her heart too sacred to be written in a diary, and she held him close whenever she needed comfort.

One night, about three months after Scruffy's arrival, I was perched on the edge of Bethany's bed for her bedtime ritual and a final "I love you," when the dog growled at her. I banished him from the bedroom in spite of Bethany's tears. The next night, he growled again. I was again ready to evict him when Bethany wailed, "Stop Mama. He's telling me his 'rar-rar's.'" Sure enough, Scruffy was talking to her in a "rar-rar-rah" cadence that sounded eerily like "I love you." After that, he told her so every night at bedtime.

Through the years Scruffy served as Bethany's unofficial, self-trained hearing-ear dog. She awakened every morning to his gentle kisses. He alerted her when the telephone rang or the doorbell sounded or the tornado siren wailed. He sat unflinching in the window each afternoon, waiting for the school bus. He lay at her feet as she did her homework and sat beside her as she read her favorite books.

Years passed. Bethany grew taller and Scruffy's muzzle grew grayer. The school bus gave way to the first car, and soon it was time for college. What a doleful day it was for the little black and white dog when "his girl" moved into the college dorm. New friends helped her now, but there was a tail-wagging, tongue-slurping reunion each time she came home.

Medical school was next and homecomings were fewer and fewer. Scruffy slept more and more, and I tried to keep him as comfortable as possible. One sad day his breathing became so labored I took him to the veterinarian. Prescribed pills had little effect, so I called Bethany to come home. Our soon-to-be-doctor whisked her childhood companion into the car. Jim drove toward the animal hospital while I prayed for both daughter and dog. As his mistress gently held him, tears streaming from her eyes, Scruffy stopped breathing. Unable to accept the inevitable, she gave him mouth-to-mouth resuscitation, and he came back to her. At the animal hospital, the vet placed Scruffy's weary head in an oxygen cone, but we all knew it was time to say goodbye. Jim and I took our turns, then stepped aside while Bethany told her childhood companion farewell. Scruffy lifted his head slightly and gave his girl one last "rar-rar-rah."

~Beverly A. Porter

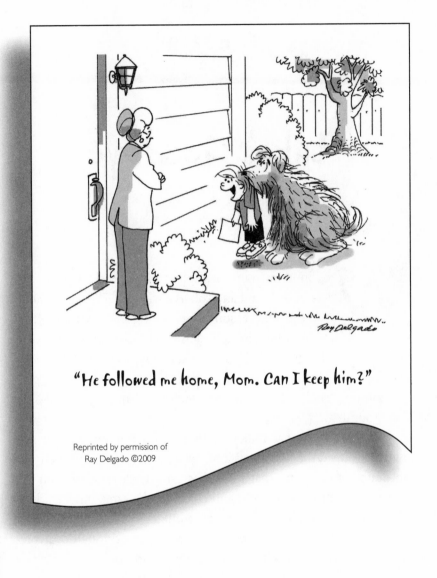

"He followed me home, Mom. Can I keep him?"

# Luke's Goodbye

*We call them animals, and so they are, for they cannot tell us how they feel,*
*but they do not suffer less because they have no words.*
*~Anna Sewell*

We found our perfect puppy through the classifieds. He was cute, blond and soft as a whisper. The whole family had different reasons for choosing Luke. Kristal, fifteen, was too old to dress him in doll clothes like she'd done with our last dog, but she gushed, "He's sooo soft. Just feel this velvety ear." Five-year-old Jeff thought his enormous feet would give him "great traction on a trail." Me? I liked the security of having a good-sized dog around.

We could see that Luke's mother was a Brittany Spaniel. Her owners claimed the father was a marauding black Lab. But there was no doubt in my mind that Luke was directly descended from Old Yeller. He had the same build and coloring, the same innocent head tilt. Same goofy smile. Same bent for trouble.

Trouble I didn't need more of. I was going through a divorce, trying to grow two kids into halfway normal adults, and running my small children's clothing store. Luke took our minds off all of that, which was just what I'd hoped.

While he was teething, Luke chewed up one of my good shoes. I was so mad that I whacked him with it, which guaranteed that he wouldn't touch THAT shoe again. The next day he chose a different pair. I must have tossed at least a dozen pairs before I learned to close my bedroom door.

The first time Luke got too close to our long-haired white cat, Max, I wasn't home. Kristal called me at work to tell me that Max had swatted Luke on the ear.

"It's bleeding all over!" she cried. "Splattering every time he shakes his head. What do I do?"

She'd tried applying pressure, but Luke wouldn't hold still. Jeff was afraid Luke was going to bleed to death. I rushed home. The vet said the cat must have sliced the blood vessel that runs around the edge of a dog's ears. He recommended trying to clot the blood with flour. He suggested laying one ear over the top of the other and tying them above his head. Yeah, right, I thought, knowing Luke would rip whatever was used for tying right off. For future reference—forget wrapping Scotch tape around a wiggly head; wide packing tape is easier to apply, but easy for big paws to remove. Medical tape lasts through two or three vigorous head shakes. Duct tape takes the hair right off with it, which has got to hurt.

Whatever we tried, Luke wouldn't stop shaking his head. Every time, things broke loose again. The kitchen walls and floor looked like a murder scene but we gave up cleaning up the blood spatters. I finally put Luke in his doghouse and left him outside. By the next day he was just fine.

Kristal babied him. She and Luke would get comfortable on the living room carpet and she'd stroke his big, thick skull and rub his belly while she told him about her latest crush or the fight she'd had with her best friend. It seemed like he understood every word of her sophomore angst.

As he grew to be a linebacker of a dog, Luke became the perfect companion for little boy adventures too. He followed Jeff and his best friend Mike as they built forts and tromped through the overgrown lot between their houses.

While doing dishes one day, I heard a crashing sound in the woods and flew outside to find foliage flying and twigs snapping. I found Jeff on one side of the vacant lot, Mike on the other. They'd been taking turns calling Luke back and forth. My young engineer had tied a big blue plastic fifty-five-gallon drum behind Luke so he would forge a trail for them. Jeff had been right about those big paws! Luke plopped down at my feet with the biggest grin on his face!

Luke was just over a year old when Kristal got sick. He kept her company while she waited out a cold, the flu and a spider bite. Before I had any idea how serious this could be, she'd probably told him she was too weak to make it to the school bus without sitting down.

The day we found out Kristal had leukemia, Luke's life changed just as much as ours did. I'm sure he worried, waiting for us to come home from the hospital that night and many other nights that followed. I often just stopped by the house to throw in a quick load of laundry during the day and we often spent weeks at a time at the hospital. A neighbor visited and fed Luke until we found a pet sitter. In retrospect, I wish I'd had the time and energy to think more about his needs, but honestly I was in way over my head. It was an awful time for all of us.

After twenty months of alternating cancer and remission, we brought Kristal home for good. She wanted to be in the middle of things, so she took up her usual spot on the couch. Luke, as always, knew how fragile she was and curled up next to her. Even heavily medicated and in and out of consciousness, her arm was always draped over the side of the couch so she could finger Luke's silky ears.

When Kristal started having trouble breathing early one morning, I had to shove Luke out of the way to hold her. He stood back, watching like a faithful sentry. Luke didn't take his eyes off her until she'd breathed her last breath and I had moved away. Then, with sorrowful brown eyes, he stepped slowly over to her still form, laid his big blond head on her chest and gave her one last kiss on the cheek.

Luke's goodbye.

~Shirley Walston

# A Dog's Last Duty

*My little dog—a heartbeat at my feet.*
*~Edith Wharton*

Whisky was a mischievous West Highland White Terrier who adored my father. My parents never needed an alarm clock because Whisky would creep upstairs each morning and lick Dad's face followed by a friendly bark and a tug at the bedclothes to remind him that it was time for a walk. Each day they kept each other company along the leafy lanes of West Cornwall as they strolled through the magnificent countryside.

Then one morning my father collapsed as he was getting out of bed. Whisky was with him and after a sniff ran into the garden to fetch my mother. The agitated barking alerted Mum that something was very wrong and she rushed into the house. Dad was barely conscious. An ambulance was called and all this time Whisky stayed by Dad's side, licking him as if he was trying to offer some comfort, and then he nestled at Dad's feet to try and keep him warm. As the paramedics arrived, my father went into cardiac arrest and Mum tried to move Whisky away in case he bit the team. Whisky refused to move and sat watching as the paramedics fought to resuscitate Dad, his eyes fixed on the scene.

"I have to move that dog," Mum said to the paramedic. "He's a Terrier and likely to bite."

"Don't worry about him," said the older of the two men. "That little dog knows what we're trying to do. He'll be fine if he stays here."

And Whisky stayed to watch the paramedics and a doctor attempt to save Dad, not flinching as machinery, drugs and other medical equipment filled the house. This small white dog stayed to the end, staring ahead through the tufts of wiry hair that Westies have and not moving as the resuscitation effort was stopped and my father left this earth. The paramedic looked at Whisky, who stared back in the inquiring way that these dogs do, as if to ask if there was anything else that could be done. "I'm sorry, old boy," said the older paramedic, his eyes moistened, and clearly moved by the little dog's devotion. Whisky glanced once more at the paramedics, licked my father a last time and then went outside and sat at the entrance to the house, his duty as a faithful companion done.

~Rachael Rowe

# Cooper and the Bride

*To live in hearts we leave behind is not to die.*
~Clyde Campbell

Cooper was her sixteenth birthday present. Ashley was ecstatic and knew exactly what she was getting into, having raised Jasper for Canine Companions for Independence. She was ready for the work, the joy, the unwavering and unconditional love of a Golden Retriever. The adorable ball of fur grew... huge... and easily became our well-loved family pet. He loved everyone in true Golden fashion, but he idolized Ashley. He stood by her side as she navigated high school, grieved when she left for college and greeted her with joyous abandon whenever she came home.

Then she left home with Gerry, the love of her life, as they pursued graduate degrees across the country. When she left this time, Cooper grieved, but Goldens are hard-wired to be happy. And he was. Of course, Ashley's dad and I bought the food, paid the vet bills, and walked him every day. We set up loving care for him if we were gone. You know—all of the things pet lovers do for the family pet. Each day when I left for work, I saw his face in the window, wearing the I-can't-believe-you're-leaving-me look. I hardened my heart and left, but I was conditioned to get home as quickly as possible. He had two cats, one to play with and one who worshiped him. He had a doggy door and a fenced yard. Life was good. But it was always better when Ashley came home.

The time came when Ashley and Gerry, now her fiancé, returned home for good. They were living with us prior to their wedding. Cooper was Golden Retriever-happy. The love of his life was home. Then one weekend my husband and I went out of town and we got the call from Ashley. Something was wrong with Cooper. It's the call none of us want. The one we know we'll eventually get, but because hope springs eternal, we keep falling in love with pets. Then they become a part of the fabric of family life and there's no going back. The vet said the cancer was everywhere. There we were—four adults sitting on the floor of the small exam room with Cooper. This loyal family member had somehow masked his pain. I had walked him the usual four miles just that morning. The vet kindly asked if we preferred Cooper's remains to be cremated separately so that he could be returned to us. Even as my heart broke, I heard my husband say that it was Ashley's decision and I knew her choice would double the bill. It did.

In our family, the path of grief we walk when we lose a beloved pet is unbelievably deep and intense at first. Then gradually, the wonderful memories soften the intensity and gentle laughter follows the sharing of each pet's unique personality. It was that way with Cooper. In fact, when the vet called a few weeks later to say that we could pick up Cooper's ashes, everyone had returned to the demands of life. I brought him home in a small wooden box and suggested that we should have a little memorial and then bury the box in the woods he loved.

"Can't do it this weekend."

"Crazy busy next week."

"Out of town next weekend."

So Cooper in his beautiful box became a sort of accessory on the seldom-used dining room buffet. Time passed. Summer came. Wedding plans took over. I secretly wondered if Ashley had forgotten her beloved Cooper.

Then came August 7th: The Wedding. Ashley and Gerry were being married at our house. The tents were up. The day was beautiful. Flowers were appearing everywhere. The harpist was practicing and the phone was ringing. We had about three hours left for approximately 9,000 tasks. Ashley walked into the kitchen and said, "I want Cooper at the wedding. We have to bury him now."

If you have had a daughter getting married, you know that on that day, you agree to anything she says. Anything. That's when I knew she had chosen the right guy—Gerry looked at my husband. He looked at me. Then he looked at Ashley and said, "Okay." A short time later, I looked outside and saw Ashley, Gerry and my husband gathered in a small circle, heads and hands down, and I knew that Cooper certainly had not been forgotten. Ashley had chosen a spot overlooking the pond, not far from the flower-covered trellis that would frame "I do." I only have a fleeting memory of that scene, given the demands of the day. But the memory snippet has come back to me so many times since.

Later, as I watched our lovely daughter facing Gerry and holding his hands, I could look between them and see the sun sprinkling through the Washington evergreens creating the most beautiful cathedral I had ever seen. The soloists sang Keith Urban's "Making Memories of Us" and my husband held my hand. Our other daughter and her husband held our grandson's two-year-old hand. I looked at my parents. Ashley wore my mother's 1944 wedding gown. My brother hovered, taking pictures. And all of our friends and other family members shared the day. The perfect scene. Then I looked past the ribbons, netting and flowers and off to the side was a slight mound of dirt. And from far away I thought I heard the joyful bark that had always been saved for Ashley alone.

~Marky Olson

# Mud-dling Through

*You can avoid having ulcers by adapting to the situation: If you fall in the mud puddle, check your pockets for fish.*

*~Author Unknown*

"I'd like to arrange a photo shoot," a newspaper editor said to me recently. I had written an article on kayaking and he wanted to include pictures of my husband, Bob, and me in our two-person kayak.

With cool professionalism, I set a date. Then, in my ever-so-sophisticated fashion, I raced to the bedroom and tore through my closet, flinging shirts, shoes, and shorts over my shoulder.

"What are you doing?" Bob asked when a T-shirt landed on his head.

"They're taking our pictures Friday!" I screamed. "You have to tell me which outfit doesn't make me look fat!"

He left the room. I could hear him muttering down the hallway, "Oooh noooo...."

Early that Friday we kayaked to a lighthouse near where we live on Cape Cod. We scavenged for mussels. We were covered in black sea mud and caked-on sand. But we had allowed enough time to go back home so I could shower, change, obsess about my hair, and decide on earrings before we had to be back at the boat landing to have our photos taken. So we didn't have to rush as we returned from the lighthouse.

As we slowly paddled back in the dwindling afternoon light, we saw the beautiful silhouettes of a woman and her dog on a distant sand bar. Then we saw the dog lay down. And he didn't get up. He looked to be a very old Golden Retriever.

We watched as the woman coaxed him and then supported his hips so he could stand. They ambled on.

"Do you think they need help?" Bob asked.

"Would we be too late for the pictures?"

"I don't know, but there's no way we'd have time to go home first if we stop."

After a few labored steps, the dog laid down again. I looked down at my muddy clothes. I hesitated, hoping he'd get up. But when I saw that he couldn't, we turned the kayak towards them and began the long paddle to the sand bar. "Can we help?" I asked, as we beached the boat.

"We're fine," the woman said, in a way that showed she was used to caring for her old friend. She extended her hand in a warm greeting. She told us she lived in one of the cottages near the lighthouse. Then she looked at her dog. "This is Dexter."

Dexter got up and took a few steps toward me; then he fell. I carefully put my arms under his belly and lifted him. "I went through this with my last dog," I said to the woman. She looked away and shook her head. I knew then, that anytime we kayaked past her cottage in the future, I'd never ask, "Where's Dexter?"

The sweet dog stood comfortably in the water for a while, which took some weight off his basically useless hips. When his panting turned into what looked like a big goofy grin, we all laughed. It was a brief moment of bliss in the late day sun. And I knew I was lucky to be there for it, as I watched the shadows cast their lengthening fingers over the dunes behind the lighthouse.

Eventually we headed back in the kayak, arriving at the landing just as the photographer showed up. "How do I look?" I asked Bob.

He put his paddle down and assessed me. I stood in front of him, smiling. There was mud on my sunglasses and my left knee. My water shoes were encased with sea muck. My clothes were soaked. My hair had coagulated into several masses of knots held together with glue-like bug spray.

He didn't see any of those grimy remnants of the day on me. He just saw, in his mind, that we tried to help a failing dog on a sand bar. "You look beautiful," he said. And in my heart, I know he meant it.

~Saralee Perel

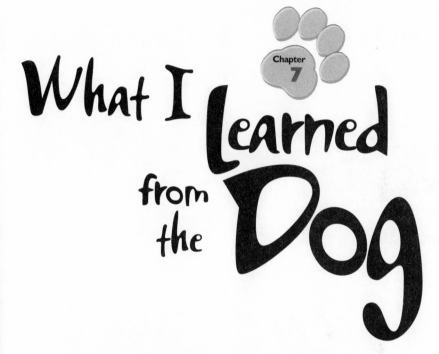

# What I Learned from the Dog

**Chapter 7**

## Learning to Put Things in Perspective

*To sit with a dog on a hillside on a glorious afternoon is to be back in Eden, where doing nothing was not boring—it was peace.*

*~Milan Kundera*

# Dog Shangri-La

*I have a simple philosophy: Fill what's empty. Empty what's full. Scratch where it itches.*
~Alice Roosevelt Longworth

Remember that old movie *Lost Horizon*? Survivors of a plane crash find themselves lost in an arctic wasteland, ice and snow surrounding them. But alas, they walk through an enchanted ice cave and enter a utopia of warmth and sunshine. They have happened upon another world, one they knew nothing of but one that greets them with new wonders and lessons.

They have discovered Shangri-La.

A few weeks ago, my son Noah and I discovered our Puggle Scooby's Shangri-La. Little did we know that beyond our home, outside our car and in a land of three acres of dirt we would discover new wonders and new lessons.

We discovered the Dog Park.

Scooby loves to run and play. We live in a very nice condo complex with several other dogs as neighbors. But the leash law is pretty strict. I let him off leash by a creek near our house sometimes, but I have to be on constant guard that he won't run off or get lost. I knew he needed a place to roam free, unrestrained and uninhibited by my constant calls of "Scooby come back. Not that far."

So we discovered a Bark Park not too far from Noah's school. We have become regulars, taking Scooby there every two or three days. He absolutely loves it. And I have found parallels between the world of dogs without leashes and the human race, for whom I sometimes think a leash law wouldn't be such a bad idea.

- Relationships take time.
  The first time Scooby ventured out with the other dogs, he was "accosted" (or humped) occasionally. He had to stand up for himself. He chose to play well with others and only "accosted" one other dog. The next time Scooby went to the park, there was no "accosting." Scooby had learned "street credibility." It takes time to find your place in your community of workmates or friends. Respect must be earned.

- Differences should be welcomed.
  The dogs play and run wildly as a pack but the moment a "new dog" comes up to the gate, they all run to welcome the arrival and sniff it. There is no profiling or racial tension. Only a bunch of happy canines barking, "New dog! New dog!" What a great world we would have if we met others with curiosity and real friendliness, instead of judgment and suspicion. But I am glad we don't have to sniff each other.

- Occasionally, special friendships happen.
  The other day Scooby came face to face with a Puggle that looked exactly, and I mean exactly, like him. Bronco and Scooby seemed to run toward each other in slow motion like in those cheesy 70s movies. They actually licked each other and then ran around together for twenty minutes. Bronco's owner and I kept getting our dogs mixed up. At the end of the play day, Bronco pooped. Scooby went to said pile and pooped on top of it. Okay eww, no lesson there, just eww!

- Never forget those who love you and feed you.
  When Noah goes outside to play, he follows the "check in"

rule obediently. When a set amount of time has gone by, he comes back to the house and yells, "Check in" to let us know he is doing fine. At the dog park, Scooby is a socializer and runs with little Chihuahuas as well as the big old hounds and German Shepherds. He knows how to play. But every once in a while, he takes his little paws and runs over to Noah and me. When he does, Noah looks at me and speaks for our Puggle, "Check in." Then Scooby goes out again, mixing it up with his "peeps" or pups. Loyalty is a trait worth cultivating. Dogs are really masters of this; we can learn from them.

- Live life unrestrained.
  Occasionally, we will witness a dog owner entering the park with a precious little princess of a dog on a leash, or worse in the arms of said owner. We watch in curiosity as the well-intended owner refuses to let the dog off the leash, or worse, out of his or her arms. Scooby and the other dogs approach said owner with an inquisitive look that says, "New dog? New dog play?" But said owner refuses, out of apparent fear. Then Scooby and the others run off and all of us at the Bark Park collectively think one thought of said owner, "Let your dog 'Dog up'!" Some people live like this. The park is calling, but they stay on the leash of fear. Running free is worth the risk.

- There is a time for play and a time for rest.
  Scooby loves going to the park and when we near it, he goes crazy in the car. But after a half hour or so, we call Scooby and he comes quite willingly, with tongue out and tail wagging. At home he finds a spot and sleeps, dreaming of other adventures at the Bark Park. It is good to be the dog. And the dog owner.

~Robbie Iobst

# 67

# Tim Russell Is in Hiding

*Yesterday I was a dog. Today I'm a dog. Tomorrow I'll probably still be a dog.*
*Sigh! There's so little hope for advancement.*
*~Charles M. Schulz*

The phone rang. I did not know it was for the dog so I answered it.

"Hello?"

"Mrs. Russell?"

"No." Usually only telemarketers called and asked for Mrs. Russell; my name is Farmer.

"Is this the residence of Tim Russell?"

"Tim Russell is my dog." I spoke the truth. Our secondary phone line was listed under our Jack Russell's name so we could avoid paying the phone company's unlisted fee.

"Your dog?" The rude person did not identify herself.

"Yes."

"I see. You named your dog Tim Russell?" she laughed suspiciously.

"Yes." I was aggravated.

"May I speak to him?"

She must be kidding, I thought, "Sure."

How was I to know she was not a telemarketer?

"Timber!" I yelled and laid the phone on the floor. Timber ran over and loudly snarfelled the receiver, expecting it to be a treat. I resisted the urge to command him to speak. Leaving the phone on the floor, I continued with my e-mails. Tim went back to his nap when he discovered the phone was not food. Eventually a tone emanated from the receiver so I hung it up. Whoever it was did not call back.

Originally I thought it was a brilliant move to list our secondary phone line under the dog's name. I got a kick out of handing it off to him when unwanted callers asked for "Tim Russell." Lesson one was never underestimate the absurdity of this world. Someday I may learn that others are more practiced at absurdity than I am.

Tim Russell is now in hiding. It is not a good idea to let your dog talk on the phone. A month after the last doggie phone chat, he received a bill from a local hospital. I laughed and then shredded the bill. Surely reality would triumph.

The next bill came from a collection agency. I wondered if I should respond. I wondered if my dog's credit rating would be ruined if I did not. I wondered if I could get credit cards in his name and run up the bills. With credit, could he get a mortgage for a luxury dog house? I wondered if a dog owner is responsible for the dog's credit because the owner is the dog's legal guardian or if it was because the dog was under eighteen. I was confused. Admittedly, I was amused the dog was getting a bill.

Out of politeness and naïveté, I called the collection agency to explain that the only hospital my dog had visited was Dr. Dan's Vet Clinic and that we did not owe him anything.

Lesson two was never call a collection agency out of politeness. I was in tears of frustration trying to explain that Tim was a dog. How many different ways can one state a simple, uncomplicated truth? He is a dog. He barks. He chews on bones. He chases cats. He even eats dog food. During the whole conversation, Timber sat and watched me intently, no doubt wondering why I kept repeating his name into the phone. I did not let him talk!

Evidently I did not do a good enough job explaining as we continued to get billed for some other Tim Russell's unpaid hospital visit.

Vainly trying to be a good citizen, I called the hospital and explained the problem. I pleaded for them to get the collection agency off my back. The billing clerk was very understanding. She even got a good chuckle from the mistake. She said she would gladly correct it.

Collection agencies are the Pit Bulls of the money world. We continued to get threats and collection notices. I disconnected the phone number listed under the dog's name but the notices continued. I wrote nasty letters to the collection agency. That did not help.

As a last ditch attempt to stop the collection agency harassment, I sent them a picture of Tim, a copy of his AKC registration and a copy of his latest vet bill marked PAID. I suggested that they call the vet if they had any further questions. Perhaps if they called Doctor Dan, he could more clearly explain that my Jack Russell Terrier is a dog and that it was unlikely he had been treated at the local hospital.

Finally, we moved. The move was totally unrelated to Tim Russell's $165 hospital bill. However, I did not request Tim Russell's mail be forwarded. Our new phone is not in his name.

I have not heard from the collection agency since. My only fear is that they will put out an arrest warrant for Tim. No doubt they will send a canine unit.

~Jane Marie Allen Farmer

# 68

# Hey Mom, We're Home

*The first sign of maturity is the discovery that the volume knob also turns to the left.*
~Jerry M. Wright

The den floor is covered with toys as the boys wrestle and roughhouse. Yelps of glee punctuate the air. But I don't have any small children at my house.

My college kids are home with their dogs.

Adam is home with Brother, a young Spaniel mix, and Emily brought her rambunctious Puggle, Otto, home for a visit. As a result, the two old Chihuahuas who live with me have been transformed from gentle, sleepy pets to tiny warriors defending their turf.

The Chihuahuas snarl and snap as the college dogs gallop through the house like two frat boys on spring break. Stuffed toys are shredded, the white cotton scattered to every corner. Slimy rawhide bones squish under my feet while tennis balls bounce about, narrowly missing lamps and pictures on the wall.

I never gave Emily or Adam my permission to adopt dogs—but, of course, they didn't ask. Both acquired their pets spontaneously. Emily called one Saturday to tell me she and her boyfriend were going to look at puppies, just for fun.

"That's like going to a bakery to look at cookies," I told her.

An hour later she walked up my front sidewalk, a tawny, black-faced Beagle-Pug mix in her arms.

Adam's dog arrived late at night while his reclusive neighbors eluded their enemies and skipped bail. Before they slipped out of the apartment parking lot they knocked at Adam's door and handed him a leash; the black dog was almost invisible in the dark. "We're moving and can't take him with us," they said.

The next day I received an e-mail from Adam with a warning, "Don't get too attached." He told me about the dog and enclosed a grinning photo of himself and a serious-looking Spaniel he named "Brother." I had seen that smile on Adam's face before. He was attached.

Emily and Adam grew up with the Chihuahuas. They loved to play with their pets but rarely noticed an empty water bowl and didn't seem to hear when the dogs barked to be let in or out. Occasionally, "a puppy" showed up on their Christmas lists, but they never seemed too disappointed when one didn't turn up on Christmas morning.

They both adjusted well to the responsibilities of college life and never implied that pet dogs would make their lives complete.

I was concerned that my son, whose bank account often hovered at $1.86, couldn't afford a pet. I knew that universities and animal shelters dreaded semester end when cats and dogs often were abandoned. I also knew other parents of college students who inherited pets that didn't work out as college roommates.

I need not have worried.

"Do you have pet insurance for the Chihuahuas?" Adam asked, on his first visit home with Brother. He was stunned to learn that his single mother of three children, two in college, did not have pet insurance.

He already had taken Brother to the vet for his shots and had him neutered for $35 at an animal clinic for low-income pet owners. With his monthly allowance from me and a part-time job, his income fell well within their range.

When we took Brother on walks, Adam was careful to keep him out of the street. Brother stayed near Adam without a leash, just a whistle stopped any wandering. When we came inside, Adam gently plucked stickers and bits of leaves from Brother's fur.

Was this the same boy who left baby Chloe crying herself to sleep in our garage just months earlier? He was Chloe's father for a day as an assignment in a high school child development class. A battery-powered baby, Chloe sounded her realistic cry when she was hungry or wet. When Adam's efforts failed to stop the crying he stashed Chloe in the garage and closed the door.

I had another worry about Emily's pet. She and her boyfriend bought the Puggle together. Emily was the noncustodial parent, her apartment didn't allow pets.

My youngest son asked the question that hung in the air.

"Who will get the dog when they break up?"

"I don't think they plan to break up," I said.

I was very fond of Emily's boyfriend, but I wasn't quite ready for the implications of joint pet ownership.

I watched as they raised Otto together, training him to sit and stay, buying him toys and nursing him through stomachaches. Together they taught him to nudge a bell by the apartment door when he needed to go outside. David wrestled with him on the floor, Emily bought him a turquoise and lime green Vera Bradley leash for their long walks. I don't think David liked the leash but I admired his silence on the matter.

They beamed with pride when they brought Otto to my house for visits, in spite of his battles with the Chihuahuas and tendency to munch on my zinnias and crash through my bed of perennials.

The college dogs quickly warmed up to me; they could see that I was the leader of this pack, but their loyalty was to their owners. When Adam left my house, Brother sat by the door, sad-faced, until he returned. Otto slept at the foot of Emily's bed when she visited and gave a low growl when I opened her door to wake her.

I've read that maturity is defined as "the ability to put another person's needs first." I would add dogs to that definition. Somewhere between tripping over the empty water bowl and her first years of college, my daughter learned to interrupt her own sleep to take her dog outside on cold mornings. Adam's bank account still hovers dangerously low, but Brother is well-fed, groomed and medicated against fleas.

Last fall Emily received an engagement ring carefully attached to Otto's collar. He was dressed in a top hat and bow tie for the occasion. Her new husband, David, is a welcome addition to our family.

Sometimes it can be hard for a mother to acknowledge that her children are growing up and starting their own lives. It took two youthful and well-cared-for college dogs to convince me that my children have taken giant steps to an important milestone — maturity.

~Nancy Lowell George

# 69

# Old Dog, New Tricks

*Could we change our attitude, we should not only see life differently,*
*but life itself would come to be different.*
~Katherine Mansfield

Every picture I've seen of my husband when he was a kid has a dog in it. So naturally, when we got married and moved to the country, I couldn't wait to surprise him with a puppy. I heard about a family who was getting rid of a Collie-mix and snagged it for him.

Right off the bat, there were two problems with Blaze joining our household. One, he was the most hyperactive dog on the planet, and two, both David and I worked constantly. That meant leaving Blaze home alone where he was forced to entertain himself by chewing on everything within a square mile and digging holes in the most inconvenient places.

Then David left town for two weeks on business and I knew I had to do something with our lonely, over-affectionate, ADHD dog. So I headed to the animal shelter convinced that what our puppy needed to vent some of his energy was a buddy. I pulled into the parking lot, got out of my car and met Biscuit. There he stood in his outdoor pen, a sturdy yellow Lab looking at me with eyes that said, "What took you so long?" The woman inside asked if I'd chosen the pet I wanted to adopt. "No," I said, "but I think one just chose me."

When I told her which one it was, she made sure I knew this was a ten-year-old dog. I thought, "That's good." He's a teenager. We probably don't need another puppy. I had no idea I was adopting a geriatric dog. As we filled out the paperwork, on one of the forms I noticed a name I knew, a childhood neighbor of mine. When I inquired about it, the shelter volunteer explained that this dog had belonged to my neighbor's father. When he died, she couldn't keep him so she was paying board at the shelter in hopes that someone would come along and adopt him.

When Biscuit and I arrived home, it took him and Blaze all of about five minutes to become best friends. I was worn out just watching them race around the yard together. I'd throw a stick in our pond and the two would sail into the water, splash toward it side by side, each take one end of it in his mouth and swim all the way back to shore, jaw to jaw, where they never tired of pulling it back and forth.

I couldn't wait for David to call that night so I could tell him about Blaze's new buddy. There was silence on the other end of the line, but after I regaled him with tales of the two dog's shenanigans, he warmed to the idea and looked forward to meeting Biscuit.

During the next two weeks, I caught myself trying to get home early from work so I could watch the two dogs play. Fetch in the pond was their favorite game. For the first couple of days, when I'd throw the stick, they were equally frantic to swim out to it so they could fight over it all the way back to shore. Their swimming styles were a study in contrasts. Blaze churned up water for a foot on either side working feverishly to keep afloat. Biscuit, being a Lab with webbed feet, glided across the water with barely a ripple, his legs moving indiscernibly under the water.

By day two, Biscuit figured something out. When I threw the stick in the water, if he stayed on the shore, he could let that young whippersnapper do all the work of hauling it back to shore where he was waiting to wrestle it away from him. The exuberance of youth versus the wisdom of age.

After a couple of days, I called the neighbor whose name I'd seen on the form at the shelter to tell her I had her daddy's dog. She was thrilled and commended me for adopting such an old dog. Biscuit?

Old? She talked about how she'd see him walking the neighborhood with her dad and laugh at how similar they were, doing the same old man shuffle. For a minute I thought we were talking about two different dogs. But the more we talked, the more I realized that this indeed was the dog she'd left at the shelter.

Apparently all Biscuit needed was the influence of a puppy to realize how much pup he still had inside. David and I worried that the newness might wear off and before long Biscuit would start shooing Blaze away to settle back into his old man lifestyle. No deal. He and Blaze were constant companions, wrestling partners, swimmers, racers and nine times out of ten, it was Biscuit who started the next tussling match.

Biscuit lived for another six years—six healthy, happy, active years. Now Blaze is the old man of the family. His face is speckled with gray and he naps more than he used to. When we go for a walk, rather than running up ahead and in and out of neighbors' yards for a sniff fest, he's content to amble along beside me. I can't help but wonder what a puppy would do in his life. Would it perk him up the way he had old Biscuit? Would it add years to his life and life to whatever years he has left? I need to run some errands tomorrow around the neighborhood where the shelter is located. I might just have to zip by there and see if anyone else is waiting to adopt me.

~Mimi Greenwood Knight

# The Magic of Second Chances

*If you don't like something change it;*
*if you can't change it, change the way you think about it.*
~Mary Engelbreit

Years of disappointing infertility treatments can leave you feeling raw inside—like an asphalt-skinned knee, or that tender place beneath an ugly blister when you peel the outer layer away. It was the kind of open wound that drove me to crazy acts. Acts like directing daggered looks at women shopping for baby wipes; and absurdly mean, but fortunately silent, comments toward unsuspecting pregnant women at the mall.

What got me through those ugly days, and what served as a bandage over that intense rawness, was this: There remained a tiny degree of hope that the next month could be different—that this time, the moon and the stars and my body would all magically align to give me what I wanted most in the world... a baby. But unfortunately, celestial magic and pregnancy continued to elude me.

Then we got the worst news of all. Our doctor called to give us some new, cutting-edge test results: Statistically, I had a much better chance of winning the lottery—twice—than giving birth to a baby. She recommended no further treatments, no further procedures. In her opinion, my body was simply not capable of pregnancy.

It was an early spring day when I got that call. Just that morning I had heard the chirping of birds outside my office window for the first time since the fall. (I liked birds; I envied their tenacity, not to mention their egg production.) But after listening to the doctor's words that afternoon—the phone pressed hard to my ear—that chirping and the traffic on the street all blurred and fell away into pieces on the floor. I remember placing the phone neatly back in its place on my desk, then doubling over in a devastating emotional pain that caught my breath in its grip and wouldn't let go.

That evening, with my husband out of town, I curled up on the couch with our Collie, George Bailey. He rested his long, Lassie-nose on my leg. He'd already secretly enjoyed the pint of butter pecan ice cream I'd opened but couldn't eat. And now he looked concerned about the growing pile of used tissues at our feet.

I rehashed the conversation with the doctor in my head, searching for something, anything that might offer a hint of optimism. But there was nothing I could hold on to this time. And her last, harsh words tumbled through my thoughts again and again. "Honestly, if I were you, I'd consider adoption."

Adopting a child? It wasn't that we didn't think it was a good idea. We thought it was great—for other people. I think in some ways, saying "adoption" out loud would've meant some kind of defeat to us—a bleak acknowledgement that perhaps we might not, in the end, conceive. And that wasn't something we could let ourselves believe.

But now, the world and everything in it was upside down and strange. I was no longer a woman who would someday see the outline of our baby's spine on an ultrasound image. I was no longer a woman who would learn Lamaze, who would fret over whether or not to hire a mid-wife, who would ask friends for their hand-me-down maternity clothes. Even our home in the Colorado mountains seemed empty and cold, the clouded moon outside more scarred than before.

I looked down at George Bailey, our formerly abused, now reformed, sweet loyal canine companion. I wanted to make sure he hadn't changed before my eyes, too. I ran my fingers through his soft, thick fur. I had to smile. George Bailey had served as a pillow, confidant, sounding board and heating pad in recent months. Now his tawny-tan coat was absorbing my tears.

We had adopted George from a rescue group two years before, his beat-up body complete with two broken legs. We'd brought him home around the holidays; the group had named him after the movie, *It's a Wonderful Life*. Both Jimmy Stewart's character and our George Bailey had been given a second chance at life.

George Bailey's dark, almond eyes stared up at me as I stroked his ears. Adoption in his case had been an easy decision. We met him online and immediately wanted to give this bruised soul a happy, comfortable home.

For George Bailey, though, becoming a part of our lives had been a leap of faith. Those almond eyes didn't always reflect love and trust.

In the beginning, he was guarded. He didn't make a sound for months. Finally, after a great deal of coaxing (not to mention treats) on our part, he decided to give us a chance. I imagine he had to overcome many doubts—and a lot of bad memories—to take the jump.

That's when I decided maybe it was time for us to learn a little something from George Bailey: Maybe it was time for us to take our own leap of faith... in a new direction.

Maybe it was my husband and me who needed a second chance.

I stayed up all night long, George Bailey sleeping at my feet, a crackling fire toasting the cabin and tossing shadows on the walls. I researched international and domestic adoption. I read blogs; I read adoptive child psychology reports. I read about state and federal laws, about laws in countries I had only previously thought of when reading ethnic restaurant menus.

That night of research set us on a journey that has transformed our lives. Within a few months, we had settled on domestic adoption, and worked on how we would fund the $30,000 bill. Within a few more months, we had completed our paperwork and passed our physicals and background checks. (Luckily, my pregnant-women-hating behavior never got out.)

By August, we were matched with a nearby birthmother and birthfather who chose us to be the parents of their unborn child.

For us, the next sixty days were a whirlwind of emotion and planning. It was a time of continued healing, and of finally allowing myself to touch velvety newborn clothes at babyGap. And it was a time of changing our ideas of what it meant to be a family.

When the time came, we held our son when he was minutes old. We cried with the birthparents, for our shared happiness, for their loss. We told the birthparents we loved them. We meant it. We brought home our baby and introduced him to George Bailey. Our Collie seemed... proud of us.

Our son is now two years old. The time between his birth and the finalization of the adoption was six months. We never let ourselves consider the fact that his birthparents had every right to change their minds during this time. We loved completely, holding nothing back—fully aware that the rawness we felt during the infertility years would be a paper cut compared to how we might feel if we lost him.

Magic, it's safe to say, no longer eludes us. Every day is filled with new words, wild giggles and watermelon-stained cheeks. And I owe it all to my sweet and gentle George Bailey, who taught me how to put the hurt and doubt behind me—and take that leap.

~Kathy Lynn Harris

# Braving the Weather with Lucky

*There is an itch in runners.*
~Arnold Hano

I lace my shoes to the mocking chatter of the rain and slosh out to the kennel. I don't want to do this, but I know that Lucky does. She is already waiting for me, turning inside out with delight and ricocheting around the yard. How that dog knows we're going for a run is a mystery. Maybe she can hear the rustle of my clothing. Maybe she can feel the vibrations my shoes make as I walk across the floor.

Maybe she can read my mind.

When I open the gate, Lucky streaks from the yard. I don't need to point her in the right direction. She knows exactly where we're going on this cold, drizzly morning. We're headed out for our training run.

I've been preparing for a marathon for the past several months, and that means running ten miles a day, without fail, regardless of the weather.

Sometimes I don't think I would do it without the company of Lucky.

Today we're running on the logging road. It's not so much a road as a crack in the woods, a narrow path that's gouged by rain and slick with mud. We are surrounded by the smell of damp trees and the close comforting feeling of a forest grown so thick your eyes can't penetrate a hundred feet.

Civilization falls away like so much sloughed skin.

At the crest of the hill is an old abandoned logging road. For Lucky and me, this is where the fun starts. The logging road is a perfect place to run. It's a ten-mile loop filled with steep ridges, roller coaster straightaways, sharp switchbacks, and the occasional leg-cramping hill that temporarily reduces me to a sucking blowfish.

Lucky gives the throttle a quarter turn and stretches out her stride. I do my best to keep up with her.

A mile down the trail and we are soaked. The rain has seeped through the seams of my jacket and turned Lucky's sand-colored fur several shades darker. I grumble about this, but Lucky doesn't seem to mind. My furry partner and I have run this trail in all kinds of weather—everything from parched summer heat to freezing winter chill. We have run in fog as dense as anything heretofore seen in a Pink Floyd concert.

Lucky will take the logging road any way she can get it.

We head east, gliding past an imposing hedge of brush, dipping a shoulder and bending a knee to avoid low limbs. The trail winds its way high and low through the woods. Here it clings to a hillside, there it meanders through a grove of redwoods. Lucky and I move along like a couple of modern-day wolves.

This isn't a place to run all out. The logging road is primitive, watch-your-step, down-and-dirty running. It's a private refuge and a reminder of some simpler era. There are no paved streets, no 7-Elevens, no angry motorists or trucks shrieking by with a suck of wind.

Our logging road is a place where lost is a rule of thumb. The trees here are the trees there. Nothing in particular, all in general. Forest folds into forest, sky into sky. The solitude bends back on itself.

This is running just the way Lucky and I like it.

Lucky ranges out, but always stays within sight of me. Maybe it's because I'm the guy who doles out her Kibbles 'n Bits. Or maybe her appreciation of me runs even deeper.

I once saved Lucky when she was attacked by a huge rawboned Rottweiler. The Rottweiler broke free from its chain as we were running by, rushed Lucky and locked its jaws around her throat. Instinctively, I delivered a testicle-crunching kick that sent the big animal scurrying for home.

Lucky has been my close running companion ever since.

For the next hour, Lucky pushes me up hills, leads me through patches of brush, and sprints alongside me past owl hoots so raw with enigma that it would send half of America grabbing for the Valium bottle. Faster and faster we move along.

At the crest of the mountain the storm breaks and the sun pushes through the clouds. Far off I can see a small town. Beyond that, all the ridges are shadow and light. A glance at Lucky tells me it's time to turn around and head for home.

We hurtle back down the road through time. Before me, blurry with speed, covered in mud, Lucky sets the pace with a fine-tuned stride. As the trail flattens, I take one last look back at the mountains. Everywhere, for miles, the wilderness is all one thing, like a great mirror, infinitely green and beautiful, always the same.

This is what we have come for, the solitude, the repetition, the dense hypnotic drone of the woods.

Plus Lucky and I both needed to get our ten miles of running in.

~Tim Martin

# Volunteering from the Heart

*The purpose of life is a life of purpose.*
*~Robert Byrne*

Are we all guided by a sense of purpose and do we live to fulfill that purpose? I am often reminded of the value of living with purpose and passion by our precious dog Toby, a seven-year-old Chesapeake Bay Retriever, who volunteers from the heart. I firmly believe that people (and animals) come into our lives for a reason and I now know the reason Toby chose us: he reminds us daily of the importance of passion, unconditional love and living with purpose.

We adopted Toby from a rescue agency two years ago. He came to us with some baggage; his original owners loved him and struggled when the time came to surrender him for adoption due to tragic circumstances within the family. Toby was about twenty-five pounds overweight when he entered foster care but when we adopted him several months later he was at a healthy weight for his size.

Several months after welcoming Toby to our family, little quirks, odd habits and strange behaviours began to surface. It was almost as if when he knew he was home to stay, he could relax enough to be himself. He began to exhibit extreme separation anxiety. When we would leave for work he would empty the front hall closet contents into the middle of the entranceway, knock things over and try and lock himself in rooms. He would also close himself in the bathroom and when unable to escape, he would crash the toilet tank lid to the floor (we have gone through four tank lids to date).

Toby is an excessive barker. Not only would he bark at neighbours, other animals and noises, but he seemed to bark just to hear his own voice. Every Monday, which is garbage day, Toby empties the hall closet contents into the middle of the floor and sometimes removes all the coats from their hangers. When it is meal time, Toby either goes outside to bark, or goes into the bathroom and bangs the shower doors with his nose or knocks the shampoo bottle into the bathtub. While frustrating at first, these behaviours and odd habits have now become somewhat amusing for our family. They are our daily reminders of Toby's individuality and personality.

Then there was what we refer to as "the incident of all incidents." My husband Christopher arrived home from work first, and by phone he described our house as a "murder zone." He explained that Toby was fine but there was blood and mess everywhere. Apparently Toby knocked a number of items off the counter including the kettle, teapot, knife block and in doing so, must have cut his foot. Then knocking over plants and the water cooler, he trekked dirt and ran through the house spreading blood and muck everywhere. It even appeared he may have tried to call for help as the phone was all bloodied.

After this incident, we took Toby to the vet as well as an animal behaviourist and trainer for help. Maggie, from Capable Canines, provided us with a range of suggestions and helpful strategies. The most profound was her conclusion that Toby was uncertain of his role — Toby needed a purpose.

Wow! What an incredible "ah ha" moment. Just like people need a purpose, so do animals. Toby and I explored the potential to become part of a volunteer team so that he could work as a therapy dog. We were introduced to the Chimo Project, a well-respected pet assisted therapy program in Edmonton, Alberta. With tremendous excitement and curiosity, Toby passed his obedience and temperament tests with flying colours. We were then accepted as volunteers with Chimo and were soon placed with Alberta Hospital Edmonton.

On the way to the volunteer coordinator's office, Toby seemed to somehow know he was "working." He walked up the steps to the building in a confident manner, stopping with me at the reception desk. Of course everyone was very interested in Toby, and he had to greet everyone by stopping in each office as we walked down the hall. Toby was curious, happy and very social with the volunteer coordinator, and slobbered all over her, just like he does with us. It was like he was saying, "I have arrived!"

Wednesday afternoons are clearly the highlight of Toby's world. The moment I bring out the Volunteer Bag (a knapsack used solely for his volunteering and containing toys, treats and his uniform), the non-stop barks of excitement begin. This makes putting on his special harness and volunteer vest an interesting challenge. The drive from our home to the hospital typically consists of Toby smiling, barking and panting with excitement. Once at the hospital we put on his special red bandana and his Volunteer Photo Badge.

When the door opens to the hospital and particularly to the unit we volunteer on, Toby's sense of purpose is evident. He greets everyone he sees with curiosity, acceptance and joy. The fascinating part is that he clearly seems to understand his purpose and proves that by interacting with each individual in the appropriate manner needed at the time. With some individuals Toby is playful; with others he is quiet and gentle. Some are blessed with his affection while others are treated with a respectful distance — Toby is intuitive enough to recognize that around some people, he must be quiet, and respectful of their need for space and distance.

His activities change each week. Sometimes patients take him for a walk or to play fetch outside. On other visits he performs tricks and shows off. Patients also help him with his obedience class homework.

Toby finds simple pleasure in things that many of us would not even notice, like a dust bunny, a leaf tumbling across the grass, a rabbit or squirrel hiding behind a tree or a dog barking in the background on the TV. When playing fetch, his sole purpose and focus is on the toy and the individual playing with him (nothing else matters to him at that moment except his purpose). And when it comes to people, Toby connects through the heart. He unconditionally accepts each and every person he visits.

As I watch my dog each week, I see the growth and change in him becoming more pronounced. Each week he lives his purpose! This program has also been therapy for the therapy dog. Since volunteering, we have noticed that Toby's barking is less of a problem as he is confident in himself and in new situations. He is more comfortable being away from my husband and me. In addition, his weekly interactions with the patients have clearly helped him grow, change and live life fully.

His story has inspired me to pursue a number of purposeful activities including developing my own Life Purpose Statement, consciously living more purposefully, and writing more about strategies for people to live a purposeful and intentional life, all based on lessons I have learned from our precious Toby.

~Charmaine Hammond

# Finding Home

*I don't think of all the misery but of the beauty that still remains.*
~Anne Frank

My dog has taught me that you can overcome a bad start in life. When he came to us he was thin and hungry and had bald spots from fleas. He had an infection. The people who had him wanted to get rid of him. He was the last in the litter and if they couldn't find a home for him they were going to shoot him. My neighbor took him so he wouldn't be shot, but she couldn't keep him. My mom and dad decided to let me have him.

We took him to the vet the next day. The vet said we got him there just in time. With medicine and shots he soon began to be the best dog ever. He is now happy and healthy and a great pet. We named him Lucky because we were lucky to find him and give him a good home.

I understand how his life has been because my life had pretty much been the same. Even though he was a dog, I understood how it made him feel to be treated that way. I was in foster care for almost five years. My first years of life were really tough. Taking care of him has helped me deal with some of my past hurt and problems.

Another thing I've learned from my dog is not to give up. I never gave up the hope for a family. I was adopted when I was eight years old. We got Lucky soon after my adoption was final. I knew I would be here forever. Lucky has helped me feel secure and reminds me that hard times won't last forever.

Taking care of Lucky made me want to help other dogs. I've decided to become a veterinarian when I grow up. For now I try to help any dogs I see that need help. So far, I've helped about six dogs find their homes. Being in your home for good is the best feeling you can have, whether you are a dog or a human.

~Alexis Joy May, age 10

# July 12th

*Turn your face to the sun and the shadows fall behind you.*
~Maori Proverb

Certain dates have special meanings. Birthdays, anniversaries, and holidays are some. There are dates filled with less joyful meanings, too, like deaths, miscarriages, and accidents. On July 12, 1995, when I was twenty-four years old, a man walked past the doorman of my New York City apartment building, took the elevator to my floor, opened my unlocked front door, and raped me. The horror that struck my life that mid-summer evening created a before-and-after event on my personal timeline.

The first anniversary of that day was the most difficult. The attack was still fresh, and the trial that put him behind bars for twenty-five to fifty years had just come to a close. By the second anniversary, much needed time had passed. Friends and family nodded from a distance, not wanting to revive old monsters. By my third anniversary I was deep in a relationship with a man who is now my husband. Although time and love have helped me recover, every July 12th a pesky shadow follows me around.

When I was six, my parents bought me, an only child, a Springer Spaniel puppy. In my six-year-old wisdom, I named her Fluffy. Despite her inappropriate name, Fluffy became my sibling, and was a faithful friend until she died — when I was twenty-one. A dog lover who has lost a beloved pet knows all about the emptiness. I wanted another dog, but the timing wasn't right. I had just graduated from college and was about to start my career in New York City. A few years later, after the rape and the subsequent rebuilding of my life, I was ready for a dog. I was ready for the commitment and more than ready to fill the hole in my life left by Fluffy's death.

My search began and ended in October 1998. I went to a breeder of Bichon Frisés that my mother knew. The breeder had had a litter of puppies in the summer, and there were two males left. She brought out a white puppy with apricot ears, and I swooned. He licked my face and took off around the room, curious about life beyond his pen. I asked the breeder how old he was, and she said thirteen weeks. When was his birthday, I asked? She looked through her paperwork and said, "July 12th."

July 12th will always remain a difficult day for me. It is the day I met evil. I still have a pesky little shadow that follows me around, but he looks a little different, and he gives me a reason to celebrate the day. Now July 12th is Scout's birthday, and his kisses help me remember how lucky I am to be alive.

~Jennifer Quasha

# We All Stoop to Scoop

*Amount of time it takes for a dog to "do its business" is directly proportional to outside temperature + suitability of owner's outerwear.*
*~Betsy Cañas Garmon, www.wildthymecreative.com*

*D*esperate Housewives* might be a lot less intimidating for women everywhere if the stars had real dogs that required real walking with real pooper scoopers. No one can be flawless if they respond to the needs of their dogs. My life was filled with secrets until I got a dog. No one outside my immediate family knew the "Before Make-up Nancy." But that was BC (before canines). Now I am the disheveled woman in the hot pink martini bathrobe standing at the paper box pleading with a Chihuahua and a Maltese to "go potty." The pooches oblige, ferociously barking at an early morning jogger, forcing me to apologize for both their rude behavior and my outrageous get-up. Polite neighbors turn their heads away as they drive by.

Dogs remind us of our strengths and our weaknesses. In my husband's case, there are the remnants of a stereotypical mother who cannot deny a child sustenance. In his world, love means never having to say "no more biscuits." My pocket Chihuahua now fits only in a suitcase. My kids are different. My oldest son is the firm parent. For him they will dance or sit and wait patiently. My youngest son's need to be an older child emerges. He worries about the canine propensity for napping ("It can't be healthy for them to sleep all day") and suggests we get them some puzzles. The optimist has high hopes for his pets, neither of whom have yet to appear on Letterman doing a jigsaw. My need to be adored surfaces. In the confines of my own home I become Sally Field because they love me. They really love me! Quietly they follow me around the house. Never do they ask for money or permission. Obviously my every move is worthy of observation. I smile a little bit more and that's a good thing.

Ever since the dogs came into my life, my flawed self has been on display for the world, or at least the neighborhood to see. I've been half dressed, overdressed and badly dressed, all for the sake of two sets of big sad eyes and respect for some oriental carpets. I walk the street with two extendable leashes tripping me every other step and a few plastic bags stuffed in my pockets as though I need to add more bulk to my body. I stopped apologizing for my look a long time ago. My canine companions have proven that mascara isn't mandatory. I still have friends and my husband never really put much stock in it.

I like to think that God made dogs so that we could escape our self-absorbed lives. Pooper scooping knows no boundaries. And how tough can you be with a tiny sleeping Chihuahua in your lap or a seventy-pound mutt who thinks she's a Chihuahua. We melt to our weakest selves when we love our pets, and sometimes become our strongest when we care for them or have to let them go. A 6'5" FBI agent friend summed it up perfectly as he spoke of the family's teacup Maltese. "It takes a big man to walk a little dog." Maybe you become a bigger person when you love a dog, and I like to think you become a better one.

~Nancy Berk

# Furring the Nest

*One man's trash is another man's treasure.*
~Kevin Smith

There's dog hair everywhere! Oh, that Bo! Why does he shed so much? I know. My fault. One look at those big brown eyes, pleading with me from the back porch, is all it takes for me to open the door. Into the house he bounds. Nose sniffing. Tongue hanging. Tail wagging.

Bo is our four-year-old golden Labrador Retriever. He's loyal, gentle and affectionate. Bo can plop his sixty-five pounds of love and fur in your lap, and lick your face at the same time. There's only one small annoyance. His thick, golden, hairy coat sheds—a lot. One morning, as I was sipping coffee and absorbing the sights of the budding trees, five little sparrows landed on the porch. Bo was in his usual laidback pose, oblivious to the feathered friends hopping around him. As my half-awakened eyes focused, I noticed something in one bird's beak.

What is it? I thought. Oh... it's Bo's hair. What's that bird doing? It's gathering some of Bo's soft fur to line its nest!

I remembered all those times I silently grumbled about his cast-off hair. Sweeping. Vacuuming. Assembling the vacuum hose and its attachments. All the times I made sure everyone had a turn using the lint roller before leaving home. Now, I'm observing a bird about to use something I consider a nuisance.

I watched it as it flew to its nest. The back porch scene I had just witnessed swayed my view of Bo's shedding hair. My sentiments were transformed from irritation to the realization of nature's superb resourcefulness. In the cycle of life, nothing is wasted. Through time, things that appear destroyed, that are shed or discarded are used again. Endings decompose and nourish beginnings.

I sat and imagined how the new hatchlings would feel as they nestled and snuggled in the comfort of their soft nest. Naked and defenseless, yet warm, secure and protected in the plush surroundings of Bo's golden fur.

~Mary E. McCloud

# My Little Diplomat

*People often say that "beauty is in the eye of the beholder," but I say that the*
*most liberating thing about beauty is realizing that you are the beholder.*
*This empowers us to find beauty in places where others have not*
*dared to look, including inside ourselves.*
*~Salma Hayek*

Nathaniel was the first dog that was entirely my responsibility. I was twenty-one when I left home and found myself living next door to a couple who had a cute little Poodle with a litter of pups. They suspected a Terrier living in the next block had fathered her brood.

Barely six weeks old when I brought him home, he was a cute little guy, but as he grew, he got uglier by the day. His coat stuck out in every direction like a bottle brush and was black, flecked with gray; not the most attractive of color combinations. He was slim but his legs were way too long for his body and his goofy-looking tail curled in an arch over his back. Literally everyone who saw him teased me about what a ridiculous-looking little animal he was. Yet, in the end, he always won their hearts. He was Mr. Personality; a homely little dog that made friends everywhere we went.

When I got him, I was just entering my hippie phase. I moved around a lot, switched boyfriends fairly often, hitchhiked when my junk heap of a car wasn't running and generally lived a lifestyle most dogs would have found difficult to accept. Not Nathaniel. I could take him anywhere and as soon as he inspected the place a bit, he would settle in with ease. Even without a leash, he never ran into the street or made messes inside and he learned to sit up and beg, which increased his appeal to everyone we encountered during our adventures. He was the perfect traveling companion and his manners were impeccable. Somehow, he always seemed to know just how to act in every situation.

He did get lost once. He followed my friend's Irish Setter when she dug under the fence to escape in search of a doggie adventure. Nathaniel was unfamiliar with the area and apparently, couldn't keep up with the bigger dog or find his way back. I was fearful and worried when the Setter came home without him. He was wearing a nametag, but he was so ugly, I was afraid no one would bother to help him.

He not only found a sympathetic soul who called me, but when I went to get him, I discovered she lived in one of the most affluent neighborhoods I had ever seen. I passed one mansion after another until I came to the address. There were iron gates and an intercom which I buzzed, even as I wondered if this could really be the right house. Sure enough, the gates parted and a voice told me to drive on in.

As I approached the house, the front door opened and there stood a woman with a cute little Yorkshire Terrier under one arm and Nathaniel under the other. She told me if he hadn't had the nametag she would have kept him because, other than her little Yorkie, he was the sweetest and smartest dog she had ever encountered. To get her attention, he walked up to her in a parking lot, barked, then twirled on his hind legs before coming to rest in his "sit up and beg" position.

"It was as if he was asking me to read his tag," she gushed, as she handed him to me.

Being beautiful can be a great advantage, but Nathaniel taught me that what's on the inside is infinitely more powerful and important than what's on the outside. Whenever I'm feeling insecure because of a bad hair day or those few extra pounds I can't seem to lose, I remember my homely little dog who managed to get positive feedback from everyone he ever met.

A couple of years ago I ran into a guy I hadn't seen for almost three decades. Within two minutes he brought up the ugly little dog he remembered was always with me and asked whatever happened to him. I told him Nathaniel had lived almost seventeen years; longer than any other dog I've ever owned.

"He sure was something," my friend commented.

He was right.

~Susanne Fogle

# Prince of Pleasure

*Pleasure is the flower that passes; remembrance, the lasting perfume.*
*~Jean de Boufflers*

When I heard the loud thud, I barreled up the basement steps, but it was already too late.

There it was: the evidence. Exhibit A was an empty Dunkin' Donuts box on the floor beside the leg of the kitchen table; exhibit B was my German Shepherd-Beagle mix, guilt-ridden and trembling, in the corner, with eyes that said, "I know I shouldn't have, but I couldn't help myself."

"Mom!" I wailed in an octave high enough to shatter glass, "Prince ate all the donuts!!"

Food. It was Prince's undoing. He loved to eat. And to be precise, any food would suffice because he never met a morsel of "people food" he didn't like. Except for iceberg lettuce. (But in all fairness, who actually enjoys iceberg lettuce?) That meant everything else was fair game, particularly if it possessed sugar, fat, or carbohydrates—a trilogy of gastric delights. This was particularly unfortunate for Prince, considering he also had been diagnosed with a thyroid irregularity for which he was prescribed medication in the form of a tiny pewter-colored tablet that we tricked him into swallowing by inserting it into a grape or tiny piece of dinner roll once a day.

But virtually nothing could stand in the way of Prince and his pleasure.

The latest casualty was a dozen fresh glazed donuts from Dunkin'

Donuts. Actually, he had devoured only eight of them to be exact, as my parents and I had savored four. In signature fashion, Prince would hover beside one of us when we gathered at the table to eat our daily meals, hoping desperately that something—anything—would evade our rhythm of plate-to-mouth. He'd drool. He'd stare at you intently should you make eye contact with him. And he'd whimper, sometimes even wince, as if it pained him not to eat. Meanwhile, across the room, both sides of his gray plastic double bowl—one side for water, the other for food—remained chock-full.

After breakfast, I completed my ritual of clearing the table as fast as I could before tending to more important matters in the basement. I was nine at the time, and my world revolved around planning fashion shows with my dolls. I had one meticulously planned—my mom's treadmill would provide the runway and I had found an industrial flashlight in the garage that would serve as the spotlight. (You become the personification of ingenuity when you're an only child.) At the same time, Prince had designs on the donut box that, in my haste, I had failed to push to the center of the table, therefore making it perfectly accessible to him should he hoist his one-hundred-plus-pound girth on his hind legs, reach with his neck, and dig in.

And that's precisely what he did.

That was twenty-three years ago, yet I remember the incident like it was yesterday.

By the time Prince reached the ripe old age of twelve (a whopping eighty-four in dog years), he had developed a growth the size of a tennis ball on his torso near his front left leg and also had a bad case of arthritis to contend with. Genetics weren't kind to Prince. Add to that the nuisance of taking daily medication and the heartache of being home alone for much of the day Monday through Friday because I was in school and both of my parents worked full time, and one might think Prince had a good enough reason to be a bit sour, if not apathetic.

But he was anything but.

All we had to do was grab the blue leash and utter the magic word—"walk"—and Prince was gung ho; he delighted in playing silly games of hide-and-seek; and he followed us upstairs each time one of us went, even though I have a sinking suspicion that, near the end, it pained him every time.

Prince lived life with the uncanny combination of gusto and compassion that only a dog can, and we as people should. Quite simply, he lived in the moment. Sure, one might think, it's easy to live life happily when you're a dog who is well taken care of. Perhaps.

But seriously, if we fail to experience pleasure, if we fail to experience excitement... don't we fail to experience life? We can't control many of the circumstances that may have a profound impact on our quality of being. But Prince taught me that it is just as easy to take pleasure in the little things in life—even if that little thing packs a ton of calories and has a hole in the middle.

Everything in moderation, right?

~Courtney Conover

# It's Not Always about the Dog

*A boy can learn a lot from a dog: obedience, loyalty,*
*and the importance of turning around three times before lying down.*
~Robert Benchley

Every Monday evening, from April until late August, for twenty-eight years, a 4-H dog club met in my yard. I taught young handlers how to train their dogs with a minimum of tears and absolutely no bloodshed. At least, that's all I thought I was teaching.

As many as twenty bright, active, eager children ranging in age from seven to eighteen hung onto the leashes of assorted ages and sizes of canines that were frequently boisterous and sometimes considerably less than enthusiastic about their owners' plans for the hours ahead.

Each spring I surveyed the collection of newcomers and returnees with one thought in mind. "How can I help this youngster succeed with this dog?"

The kids started out with great goals for the summer, but their attention often flagged with the repetitious basic obedience. They had to master "sit" and "stay" and the other exercises that gave them control over the dog. I coached them in patience, perseverance, and commiserated with their frustration. They knew that the reward for enduring several weeks of the monotony of "heel," "down," and "wait" was the exciting introduction of low jumps, barrels, tunnels, and a seesaw for an obstacle course.

In short order, "My dog won't do that" was replaced with shouts of "Mom, watch us!" when the family cars arrived to retrieve kids and dogs.

In addition to the training, the members had to keep expense records to appreciate the cost of maintaining a pet. They had to demonstrate that they could trim toenails, clean ears, and inspect for fleas. And the written records were displayed at the county fair. They didn't get a ribbon if the project book wasn't completed.

On the last page of the book was the question, "What did you learn in dog training this year?" The rest of the page was blank in anticipation of a few sentences or a story.

The most memorable stories ranged from the hilarious to the poignant.

From an eight-year-old boy: "I learned to use the pooper scooper and that Mrs. Vitale doesn't like messes in her yard. But now that I know how, my father makes me do it at home even if it's my sister's dog."

From an eleven-year-old girl who began the year giving commands to her dog in a timid, barely audible voice: "If I hadn't been in 4-H Paws and Tails and showed my dog in a show, I would still be too shy to do anything. Now I pay for my own ice cream cone instead of making my sister do it."

One of a trio of sisters whose parents were going through a difficult divorce wrote: "When my mom and dad start yelling at each other, I take my dog and go to my room and sit on the floor and hug her. I can cry on her and she doesn't mind."

And the most intriguing from a sixteen-year-old boy, who spent four years lackadaisically hanging out at dog club with his Collie, but didn't show much concern with advancing his training skills: "What I learned from Mrs. Vitale in several years of dog training helps me when I teach Red Cross swimming to the little kids."

I wasn't sure I wanted to know exactly how training collars and leashes translated into teaching swimming to primary school children.

When I crossed paths with him one day, I asked what he meant by that sentence.

"I saw," he said, "that sometimes when you demonstrated something to the whole group, some of the kids got it and some didn't pay attention. Then you would go and give them directions individually. And some didn't get it even then and you had to take their hands and help them hold the leash right. I do the same thing when I teach the little kids. Some get it when I show the group how to do something, some I have to talk to one-on-one, and some I have to move their arms to show them how."

For the kids, the blue ribbons and the accomplishments of getting a pup to walk the teeter-totter, or a hyperactive Terrier to stay in place for five minutes, satisfied their goals for the year. They didn't know that the dog was a vehicle. That sometimes, what they learned wasn't about the dog.

~Ann E. Vitale

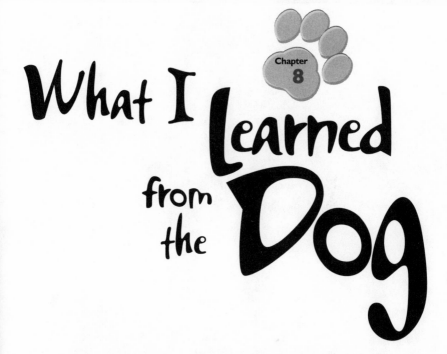

## Learning to Be Kinder

*One can pay back the loan of gold,*
*but one dies forever in debt to those who are kind.*

*~Malayan Proverb*

# Pay It Forward

*If it weren't for my cat and dog, I think I could not live.*
~Ebenezer Elliott

Kodiak, a beautiful, gentle Huskie mix, was dying. She was anemic and only a blood transfusion would give her a quality-of-life extension. Her veterinarian in Coeur d'Alene, Idaho drove to his home, gathered his own two dogs and took them back to the clinic. There, he withdrew a unit of blood from each of them and gave Kodiak a gift of life. She responded almost instantaneously and lived another year of an active life.

This was my "granddog," to whom I would send brightly wrapped Christmas presents. We talked on the telephone. She would howl with delight—at least, I hope it was delight—when she heard my voice. She watched with rapt attention as the contestants on the Westminster Dog Show paraded across the TV screen. She voiced her approval, in a loud "woo-woo-woooo," for the ones she felt should win. Her antics never ceased to make me laugh.

As Kodiak regained her health and spirit, we celebrated the gift that had been given us. It was a blessing that we would not take for granted. Kodiak had a lesson to teach her "mother," my daughter Kim Clark, that day in 2006. "Pay it forward," she seemed to say. Kim, through her tears listened. Dogs give so freely of their affection, demanding nothing except to have their basic food and shelter needs met. Kodiak gave that unconditional love and was lucky enough to have it given in return.

She graced this earth with her presence for another year. My daughter treasured every minute. When the time finally came to say goodbye and she gazed into those soft brown eyes of sweet Kodiak, she knew that someday she would give back to someone what had been given to her—a dog's love.

Kodiak had benefited from a relatively new concept in the U.S.—animal blood banks and donor programs. Veterinary science is now applying the same technology and equipment used for human blood donations to our four-legged friends. There are requirements for age, weight and disposition for a dog to be an acceptable donor. If these criteria are met, dogs can give so much to their comrades in paws.

Owners, too, must meet certain conditions. Are they willing to commit to having their dog available to give blood? Certainly, there are financial compensations for the owner—pet food, exams, vaccinations—but, the biggest payoff of all is helping other dogs.

Kodiak is gone now, but she will never be forgotten. Kim remembers her promise to that sweet girl. "I will pay it forward," she says to the photograph that sits on her mantle.

And she has. Her canine companion now is Timber, a one-hundred-pound-plus bundle of St. Bernard/Boxer energy. Timber is, of course, a blood donor. He meets all the requirements, including the gentle nature that enables him to endure the blood drawings process without a whimper. Perhaps he hears Kodiak whispering to him: "We are comrades in paws."

Kim is pleased to have Timber in the blood donor program. "I want to help someone and their dog by giving back a little of what was done for Kodiak... and me."

Give Blood, Give Life.

~Susan E. Tornga

# Trusting Soul to Soul

*Those who deny freedom to others deserve it not for themselves.*
*~Abraham Lincoln*

Two pairs of longing eyes, and an abundance of restless energy told the story. My two dogs, Milo, a twelve-year-old male Border Collie Duck Toller and Vallee, a two-year-old female Border Collie sorely needed to get out of the house and have an adventure. On this day I decided to collect Milo's mom, Nellie, who was thirteen and deaf, to join us. When I picked Nellie up I was told repeatedly to keep her on leash because she had a tendency to wander off into her own little Duck Toller world. And because she was deaf, she'd never hear me call her, and would surely get lost.

The sun shone on this blue sky day as we drove up the mountain. The road was lined with giant fir trees laden with snow, looking like majestic sentinels. When we arrived at our destination—a small pull-off on the side of highway, I circled around to the back of the Jeep and lifted the tailgate very slowly. I knew the three dogs wanted to explode out in a burst of excitement, but I wanted to let them out in an orderly fashion, one at a time, so they wouldn't get disoriented and run onto the road.

One by one I let them down. When it was Nellie's turn, I picked up her leash and was about to snap it onto her collar when I looked into her eyes and just stopped. For many seconds we just stared at each other while I clearly received her request. She did not want me to put the leash on, and she promised to stay nearby. I could only agree. Taking a deep breath, I invited her down, and then three happy dog souls and I set off on the trail into the woods.

At first I was acutely aware and a bit fearful that maybe she would wander away, and if she did veer off into the thick forest, I wouldn't be able to catch her or find her. Then she really would be lost. Was I being irresponsible? I watched her like a hawk as we made our way along the snow-packed trail. She would run along ahead and suddenly disappear, sometimes several yards off the path and out of sight. Each time I had to remind myself to keep trusting her. She would be okay. Surely the presence of Milo and Vallee would keep her from disappearing altogether. Each time she was out of sight, I'd wonder if this time she was gone. And each time I'd begin feeling anxious she'd bound back to the path, all smiles and wagging tail.

And then, quite unexpectedly, a sense of calm swept over me. I got it. Instead of spending this precious time worrying, I should pay attention to being with these loving dogs and enjoying this beautiful day we were sharing. The fear of losing Nellie was replaced by the joy of loving her. We had made a deal to share this adventure together. I was grateful and happy for her to be having this experience in her later years, being free to go where her heart took her. And she didn't break her promise to stay near.

Nellie was having fun and being responsible for her own safety. She was checking in with me from time to time to see where I was. And to my great joy, she romped along like a puppy for a good portion of our adventure. Her grateful smile confirmed we had made the right decision. We had trusted one another soul to soul.

This was such a good wake-up call for me to get out of my head and listen to my heart. Nellie helped me trust that inner voice that said, "All will be well." When I reach old age, I hope there will be those nearby who will understand my need for freedom, and trust me to do what's best for my own safety. Perhaps we need to let each other off leash, and instead of trying to control one another, we need to trust our inherent individual right to freedom.

~Rae Armour

Chicken Soup for the Soul

# A Delightful Afternoon

*No one appreciates the very special genius of your conversation*
*as the dog does.*
~Christopher Morley

"Hey lazy bones, it must be nice to sleep on the job."

As the owner of a small book and gift shop, I was addressing the most popular member of my staff. She lifted her head slightly to peer at me with her large brown eyes. Sensing that I wasn't initiating a snack break, she lay her head back down on the oval bed secluded under my desk. Rather than going back to sleep, my one-year-old Pug gazed at me contentedly.

"I love you too, Guinevere."

Having a canine employee has many benefits. How many bosses can say they have a staff member who loves them unconditionally? There is never a complaint about being paid in biscuits rather than cash. Break time is a refreshing gossip-free walk together around the block. There are never reprimands for a poor attitude, as my four-footed employee views every day on the job as an exciting new adventure. And as any business owner knows, the hours can be long and lonely when doing the less glamorous behind-the-scenes work. The companionship of a devoted furry staff member is priceless.

Guinevere loved going to work with me and if she thought she was going to be left at home, she would try to climb into my soft leather briefcase. She took her job to heart and quickly acquired a fan base among my customers. She greeted every one who entered the shop with a wag of her tightly curled tail and listened intently as they spoke to her.

Dogs tend to be non-judgmental toward humans, but Pugs in particular love everybody. Guinevere accepted everyone for just being themselves and she had the gift of making everyone feel special when she focused her attention on them. Guinevere's presence brought out the best in many of my customers. Even the shyest customers became more loquacious when talking to or about my little canine ambassador.

One afternoon a woman came into my shop with her teenage daughter who was mentally challenged. The daughter was delighted by the sight of my Guinevere peering at her through the glass jewelry case.

"I have a Dalmatian," the girl said excitedly.

"My dog's a Pug," I shared.

Guinevere sauntered over to the baby gate that kept her contained within the employee area, which was formed by the jewelry case, my desk, and the checkout counter. I kept a chair by the gate so that Guinevere's admirers could sit and be with her and she never denied anyone an audience. Sometimes a weary customer just needed to sit for a short rest, only to find themselves reenergized by interacting with my furry staff member. Petting my Pug's luxuriously soft fawn-colored coat or stroking her black velvet-like ears was an instant stress reducer.

After letting the mother know I was available if she had any questions or needed help, I addressed her daughter.

"Would you like to see my dog? Her name is Guinevere."

As I pointed to the chair, the girl happily accepted my invitation to sit with my Pug. Guinevere, always the hostess extraordinaire, stood on her hind legs with her front paws resting on the girl's lap, her tail wagging furiously, and her tongue at the ready to dispense Pug kisses.

"My name's Dianne. What's yours?"

"Ellen," the girl replied.

Ellen's mother gave me a smile and continued shopping as her daughter and I swapped dog stories and compared the similarities and differences between the Dalmatian and Pug breeds. Guinevere listened to Ellen with rapt attention, occasionally cocking her head to one side or the other as if to absorb this new information about something called a Dalmatian. Ellen's enthusiasm eclipsed all appearance, both mentally and physically, of being a mentally challenged person.

It was a slow afternoon and no other customers had come in so I hadn't realized how long Ellen and I had been talking and laughing until her mother came over to the checkout counter.

The mother's eyes teared up as she said, "Thank you for taking the time to talk to my daughter. She's extremely shy and rarely talks to anyone but family and close friends."

"It was my pleasure," I responded. "We both enjoyed talking about our dogs."

As I said these words, I thought of the other mentally challenged folks in my town. I always smiled and said, "Hi," and perhaps added a little small talk. But like any stranger or someone I knew only by sight that I passed by during the course of a day, I didn't know their hopes and dreams, their hobbies and passions, their abilities and talents. My furry little ambassador had bridged the conversation gap, allowing a woman with a Pug and a teenage girl with a Dalmatian to discover their mutual love of dogs. This simple connection gave us the gift of spending a delightful afternoon enjoying each other's company.

~Dianne Bourgeois

# Mourning Murray

*A friend is one of the nicest things you can have,*
*and one of the best things you can be.*
~Douglas Pagels

To say that Huey was boisterous would turn out to be an understatement. This black and white American Cocker Spaniel had been hand-picked by four members of our family and paw-picked by the remaining member, six-year-old Murray, our easygoing, "I love everybody" tan Spaniel. Murray might be a bit lonely, we had been thinking, and in need of a companion. And that's as simple as it was—Huey was to fill what we thought might be a void in Murray's life.

We responded to an ad in the newspaper and headed out on a cold, snowy day in March to look over a litter of pups. Since Murray naturally was a part of this important decision we'd brought him along for his stamp of approval. On arrival, the breeder immediately invited all five of us down to the basement where she introduced us to seven adorable creatures all vying for our attention. There was an array of black, white, tan and variously spotted pups. At last, lucky number seven turned his attention from the toy he was pulling apart and raced over to greet first Murray, and then the rest of us. This male was a lovely black Spaniel with a white chest and white front paws. He was absolutely beautiful: charming, funny, ingratiating and he knew that he was utterly irresistible. Not only did the pup cuddle up to us, he gave Murray a thorough kissing and cleaning. He wedged himself into the middle of our family and our hearts. Who could not want this puppy? Certainly not this family, and so, the deal was sealed and we headed home.

Life with the two dogs began well. Huey was a quick study. He was a dog with humor and he loved to play. He was a dog in motion, constantly dancing and prancing: without question, an extrovert to Murray's more introverted personality. I can still picture Murray lying in the corner of the family room sofa simply watching—watching Huey whirling and scampering around, a toy in his mouth, in search of a human playmate. Murray, head moving from side to side in order to keep up, seemed to be sitting there thinking to himself "What are you doing, you crazy dog—relax, be cool, lie down and sleep, eat, pee, take a walk, sleep, eat, you know, be cool."

But Huey saw life differently, definitely getting involved on all fours and convinced that Murray should do the same. He would pounce at Murray in an attempt to pry him loose from his favorite spots on the couches and easy chairs in our family room. Occasionally Murray was game to play and was usually up for a good walk, but would often retreat to a hideaway under a desk or other quiet site removed from Huey's view. This was pretty much the pattern in our household for the first year. At about that time Murray suffered a mini-stroke which left him with nerve problems on the right side of his face, particularly in his eye. Murray learned to cope with the residual difficulties and for the next five years he functioned perfectly well. When Murray was about twelve, a serious eye problem occurred and it became necessary to have the eye removed. Miraculously, Murray healed better than new; his energy level rose and his spirits lifted. Clearly pain that we'd been unaware of had now been alleviated. Murray was rejuvenated and he and Huey became true pals.

Chasing each other up and down the stairs, sleeping end to end and sharing the food in each other's bowls became their way of life; the two dogs even became well-matched when it came to fun and games. Later, as Murray's hearing began to fail, Huey helped him out in subtle ways, with a nudge here or there. When it finally went altogether, Huey took charge. Unless he actually saw the leash,

Murray was unaware that it was time for a walk. It was Huey who saw to it that Murray was alerted: he would jump at Murray's backside to give him a push. You could practically see the light bulb go off: "Oh, a leash—yup, must be time to go." This applied to any activity; trust Huey to take a flying leap at Murray and the two of them were pumped and ready for action. And so it went; Huey became Murray's ears and probably to a lesser extent, his eyes.

Inevitably, Murray's age won out and it was with great sadness that we were left with no choice but to put our beautiful blond Cocker Spaniel down two years ago. As difficult as it's been for Murray's human family, his "brother" Huey has been at a loss. A few weeks ago, with Huey along for the ride, we stopped at the vet's office. Huey stood on the seat, staring at the front door: was he expecting Murray to exit and finally come home?

I see how I had taken the dog relationship for granted and now I recognize that Huey's exuberance, or pushiness, was a demonstration of his love. Huey was Murray's caregiver as well as his best friend and now his loss is so big that the sadness spills out of his eyes. I think that we'll begin looking for a new pal for Huey soon, but of course, only one that meets with his approval.

~Janet Caplan

# Matty, the Cat Chaser

*The average dog is a nicer person than the average person.*
~Andy Rooney

Matty was a sweet, lovable, easygoing yellow mutt that I adopted from the pound when he was about a year old. Of course, none of the neighborhood cats would agree with the attributes I bestowed upon Matty. You see, Matty loved nothing better than to chase any cat that dared show up in our yard while he was outside. Indeed, Matty seemed to think this was a wonderful game and that the cats loved it as much as he did. The goal of the game, according to Matty, was to chase the cat up one of the many trees on my property. Then he would give his loudest, most vicious victory bark, declaring himself the winner, before retreating to let the terrified cat "escape." If a cat chose to flee instead of climbing a tree, Matty would chase it as far as the edge of our yard, and then stand watching the retreating cat with a look of deep disappointment on his face. He clearly thought the fleeing cat had not played by the rules. After all, he wasn't allowed to leave the yard, so he lost the game by default.

Matty clearly loved the macho feeling he got from frightening the cats and watching them run in terror, but his goal was never to actually catch one. If he came too close to overtaking a cat, he would back off a bit while continuing to growl and snarl so the chased cat would not guess what a softie he really was. As if he could read my thoughts, Matty sometimes ducked his head sheepishly when he saw me watching him from the porch as he walked back toward the house and allowed the latest treed cat to safely escape.

Once, to Matty's surprise and alarm, a large orange tabby stood his ground, hissing and slapping at the stunned dog. Too overwhelmed to retreat quickly enough, Matty got raked across the nose by the cat's claws. I ran toward the two animals, not sure what Matty would do next. But Matty, shocked, ran to me, whimpering, seeking comfort. It never occurred to him to hurt the cat, which, in Matty's mind, had cheated him out of a victory.

One afternoon I went outside with Matty to play ball. I watched the red rubber ball sail through the air and land in front of an evergreen bush on the far side of the yard. Matty yelped in glee and ran after the ball. Instead of bringing the ball back to me, his attention was caught by something in the bush. Guessing it was a cat, I figured our game was over for the time being. I heard Matty give one deep, loud growl, and then grow silent while peering beneath the bush. I walked closer and saw a slender gray cat hiding under the bush. The cat didn't make a move to run, but its eyes were wide with fright. Matty hunkered down and stared at the cat, woofing softly, as if to coax the cat into playing the game with him. Unlike the orange tabby, the gray cat showed no signs of aggression. It just lay still and watched Matty warily. Matty looked back at me, confused. This one wasn't going to run and it wasn't going to fight.

I reached the bush and squatted down to see if I recognized the cat. It was scraggly and thin, obviously a stray. The cat looked as if it had come out badly in a fight, with one ear torn and one eye swollen almost shut. "Let it alone," I said sternly to Matty. "This one is in no shape to run."

Reluctantly, Matty picked up the ball and dropped it in my hand. Although he chased the ball willingly, he frequently stopped by the bush, hunkered down, and gazed at the cat, woofing softly.

When it was time to go inside, Matty hesitated, looking back at the bush beneath which the injured cat lay. He looked up at me, his soft brown eyes almost pleading. He clearly thought I should do something. "He'll be fine," I told Matty. I made up my mind to call

Animal Control if the cat was still here in the morning. With one last backward glance toward the bush, Matty lowered his head and obediently followed me inside the house.

I gave Matty his dinner in the kitchen and settled down in the living room to watch the evening news. I heard a whimper and looked up to see Matty standing at the door with his dish of food in his mouth. He had not eaten a single bite. Astonished, I could only stare in disbelief for several seconds. Matty's intentions were perfectly clear. I took the dish from Matty's mouth and we both went outside to the bush where the gray cat still lay. The cat raised his head and watched us approach, the apprehension in his eyes giving way to hope as he smelled the food in the dish. I placed the dish in front of the cat and stepped back so he wouldn't feel threatened. Watching Matty and me warily, he took a small bite. Then, unable to contain himself, he gave in to his great hunger and stuck his head in the dish and ate greedily.

Watching the cat as it ate almost in a frenzy, I suddenly felt ashamed. Matty had shown more concern for this poor, hungry, injured creature than I had shown. I thought of how I would feel if it were Matty, lying under a bush somewhere, at the mercy of strangers. I would certainly want someone to show compassion for him.

I bent down and hugged Matty, blinking back tears. If not for Matty, I would have called Animal Control in the morning, hoping that they would find a home for the unfortunate cat. I was humbled to realize that a dog had a kinder heart than me. I once thought that I had done a noble thing when I rescued Matty from the pound. My actions paled considerably when compared to Matty offering his dinner to a stray cat. And I was supposed to be the superior creature.

I retrieved a towel from the bathroom to wrap around the cat, in case he panicked when I picked him up. I carried him inside the house to tend to his wounds as best I could. In the morning I would take him to the vet for a checkup. After all, if I was going to allow Matty to have a cat, I had to make sure it was healthy.

When I asked Matty what he wanted to name his cat, he only said "woof" so I called him Wolf. The love this dog and this cat have for one another is remarkable. Remarkable is also a good word to describe how I came to learn kindness and compassion from a dog.

~Joe Atwater

Reprinted by permission of
Off the Mark and Mark Parisi ©2000

# Angel Without Wings

*It is not known precisely where angels dwell—
whether in the air, the void, or the planets.
It has not been God's pleasure that we should be informed of their abode.*

~Voltaire

I walked down the hall of the nursing home, nodding to all the aides and nurses, as I made my way to visit ninety-three-year-old Ruth.

I stood outside her door and listened to the quiet before entering her room. She was in her wheelchair, her head drooped forward and her eyes closed. Gabe, her faithful chocolate Lab was at her feet.

"Ruth," I said softly.

She lifted her head, smiled, and motioned for me to take a chair opposite her.

"I wouldn't have come here if they didn't take Gabe." She told me many times how her family had searched to find a nursing home that would allow Gabe.

Ruth liked to talk about her childhood. She couldn't recall what happened recently, but she could remember her childhood days vividly.

"How are you today?" I asked.

"I was thinking."

"About what?"

"Why I've always loved dogs."

Ruth had the reputation for rescuing dogs and taking in strays up until the time she moved to the nursing home.

"Why do you love dogs, Ruth?"

"I remember my sister was to pick me up at the library. I'd gone there to do my lessons."

"How old were you?" I asked.

She shrugged her wee shoulders. "Maybe about nine."

"Did she get you?"

She giggled softly. "You didn't know my sister. Sally would take Dad's car and take off with her friends and forget all about me."

"That was eighty-some years ago and you still remember?"

She nodded. "Some things you can't forget."

"What happened?"

"I was standing on the library steps waiting for her; it was starting to get dark. I knew Sally wasn't reliable, so I decided to walk home."

"How far was it?"

"A few blocks. I was afraid because a little girl had been kidnapped and murdered in California. I remember thinking about that." Her voice trembled.

"A good reason to be afraid."

"I was walking along when all of a sudden this car came down the street and slowed up. It drove right along beside me. I tried to walk faster, but the car kept up with me." She paused, swallowing hard. "Out of the corner of my eye, I saw two men in the car, but tried not to look at them." She paused to take a breath. "They started calling to me. They said things like 'hey, little girl, you want some candy' and 'come here pretty little girl.'"

"What did you do?"

"I said a couple prayers." Her voice grew weak. Tears appeared in her eyes. "All of a sudden this big dog, like Gabe, came running out of a house. It looked up at me, nudged me, wagged its tail, and walked along beside me." She smiled. "That dog walked me all the way home."

"What about the car?" I asked.

"It followed us for a bit, but then drove off." She sniffled.

I reached over and clutched her small trembling hands.

"I remember following the dog to my porch. He knew where I

lived. He sat down, looked up at me and wagged his tail." She closed her eyes. "I can still hear his tail slapping on that old wood floor." A tear slid down her cheek. "I hugged him and whispered 'thank you,' then went in the house."

I must have had a look of doubt on my face.

"It's true and that's not the end." She shook her finger at me.

"Okay," I said, hearing the skepticism in my voice.

"The next day I went to that house to see the dog. I knocked on the door and a young woman answered. I asked if her dog was there. She said they didn't have a dog."

She looked deep into my eyes. "Then I got the strangest feeling." She reached down to pat Gabe. "In my mind, I can still see that dog. But there wasn't any."

"Maybe the dog came from another house," I said, still doubting the tale.

Her hands were folded as if she was praying. "I know it was that house. I prayed for help. God sent that dog. He was an angel dog, an angel without wings."

I looked at her questioningly.

"Angels come in all forms." She sniffled. "That dog saved me." She wiped away a tear.

"Maybe so," I said.

"And when I get to Heaven, I know the good Lord will have a dog waiting for me."

I took her little hands in mine.

"Gabe is short for Gabriel, you know, the angel." She glanced down at the dog.

Gabe's head rested on her knees and his soft brown eyes were gazing lovingly at Ruth.

Ruth smiled. Her eyes closed, her head nodded, and drooped forward. Gabe curled up at her feet.

I hugged Ruth gently, then started to leave the room. I turned to look at her and saw Gabe observing me.

"Gabe," I said softly.

If I didn't know better, I would say Gabe smiled at me.

Back in the hall, I grinned to myself, and decided... maybe Ruth's story was true.

~Carol Kehlmeier

# An Unexpected Blessing

*We long for an affection altogether ignorant of our faults. Heaven has accorded this to us in the uncritical canine attachment.*

*~George Eliot*

Bear arrived in our lives when our family was going through a very difficult time. Our schedules were hectic, our relationships strained, and our emotions guarded. The last thing we needed was a dog.

After much persistence from our daughter, my husband and I finally relented. Finding a dog which would meet our needs, however, would not be easy. Our son had always been very wary of dogs and our daughter suffered from asthma.

After seeing a puppy that belonged to a friend, my daughter was convinced this type of dog would be perfect for our family. After praying about it, we decided if the owner still had puppies available, we would get one. The puppies were located approximately one hundred miles from where we live, so my sister offered to pick out the puppy and deliver it to us. My only request was that it be a girl. I was surprised then, when she arrived with a boy.

Regardless, in a home filled with tension, Bear became a welcome distraction. Sensing our individualities, he began to reach out to us in different ways. To Matt, our son, he'd deliver his favorite toy, hoping for playtime. With Emily, our daughter, he'd take things from her room so she'd chase him. He'd steal a sock from my husband, only to return in a few moments flaunting his treasure. And, to me, he'd simply follow me around from room to room, or sit at my feet.

Recently, after an unusually frustrating day, my daughter asked, "Why are you nicer to Bear than you are to us?"

"Well let's see," I replied, "Bear doesn't care what, or when I feed him, he doesn't complain, he never talks back, and he's always happy to see me."

Even though my response was spoken out of frustration, it made me realize how we, as a family, had started to treat one another. In our hectic lives, we had begun to take each other for granted. We were so caught up in the world, and its acquisitions, we failed to appreciate the blessings God had already provided. Bear had become a welcome reprieve. He offered us the opportunity to feel loved and appreciated without placing large demands on us personally.

Later, as I considered Emily's question, and my response, I thought of how Bear reacts to us—loving us individually, yet unconditionally. I thought of his inability to hold a grudge. A sharp word directed at him and he'll scamper to his bed, where he'll sit, head hung so low his nose touches the pillow. Once his name is called, however, he runs back, all is forgiven, and perhaps most importantly, forgotten. I considered how his contentment is based solely on the safety and love he feels from his family, unlike us, who often search for contentment in other ways.

I believe there are times when God hears our prayers, but rather than give us what we ask, He instead gives us what we need. I think this is the case with Bear. Although, I'd asked for a female dog, we were given a male. Still, I could never have imagined a better match for our family. God has used him to help bring a balance back to our lives. In fact, Bear has helped draw our family closer together. He has been used to teach us some valuable lessons about love—the giving and receiving. Bear has taught us that sometimes, a gentle touch, a kind word, or a smile is really all we need.

~Marcia Hodge

# Lost Dog

*People who are homeless are not social inadequates.*
*They are people without homes.*
~Sheila McKechnie

He looked like a little lost sheep. I saw him down the road as I pulled into my driveway. Seen from a distance his funny gait caused me to wonder just what kind of animal he was. I figured he had to be a stray dog—one I hadn't seen in the neighborhood before.

I saw him again an hour or so later when I stepped into the garage—he was eating our kitty's dinner, much to her obvious annoyance. He didn't even hear me approach, testifying to his advanced age. His dirty, grizzled fur of uneven length, cloudy eyes and arthritic limbs all seemed to confirm my belief that he'd traveled a long time on this earth and didn't have many miles to go before reaching his journey's end. Because of a bad leg he hopped a little with each step, causing his ears to flop and making me think of a lamb—that and his facial markings—a black snout surrounded by a white mask.

A broken fastener attached to his collar indicated that he'd belonged to someone at some time. Sadly, there was no identification tag. How I'd have loved to relay the message to someone that their dog had been found! I wondered how he'd come to be wandering, my imaginative mind picturing him swept away from his familiar surroundings in the recent flash flooding.

I'm not normally drawn to stray animals—especially dogs. I fear disease, dog bites... even possible adoption and another mouth to feed. Our house is already home to more animals than humans. I didn't want to appear too friendly.

But for some reason, his pitiful appearance broke my heart. Maybe it was the way he cowered when I reached to check his collar—I wondered what abuse he'd been subjected to in recent days. He didn't seem to be the kind of animal most homeowners would welcome around their yards and garages. Maybe it was his limp that caused me to pity him, wondering if those shaky legs would ever carry him back to the life he once knew. Or maybe it was the loss of our own old soldier just months ago—a wound just barely healed that was reopened at the sight of a brother in similar straits—one sure to soon walk the path our old friend had so recently trod. Even as he sniffed around the yard I couldn't get past the notion that he was looking for a place to lie down and die. He reminded me of a traveling hobo, looking for nothing more than a meal and a place to spend the night. Surely I could offer him that much.

Sometimes people are treated as poorly as the stray animals among us. I wonder how many of the homeless out on our streets have found the same reception as had this old dog. Many once had fine homes and families that loved them. But somehow they came to be lost, swept away by circumstances over which they had no control. Many of them still carry wounds of one type or another from the storms that washed them away from the lives they once knew. And now their appearances often scare away any who might be able to help. Too often these aren't the type of people we want around our homes, our lives... our churches. We fear disease. We're afraid of being hurt. We don't want to risk involvement and any possible future dependence on us that our overtures of assistance might create. And so we keep our distance, when all these fellow travelers are looking for is a meal, a place to spend the night... and maybe some direction as to how to find their way Home.

Maybe God has them cross our paths in the hope that the

welcome they find in our hearts will cause them to see that which has always existed in His. After all, to Him they look a lot like little lost sheep....

~Elaine L. Bridge

# Back in the Game

*It is astonishing how little one feels alone when one loves.*
~John Bulwer

Who says a therapist has to be human? I have found that canines can do the trick very nicely.

Belle, a long-hair Chihuahua, came into my life approximately a year ago. I found her online, residing in a rescue home sixty miles away, in Ponca City, Oklahoma. According to her electronic profile, Belle was a special needs dog; she'd been born with a curved spine which left her "slightly" crippled. That was the extent of the details given. When I first saw her, however, I noticed that her right back leg was longer than the left one, which she kept curled up close to her body. This deformity caused her to hop, not really walk. The rescue worker also confided to me that Belle, the runt of her litter, hadn't been expected to survive to adulthood. Yet somehow, she had grown to maturity, although at just under three pounds, she was the tiniest dog I had ever seen.

I also learned that a steady stream of clients had already rejected the Chihuahua. The rescue worker told me that several people had dropped in to see the cute little mutt, captivated by her online picture; but when they saw her in person—and the full extent of her disability, they declined to take her home.

"Everyone said she'd be too much trouble," the woman told me.

There was more bad news. I learned that because of her disabilities, Belle tended to prefer seclusion, and, as a result, suffered from severe bouts of depression.

"So don't become worried if she balls up in a corner and refuses to come to you, even if you call her name."

Could this get any worse?

Staring at the dog, however, my heart melted. Who could turn their back on this tiny, crippled canine? Besides, if she stayed here in the rescue home much longer, she would run the risk of being euthanized—an unacceptable possibility.

I'd like to say that Belle ran up to me at our first meeting, and, with kisses and wagging tail, picked me as her new "companion." Truth was I had to make the first move.

After many months of rejection, which, no doubt, added to her depression, Belle was naturally cautious toward a stranger like me. She stayed pressed against the wall, hopping back and forth between the rescue worker and a bowl of dog food. In an effort to break the ice, I dropped slowly to the floor and, in a sitting position, held out my hand and softly called her name. I was thrilled when, after several attempts, she responded by inching over and sniffing my hand. She then cautiously licked my fingers and crawled into my lap.

It was a slow beginning, but for me, the bonding was already in motion. Once Belle looked up at me with those huge, sad eyes, I knew my life—and hers—had changed forever.

For me, at least, the future suddenly looked brighter. Until that dog crawled into my lap, I was lonely and needed the companion-ship of someone or something to make me feel alive. Like Belle, I felt bruised in life. A slew of personal and career disappointments had left me depressed and very distrustful. Although employed, I had been rejected from a series of interviews that would have allowed me to advance in my field as a caseworker for the State of Oklahoma. My confidence and hope shattered, I continued to work without any energy, and after dragging myself home from the office every night, I seldom went out. I more or less hibernated on the weekends, losing what few friends I had. Withdrawn from the world, I was convinced that I didn't deserve any better, that the best years of my life lay behind me.

Soon after bringing Belle home, however, I began to notice life changing. Even the setbacks no longer bothered me—for long. The turning point occurred, ironically enough, when an ice storm struck two days later and left my home without power for a week. The arctic temperatures forced me to bring Belle to work with me. Clients, co-workers and even visiting administrators were charmed by the miniscule pooch and stopped to chat with me while petting the new four-legged office resident. As a result, both Belle and I made a whole legion of friends. Plus, I received useful information that led me to my subsequent promotion and generous increase in pay.

Later, my depression gone, I decided to throw a Christmas party. Although I was the host, Belle received the most attention, limping quickly from guest to guest and establishing herself among my friends as the quintessential canine social butterfly!

Belle had definitely come out of her shell. She now seemed to enjoy life, and to play and trust again. This was no easy transition, considering the difficulties of re-establishing trust when one has been hurt—a challenging journey which I knew only too well.

Inspired by Belle's renewed faith, I have abandoned my own reticence and no longer wait until someone shows me a bit of kindness. I now feel confident that I can make that kindness happen, that I can trust again.

Strange how a tiny, "special needs" dog can make one feel better about oneself and others. Because of Belle, I am back in the game, ready to take risks and enjoy life to its fullest.

Talk about a surprise shot in the arm!

But then, who knows where fate will lead us? In my case, it just happened to be a rescue home in Ponca City, Oklahoma, where a tiny, emotionally and physically scarred Chihuahua waited for someone to take her home and give her a new life.

~Al Serradell

# Paw de Deux

*You can dance anywhere, even if only in your heart.*
*~Author Unknown*

I look down at my almost-thirteen-year-old dog, Buddy, and smile. It looks like someone has taken a magical paintbrush and traced white around his most beloved features for emphasis. To me, these are the best years. I think of them as the years of the Dance of Devotion.

The Dance is choreographed slowly by our subconscious minds. What began in tentative, gentle steps has melded over the years into a graceful pas de deux. We've learned, Buddy and I, how to move around each other in that symbiotic sway of companionable souls.

The Dance became clear to me the morning after my last dog died, when I stepped out of bed and realized for the first time that I wasn't putting my feet on the floor, but gently tapping with one toe to make sure I didn't step on my beloved companion... the one who should have been lying in the spot that was now so cruelly and profoundly empty.

In the days that followed, I learned just how many steps there were to that dance. I drew my feet up when I sat at my desk to make room for the dog that should have been under my chair. I reached for an invisible head in my lap. I hesitated for him as I moved about the house and waited at the door for the one who was normally there before I even knew I was leaving. I missed him over and over and over, until I finally realized I had spent more time in close proximity to that dog than I had any other being in my life.

Now, years later, I find myself dancing another duet. It happens when I put on the gardening shoes that mean we are going outside, or when I walk in that purposeful way that means I'm leaving for work soon. Or it happens on those rare occasions when Buddy needs to be let out in the middle of the night, and he knows how to bark in an apologetic whisper.

It's delicate and gracious and so very subtle, this dance. I suspect to a seasoned old gentleman like my dog, it's somewhat crass to bark loudly, so instead, he stands by the door and shifts from side to side when he wants to go out. Click click, go his toenails on the wooden floor. Click click. It is a patient, benign sound, barely audible. Yet I find myself headed for the door when I hear it.

We move to the rhythm of our routines. Dozens and dozens of cues, signals, exchanges, every day. Step, sway, tap, glide.

Like most of us, it takes a dog a lifetime to get truly wonderful, and the dance is a hard, hard thing to let go. When it's that time that every devoted pet owner dreads because it comes much, much too fast, we shouldn't feel silly because we are grieving for a pet, but honored. The enormity of the grief is testimony to the greatness of love.

To love a pet is to know a universal truth at its most elemental: True love is not confined to mere species. Love transcends.

I look at my friend again and smile as his tail thumps. Someday the final bow will come, but I will always hold what I learned from this gentle, humble creature. True love is, after all, nothing less than the embrace of souls.

~T'Mara Goodsell

# Clover and Bear

*It is not so much our friends' help that helps us,*
*as the confidence of their help.*

*~Epicurus*

The first day of March, 1997 turned out to be a very unusual Saturday. Unseasonably steamy, the air had a tangible unsettling feel to it. Weather stations warned that a quickly advancing cold front could cause some serious turbulence. Though it was not out of Arkansas' character for thunderstorms to display tornadic strength, it was markedly early for such volatile weather even in a state that averaged just over twenty tornadoes a year.

As I watched, pregnant thunderclouds darkened the late afternoon sky. The morning breeze now whipped at the forty-foot pines in my yard, whispering warnings of things to come. The alerts, which had been beeping across the top of the television screen for several hours, advised that fifty-eight of Arkansas' seventy-five counties were in the path of seriously unstable weather. Moving from window to window, I kept a watchful eye on the skies amid glances at Doppler radar screens flaming with red and orange in what seemed like every area of the state. When the shrill siren finally screamed through southwest Little Rock, I gathered my menagerie into the downstairs bathroom and wondered why I had to fall in love with a house nestled smack in tornado alley.

When the blare of the warnings finally subsided, the house was still standing and seemingly none the worse for wear though a dozen or more heavy limbs littered the yard. We were lucky. Incredibly lucky. By morning fifteen major tornadoes had blasted across the state; over two dozen people perished. According to experts, twisters rarely stay on the ground more than a few miles, but several of these storms left paths of devastation over fifty miles long. The storm that had skirted my home, set down originally in Arkadelphia, a town about sixty miles to the west. The twister carved a half-mile wide strip of destruction through four counties, as it barreled east into the southern part of Arkansas's capital city. Authorities reported the storm's intensity to be up to the F4 level, with winds over 200 miles per hour, along the way. The damage left in its wake was profound.

A late-night call changed my plans for a lazy Sunday and ended up changing my life. Gray and drizzly with an unexpected bite of winter, the second of March was the kind of day that chilled you to the bone. Adorned in boots, jeans, sweaters, and backpacks, animal rescue volunteers gathered at a local shelter and waited for word from the police that we could begin our search for injured and displaced animals.

My team ended up in Sardis, a residential area just southwest of the city. Bone-chilling mist was made worse by the fact there were still downed electrical lines emitting sparks from place to place and reports of active gas leaks. Parking at the perimeter of the devastated area, we started our hike not knowing what we would find. As we neared what had been a tract of about a dozen homes, a sense of otherworldliness invaded my soul. Collapsed skeletal structures rose like gravestones where homes once stood. It was impossible to tell which shattered piece of furniture belonged to which demolished house. Cautiously feeling the way over dangerous blown out walls, broken glass, downed trees, and unidentifiable debris, my brain had trouble processing the errant baby shoe lying in the mud or the golden-gowned doll protruding from beneath a cement block. The sheer magnitude of loss sent me reeling.

Owners plodded around in shock and disbelief—some in tears, most stunned into abject silence. When they learned who we were, more than a few pleaded for our help to find their furry companions, desperate to salvage at least their dearly loved animals. We reassured them as best we could and began the daunting task of cajoling scampering dogs and furtive felines—all unnerved by the trauma—into trusting we were friends. By afternoon, we were cold, wet, hungry, and exhausted, but we had rescued a good number of animals and knew many more would surface in the days to come as hunger replaced fear as the primary instinct.

As we plodded toward our vehicles to head to another location, we spotted two dogs haphazardly making their way down a dirt-packed road. As the canines approach, the smaller dog kept bumping and pushing her larger companion this way and that. What in the world was she doing? Responding to our welcoming calls, the dogs ventured closer, barking with relief to find friendly humans. Chow mixes with fuzzy tails that curled above their hind ends, the duo enthusiastically greeted us and we quickly realized the larger dog's eyes were closed and crusted over. As my dog-lover colleagues slipped leashes around the necks of our newest rescues, it became clear that the smaller one had been nudging her friend to keep him on a trail that he could not see.

After a day amid indescribable devastation and hundreds of traumatized people, these two canine comrades—quickly named Clover and Bear—had come bumbling into our path. What a symbol this doggie duo was of the undaunted spirit of those who survive disastrous situations. Without Clover's continual correction, Bear would have been lost in the havoc resulting from the relentless storm; he could easily have starved to death if not discovered by some kind soul. Instead of seeking safety and solace, Clover refused to leave Bear's side, instinctively knowing he needed her guidance to survive.

Clover and Bear were two of nearly three hundred animals rescued in the aftermath of those terrible storms. While some badly injured animals didn't make it, Bear was one of the lucky ones. His eye trouble was caused by a painful condition called entropion, in which the eyelid rolls inward causing the eyelashes to irritate and possibly damage the eye. After surgery enabled Bear to see again; he and Clover remained the best of pals and favorites of everyone they encountered. Almost sixty percent of the rescued animals were eventually reunited with their human families. Like the other animals whose owners couldn't be found or could no longer keep them, Clover and Bear were placed into adoptive homes—our heroes went together, of course.

Disasters push people and animals into places they have never been emotionally, physically, mentally, and spiritually. More often than not, they bring out the best in survivors, enabling them to uncover hidden strength, to forge relationships they might never have known, and to rediscover what is truly important in life. That's exactly what these furry friends on four legs experienced. Clover and Bear, two funny dogs with curly tails, made their way from disaster to safety and new lives by sticking together.

~Nancy Sullivan

# What I Learned from the Dog

**Chapter 9**

## Learning about Unconditional Love

*I think dogs are the most amazing creatures; they give unconditional love. For me they are the role model for being alive.*

~Gilda Radner

# 91

# Close Encounters of the Canine Kind

*If opportunity doesn't knock, build a door.*
~Milton Berle

My dog, Tiffany, a white Samoyed, greeted me at the door as she always did, with her leash in her mouth. I was already drenched from the storm we were having. It had been raining for days with no end in sight. My hair was matted down, and all I really wanted to do was jump in the shower and warm up. However, walking Tiffany was necessary and part of the responsibility that came with dog ownership, although it was not what I wanted to do at the moment. I attached Tiffany's red leash and rushed her downstairs in the elevator hoping we would make it to the curb on time without my excited dog having an accident. It was embarrassing when that happened.

Typical of my dog, when it was raining, she took the most time to find just the right spot to do her thing. I kept saying, "Hurry up, Tif! I'm freezing. Look at my hair! I'm drenched. Come on, Tiffany. Get done already."

Just then, I saw Sam's car coming down the boulevard. We had been introduced by mutual friends who lived in the same building as we did. Nothing had come of it, but I thought I saw a hint of interest in him. I was definitely interested. He was handsome and tall and from the few words we exchanged, he seemed intelligent and interesting. I tugged Tiffany back behind a bunch of trees and hid. "Come on, Tif," I said quietly. "I like this guy. I look horrible. Help me hide. Don't bark. Shhhh. Be a good girl." Together we spied as Sam parked his red Honda at the curb and ran toward our building with his attaché case held over his head.

That's when I formulated my plan: I was going to "accidentally" bump into Sam while I was running out of the high-rise apartment building to the curb with Tiffany while he was parking his car. Only this time, my hair would be perfect and I would not be sopping wet.

I began my vigil from my 18th floor apartment window on the first sunny day after the storm. I arrived home from work and waited for Sam to pull up to the curb. As I saw his car approaching, I ran like a maniac to the elevator with Tiffany. No matter how hard I tried, I kept missing him. I would get to the curb and see that he had parked his car and was nowhere in sight. We never bumped into each other. Time after time, I would grab Tiffany's leash and attach it, but the elevator was just too slow for me to accidentally run into this guy I liked and wanted to get to know better.

I decided it might be more effective if I were already walking Tiffany when he parked his car. I sort of knew what time he got home. Tiffany had to be walked anyway. What difference did it make, as long as my hair looked good? I would call to him, "Sam, hi. We were introduced by Jerry and Maddy at their party last month. Remember?"

Unfortunately, that didn't work either. I walked Tiffany for hours and never timed it correctly. It seemed Sam's schedule had changed, or maybe he had a business meeting—or a new girlfriend who was eating into my time with him.

Then, one day, as I was taking Tiffany downstairs for a walk, the elevator stopped on the fourth floor, and Sam stepped in. He was as handsome as I had remembered.

"Hey," he said. He seemed genuinely happy to see me again.

"Hi!" I responded, totally forgetting my planned remarks.

"What a great dog. What's her name?" he said.

"Tiffany," I said.

With that, he bent over to pet her. "Hey, Tiffany! You are a pretty girl. Is Mom taking you for a walk?"

Tiffany jumped up and grabbed onto his leg. The elevator stopped at the lobby where we both were planning to get out, but Sam couldn't move. My dog would not let go of his leg. I kept apologizing. He kept saying it was okay. And Tiffany held onto Sam's leg, not letting him move an inch.

Then the door closed, and the elevator started going up again.

At this point, Tiffany let go of Sam's leg and rolled on her back.

"Bad, Tiffany!" I said with a complete lack of sincerity.

"It's okay," Sam said. "I guess she didn't want me to leave." If he only knew!

Sam and I rode the elevator up to the eleventh floor. Other people got on. When we reached the lobby again, Tiffany pulled me off. Sam followed. We walked together for a long time on the boulevard that afternoon. At one point, Sam asked for the leash and he ran with Tiffany, giving her a great workout.

We were married several months later.

That was twenty-five years ago. When asked how we met, Sam tells people, "Get this! We met on an elevator. Her dog grabbed my leg and never let go." I have never let on that this was a planned canine encounter.

~Felice Prager

# 92

# Growing Up and Old Together

*It takes a long time to grow an old friend.*
~John Leonard

Houston relaxes in my arms as I carry his arthritis-crippled body downstairs to the yard. Our three-story urban townhouse with slippery polished wood floors isn't easy on an old dog with a weak bladder and achy joints. But Houston doesn't complain—he smiles with his eyes though he can't wag his tail without losing his balance.

We met on the porch of a double-wide trailer in rural Illinois. He was a scrawny pup with downy black fur, perky ears, and a long, crooked tail. I was an overworked graduate student in a dead-end romantic relationship. Human affection felt fickle; I needed a dog's love.

The ad read, "Free to good home, Collie-mix puppies, eight weeks old."

There were ten pups in the litter, and the mother—a blond Collie-mutt herself—looked tired. I watched for nearly an hour as puppies wrestled, nipped, and chased each other. Some splashed into the swimming pool with muddy paws and emerged sopping wet and ready for more tussles in the dirt.

"So, which one do you want?" the owner asked.

Surveying the litter, I pointed to a pup that had snoozed on the porch the whole time I'd been there. "He's just my speed," I said.

The puppy nestled into the backseat of my worn-out Honda. "We're going to be good friends," I told him, "but you need a name." I tested names and watched his expressions in the rearview mirror. Maybe the country music on the radio brought Houston to mind, I don't know. When I said it aloud, it fit.

I took Houston home to our rambling ranch, where he chased deer in the yard and played in the snow. His company kept me from losing my sanity that year. When I mustered the courage to leave my boyfriend, I rented a 400-square-foot apartment in a not-so-safe part of town. It was the only affordable apartment that would allow a dog. And this is how I learned that home isn't a place: home is wherever you're loved.

The next year—degree in hand—I took a college teaching job in upstate New York. The dog-friendly campus was my favorite perk: Houston could come to work with me. I bought a baby gate so he couldn't wander from my office when I went to teach class, and I stocked my desk with dog treats.

Each morning, I'd ask, "Do you want to be a working dog?"

Houston yelped his reply as he ran at me full-speed and jumped up on my good clothes. He loved going to school, and my students loved him, too. They'd stop by my office to take him for walks or play fetch in the hall. It was a full life for a dog.

But that fall, Houston got sick. Chronic digestive problems left him weak and in pain and our veterinarian's treatment wasn't working. After months of quiet compliance, I couldn't bear his suffering any longer. Though he had seen the vet on Friday, I begged another doctor for a last-minute consultation on Saturday morning. He agreed.

The veterinarian's expression grew strained as he examined Houston. Tears rolled down my cheeks; I could tell the situation was dire. He said the problem had been misdiagnosed and Houston had two gaping hernias. He wasn't sure they could be repaired.

Overwhelmed with grief, I blamed myself for waiting so long for a second opinion.

"What you need," he counseled, "is someone who will treat this very, very aggressively."

He referred us to a veterinary surgeon an hour south in Ithaca. Over the next year, his team performed six surgeries to repair Houston's hernias. The surgeon likened it to sewing together strands of spaghetti—the thin muscle fibers couldn't hold stitches. Within weeks the hernias would re-open.

Houston lived at the clinic for much of that year, and it became my second home. When I visited each day after work, I'd sit on the exam room floor and Houston would lie in my lap, his head in my hands. He whined loudly as I petted him as if to say, "It hurts so much. I needed your touch." I felt the same way.

Between surgeries, Houston came home. He looked like the ghost of a starving lion, with thick black fur on his neck and feet, a pouf at the tip of his tail, and short sleek hair in between where they'd shaved him for surgery. His weight dropped from fifty pounds to just over thirty.

We slept together on the pullout sofa in the living room because he couldn't climb stairs in the cone-shaped collar that kept him from licking his wounds. I worried the stitches would tear if I carried him upstairs and down.

Thanks to the surgeons' skilled persistence and creativity, Houston recovered. Though he still suffered terrible digestive problems when stressed, over the years I learned to manage them with diet and swift intervention.

Our lives have been intimately interconnected for fourteen years now. College, my career, and a military marriage haven't given me many chances to put down roots. I've lived—with Houston—in nine houses in six states: Illinois, New York, Colorado, Utah, California, and Virginia. Each one feels like home as long as Houston is in it.

I've grown up with Houston, from college student to fledgling professor to successful professional. I became both a wife and a mother. At the most trying times, Houston's love sustained me.

When my husband deployed to Iraq, I sobbed into Houston's long black fur. He walked with me on the mountainous trails near our house, never questioning my need to keep moving. He stayed by my side. When that deployment unexpectedly led to another (in Afghanistan), I moved home to California with Houston riding shotgun. At the time I was seven months pregnant.

Houston kept me company through countless middle-of-the-night feedings, watched over my son when he napped, and alerted me when he awoke. He nuzzled against me when I was sad and angry that my husband missed our son's first smile, first steps, and first word. I never asked him to comfort me, but I didn't have to. Dogs know love is a verb.

While I grew up, Houston grew old. Arthritis limits his mobility, and deafness invites anxiety. His world is smaller. Though he still likes to follow his nose in nature, he can't venture far. When the hundred yard walk to the mailbox is too much to complete, I carry Houston home with the mail pinned under my arm. We're in this thing together.

As Houston's health has declined, I realize he's taught me the fundamental lesson of love: that it's okay to need people. Accepting help is hard for me. Really hard. But even a staunch do-it-yourselfer like me can take canine comfort—because dogs don't judge our needs, they just love us through them.

Now, my son is a walking, talking, tail-pulling toddler and kind, sweet Houston is frail and dependent. When he fell down tonight on the slick wood floor in our dining room, my son wrapped his small arms around Houston's belly and tried to help him up. It made me proud.

I'm teaching my son that needing others doesn't diminish us—it expands us—because it opens us to love.

That's what I learned from Houston.

~Heidi Smith Luedtke

# 93

# Yuck! Dog Germs!

*The nose of the boxer has been slanted backwards*
*so that he can breathe without letting go.*
~Winston Churchill

My mother loves to tell the story of my dog Skippy, who protected me in my playpen when I was a toddler. She claims I would often share my treats with Skippy, licking my ice cream cone, and then allowing Skippy a lick. I have no memory of these events; however, I have no reason to doubt my mother's word.

Allow me to clarify my personal feelings about dogs during the first fifty years of my life, at least in my own memory. "Yuck! Dog germs!"

I have never truly liked dogs in general, although there were a few I was faintly fond of. We had a St. Bernard named Tonka that was a beautiful, kindhearted creature. Unlike my siblings, I did not care to have Tonka kiss or play with me. I suppose my attitude towards most of the family dogs was one of detached amusement.

My mother had a Pekingese for a few years when I was a teen. It was the only dog we ever owned who lived in the house. I tolerated Tippy, as long as it stayed out of my room. I apologize for the pronoun, "it," but I don't recall if Tippy was a male or a female.

My favorite line in regard to dogs was from the Peanuts character, Lucy. I remember Snoopy licking her face, and Lucy responded with, "Yuck! Dog germs!" My thoughts, exactly. I thought of dogs as bad-smelling, germ-carrying, hair-shedding, lawn-defecating nuisances. My husband was no dog lover either, so I had support from him when my older daughter would occasionally plead for a dog.

My daughter grew up, moved to another state, bought her own house, and promptly adopted a sixty-pound Boxer named Tyson, who was in danger of being sent to the pound. She called me with this news as if I were going to share in her rapture. "What does a Boxer look like?" I asked. "Where will you keep him? How are you going to pay for his food and veterinarian bills?" None of my questions deterred her enthusiasm.

She proceeded to e-mail me pictures of Tyson, announced that he was an "inside" dog, and assured me that she would be able to give him proper care. I responded with typical motherly comments like, "You must not want me to visit anymore!" and "Does he bite?"

These were followed by such thinly veiled threats as, "I don't want dog hair all over my good clothes!" and "Your house is going to smell like dog!"

I briefly considered boycotting my daughter's home, for a fleeting moment thought of forcing her to choose between this dog and her mother, and had I been extremely wealthy, I might have threatened her with writing her out of my will. This last idea was quickly discarded as being totally ludicrous, as I had neither a will nor wealth.

The holidays were approaching, and my husband and I packed for our first visit with my daughter and the new addition to her family. I distinctly remember packing clothes that were not my favorites, in case the dog shed or drooled on them. I left at home anything silky that might easily snag and anything light in color. I believe most of my wardrobe during that visit consisted of jeans and sweatshirts.

My first impression did little to change my opinion of dogs. Tyson is a typical Boxer, excitable by nature, and his desire to jump and lick me in the face reinforced my "Lucy" instincts immediately. "Yuck! Dog germs!" My daughter attempted to calm him down and had me sit in a rocking chair from which I could pet him without worrying about being knocked off my feet by his exuberance.

I would like to say that I was immediately won over by his sweet brown eyes and his wriggling short stump of a Boxer tail. I would like to say it, but it would not be true. It has taken several years to win over this "Lucy." I am now, however, the woman in Wal-Mart with the box of Milk-Bones, the lady in Target with the large doggie stocking, and the tourist in the doggie bakery with a bag of gingerbread men dog treats.

I was not won over by the sweet brown eyes or the wriggling stump of tail; I was won over by the love and comfort this devoted canine companion brings to my beloved daughter. He is her shadow. He is her friend. He is her protector. He is my granddog. Dog germs? Who cares?

~Kim Seeley

Reprinted by permission of
Off the Mark and Mark Parisi ©1998

# 94

# Dirty Harry

*Courage is almost a contradiction in terms. It means a strong desire to live taking the form of readiness to die.*
*~G.K. Chesterton*

He was a downright plain, homely dog. A big old mutt with matted, orangy-brown hair hanging over his eyes and tangles all over his skeletal body. His breath reeked of rotted meat, onions and other garbage he'd been scavenging from the community dump where, my husband and I guessed, the aging animal had been abandoned when his callous owners moved away from the small northern community where we were living.

Remembering back, I didn't want to keep the mangy stray who limped into our backyard and sprang into my kids' hearts faster than I could say "no." But what's a mother to do when her three children are bawling their heads off to save a pitiful animal from certain death? After all, the pathetic dog had already been wounded by a gunshot to its hind leg—an indication that someone was trying to put the nuisance beast out of its misery.

So there came to our family a dog the kids named Dirty Harry. After a costly trip—more money than we could afford—to the vet in town to get the bullet removed as well as shots, pills and papers, Dirty Harry was on the mend.

I laid down the law. Dirty Harry could live in the garage and that was that! I don't know how it happened, but within days he was snoozing on the porch. Next thing I knew he had graduated to the laundry room. From there he took over the whole house. Sleeping, for that's mostly all he did, anywhere he wanted. Of course, by then, he had weaseled his way into our lives and there was no turning back.

At first I didn't think Dirty Harry liked me very much, for let's face it, it was I who had to do all the scolding when he chewed up the vacuum hose, ate carpeting or gnawed the runners off my rocking chair!

One late spring day when my husband was at work and the kids were in school, I decided to take Harry along with me up the hydro line that ran for miles through the woods behind our house. I had to do a photo shoot of some wildflowers and figured the walk would do him good.

I usually went alone on my picture-taking outings, but since the vet warned us that Harry was getting fat and needed more exercise, I coaxed him along.

That's how he happened to be with me on the trail that fateful day. And that's how he came to save my life. I was about a mile from home, kneeling on the ground trying to get a good close-up of a rare Pink Lady's Slipper. Dirty Harry had gulped his fill from a muddy puddle and, exhausted, had laid down in the shade to snooze.

In the quietness of the forest, I sensed something behind me and slowly rose and turned around. To my horror, not more than a few feet away stood a huge mother bear on her hind legs with two cubs romping playfully at her side.

The bear let out a roar, looking like she was ready to charge. I froze, too frightened to breathe. Usually Harry could sleep through anything, but the ferocious roar woke him up and, out of character, he sprung to his feet. In an amazing burst of speed, Dirty Harry dove at the bear.

The bear swept her huge paw at Harry and sent him flying and yelping through the air. He landed with a loud thud but, miraculously, was back on his feet and snarling at the bear with a protective viciousness I never knew he had.

After tossing the old dog a few more times in the air, the mother bear decided she'd had enough. The cubs had already disappeared into the gully and, after a final loud warning roar, she turned and took off.

I managed to catch my breath and ran to Harry. There was a huge gash in his shoulder and his stomach was torn and bleeding. He was whimpering but licked my hand when I laid it on him.

Until that moment, I had never shown the homely old dog much affection. For after all, I never really wanted a dog! But there I was, praying with all my heart to keep him.

I laid my face on his shoulder. He licked my cheek. Then he was gone. Dirty Harry taught me one of life's most valuable lessons: Only in love do we see true beauty.

~Linda Gabris

# 95

# My Furry Angel

*We derive immeasurable good, uncounted pleasures, enormous security,*
*and many critical lessons about life by owning dogs.*
~Roger Caras

In the spring of 2001 I completed a year of cancer treatments and was pronounced "in remission." Little did I know that it would be a short-lived victory. It was a triple-digit hot Saturday afternoon in July when a dog changed my life forever. We were out of milk so I jumped in the car, blasted the air conditioner, and drove to the corner supermarket. My goal was simple: Buy milk and channel surf for the rest of the day inside the coolness of my home. That's not what happened.

Outside the supermarket a dog adoption was in progress. In order to get inside the store I had to walk through a maze of orphaned, furry angels. About a dozen or more dogs of all types and sizes were in need of loving homes. A black, male Labrador Retriever instantly caught my attention. "He doesn't belong here," I thought. None of them did. But, this dog (Buddy) stood out among the pack. The vet estimated his age to be about three or four years old. When I looked into his soulful brown eyes I felt a connection.

As a cancer survivor, I knew what it was like to want a second chance at life. I knew what it was like to want to run, play, and feel the sun and wind on your face. I imagined that Buddy wanted the same. Before I knew it I was asking the volunteer about him and why he hadn't been adopted yet. Adopting a cute puppy was always easier than an adult dog, they told me. Buddy's large size and color is often associated with "dangerous dogs," but when people realize how friendly he is, their few seconds of fear seem laughable. As I continued to ask questions I took notice of Buddy's behavior. He had a quiet disposition and didn't incessantly bark like the other dogs.

"I want to adopt him," I said to the volunteer. "But, before I do I have to at least discuss it with my husband. I know he'll say yes. I live two minutes from here; give me fifteen minutes to go home and talk to him." To show that I was sincere I paid for the adoption in advance and rushed home.

Bill and I had discussed getting a dog many times, but for one reason or another we never did. Bill happened to be in the front yard when I drove up.

"We have a dog!" I began telling him everything but I was so excited my words sounded like incoherent babble.

Bill stopped me, "A Labrador Retriever? You wanted a guard dog."

It was true. I had talked about Dobermans and Rottweilers. I knew nothing of those breeds except that they would protect me. I knew nothing about Labradors either.

I started to cry. "Oh, wait until you see him. He's beautiful and I've already bonded with him."

I never got milk that day.

We later learned that Buddy's days at the shelter were numbered and his situation was desperate. If not adopted soon he would have been euthanized. When I brought Buddy home, Bill said, "I know this dog!" A few months earlier, a stray dog (Buddy) trotted through the neighborhood while Bill was in the front yard. The dog was thin, wore no collar, and didn't want to leave Bill's side. This was the first I had heard of this incident and it was then that I realized divine intervention was at work.

Within a few weeks of living with us, Buddy was housetrained. His belly had healed from being devoured by fleas and ticks, and his coat was improving, too. Though he has never chewed our wood-work or furniture, he has claimed numerous victories over bakery items left on the kitchen countertop and there was one particular incident involving a cherry pie.

One day after a few hours of running errands, I thought I'd reward myself with a piece of pie and a cold glass of milk. I couldn't find the pie. Buddy had taken the pie box from the countertop without disturbing the myriad of paper piles surrounding it, carried it to his bed, neatly opened the never-opened box, and eaten the entire contents. I phoned Bill at work and was doubled over with knee-slapping laughter. "This could have been so much worse," I said and imagined cherry filling all over the house. Buddy had eaten every morsel. Not a crumb or a speck of red, in any shade, could be found on our light gray carpeting and white walls. Except for the box and tin there was no evidence that a cherry pie ever existed.

Bill's work days are long. We'd check in by phone, but during the day my constant companion was Buddy. It's because of Buddy that I got out of bed at all. He couldn't pour a bowl of kibble or get fresh water. He couldn't open the back door to relieve himself in the yard. My love for him forced me to maintain a routine and revived my spirits. My question about his ability to protect me was challenged one afternoon. I'd been lying on the couch, my head felt like a smashed watermelon, and because of chemo I could barely walk across the room without holding onto the walls for support. I heard a delivery truck drive up and a few seconds later the doorbell rang. Buddy leapt over the couch like an Olympian, barking and growling in a ferocious voice that I'd never heard as he approached "the intruder." He blocked me so that I couldn't open the door, and given his demeanor it was best that the door remained closed.

Buddy reminds me to live every day to the fullest, and though he has never caught a rabbit, his passion for chasing them inspires me to never give up in my own quest to beat cancer. He's about twelve years old now. His paws, eyebrows, and muzzle have grayed and mild hip dysplasia causes him to move slower than an old man easing into his rocking chair.

Last year, we adopted our daughter, Elizabeth, and became parents. She was two days old when we brought her home. The noise level in the house has dramatically increased ever since. Having a baby has been a big adjustment for everyone, including Buddy. He is gentle and patient with Elizabeth, his human sister. This is impressive considering she takes his rawhide chews, uses him as a pillow, a pull-up device, and tugs his whiskers. Buddy doesn't seem to mind these intrusions of personal space and it has given us the opportunity to teach Elizabeth about caring for others. So, instead of pinching and pulling Buddy's ears and hair, we've taught her about "nice touch" and now she pets and cuddles with him nicely. In the final years of his life, my furry angel has renewed purpose, and we are blessed that long ago he crossed our path, twice.

~Michelle L. Miller, Ph.D.

# 96

# For the Love of Ruby

*I have found that when you are deeply troubled,*
*there are things you get from the silent devoted companionship of a dog*
*that you can get from no other source.*
*~Doris Day*

Forty-five days of rehab, months of daily A.A. meetings, professional counseling and innumerable attempts at "finding God" should have made it easier, but instead each day of sobriety became a tougher battle to fight. I had been a daily drinker. Now, facing the world without some artificial form of confidence was agonizing. Fear paralyzed me. Despite the support of counselors and fellow A.A.'ers, it seemed all hope was gone. I resigned myself to the fact that I was a lost soul bound to go through life angry, alone and afraid.

The last place I expected to find salvation was in the companionship of an unwanted dog.

I hadn't expected life to turn out this way. The plan was to graduate from college, start a career, get married and settle down in a house complete with a white picket fence, and kids and dogs running around. That was the plan anyway.

My addiction had other ideas. As with any unhealthy relationship, alcohol had no intention of sharing my time, my money or my attention with anything or anyone. Within two years after graduating college, my drinking had spun out of control and I found myself bouncing from state to state. In early 1990, after being rushed to an ER with a near fatal case of alcohol poisoning, I was forced into treatment.

The advice of well-paid counselors and well-meaning friends could not break through the loneliness and frustration that continued to threaten my sobriety on a daily basis. After five months, the only progress I could claim was that I hadn't been fired or committed a homicide and I hadn't had a drink. The likelihood that I could go much longer without one of the three happening was seriously in question.

"You need to get a higher power," they would say. "You need to believe in something greater than yourself."

As far as I was concerned, God had long since left me behind. I felt truly alone.

Then a co-worker came to work one day chattering about her new litter of Labrador Retriever pups. Week after week, she gave updates on the litter. They were registered Labs with strong blood lines and all had high hopes for being adopted into homes where they would be given first-class treatment as AKC champions.

All except for one.

It soon became obvious that the smallest of the litter would not find a home. The "runt" was bound for the pound.

"I can't afford to raise a dog that won't provide income someday," was her reason for disposing of the flawed pup. My heart broke. I knew the cold isolation of being shunned because you fell short of some impossible standard. I had to see this little outcast for myself.

As soon as I walked into the yard, I saw the shy little "runt" sitting alone in the corner, obviously frightened by the other dogs that were bounding about excitedly. She looked awkward and unsure, innocent and afraid. In an instant, I knew we belonged together.

That evening, I scanned the parking lot of my apartment for any sign of management. A dog could get me evicted, and with my financial situation I didn't have many options. When the coast was clear, I bolted up to my third-story apartment with Ruby tucked inside my shirt. Getting the bed, an array of puppy toys and a forty-pound bag of dog food up proved a far greater challenge.

Protecting her became my sole focus. I trained her, spayed her, fed and clothed her (a prospect she learned to hate). Within weeks, she grew to a point that she was no longer easy to conceal. Walks became covert operations as we played a daily game of "dodge the manager."

I was more in love with that dog than I ever had been with another human. This fact became terrifyingly obvious to me one day as I was sneaking her home after one of our clandestine outings. I dug frantically for my key. A cold space opened in the pit of my stomach as I realized I had locked myself out of my apartment. How would I explain her to the manager? I didn't think "seeing-eye dog" would fly.

If Ruby couldn't live in the apartment with me, we would live in my car together. I would not abandon her—not at any cost. I knew then she had changed me. I finally found something that mattered to me more than myself.

I had found a Higher Power.

The next day I called a real estate agent and a bank—a prospect that six months earlier I would have never considered. Within a year, I had realized a dream—I finally had a home of my own. With Ruby by my side, taking those first steps towards a fulfilling life was no longer such a daunting prospect.

Somewhere along the way, she taught me to love myself. To Ruby, I was always beautiful and fun, always smart and strong. Her love was unwavering even when I didn't feel deserving of it. When bouts of deep depression would drag on endlessly, she waited steadfastly by my side. When I desperately wanted to go to sleep and never wake up, her big brown eyes pleaded with me not to let go.

In my darkest of days, I hung on for no other reason than for the love of Ruby.

In just two years' time, I had gone from an angry, depressed recluse to a socially well-adjusted member of my community. Ruby gave me courage to live again. She gave me a reason to take care of myself and to tackle problems that once overwhelmed me. She took the edge off my fear and gave me a safe, comfortable place to start my recovery.

I have since moved back to my home state of Texas and put to rest the ghosts that had me on the run for so long. I have a career, a wonderful husband, a beautiful home and, of course, a yard full of dogs. With the help of a little black pup that was written off as a "runt," I now have the full and happy life that eluded me for so long.

And nineteen years later, I am grateful to say I have not taken a drink.

In the early days and months of my sobriety, I was too self-centered and too cynical to believe in most things I could see. I wasn't about to turn my will and my life over to the power of something I couldn't see. God understood that the best way to reach out to me was in a form I could love and understand — a helpless and unwanted dog.

It has been nine years since Ruby peacefully passed away. I feared that without her there for support, my world would collapse around me. That didn't happen. The life lessons she taught me carried me through.

And to this day, her loving spirit still lives in my heart.

~Stacy Murphy

# Magic

*Happiness is a warm puppy.*
*~Charles M. Schulz*

I'm devastated. How can I possibly have breast cancer? I'm only forty-four years old. There's no history of cancer in my family. I exercise, eat healthy, and pride myself on looking younger than my years. Cancer's merciless disregard for my proud arguments is frightening. How did I end up being one of the women diagnosed each year in our country with breast cancer? How am I going to face this—the betrayal of my body and my own mortality? How am I going to face the next five minutes, knowing—and not knowing—what's next?

Add to that this crazy new puppy. What a maniac! I'm not even sure I like him. I hear him running in and out of the doggy door. Ugh. Soon he'll be back in here running in circles. It's what we call "puppy frenzy." He smiles, puts his head down and his bottom up, and positions himself to catapult around the room. I'm lying on the couch in absolute despondency as he circles the room. Suddenly, he jumps on my chest and uses my body to launch himself halfway across the room. Tail high and proud, he lands and looks for praise. All I can say is, "Chaco! For pity sake, settle down!" He's heartbroken that I don't appreciate his antics and goes to his bed. His sigh fills the room as he rolls over and accepts my rejection.

I learn that my cancer is early stage and small, but very aggressive. As such, the treatment will also be aggressive. First, a lumpectomy followed by four rounds of chemotherapy, and then six weeks of radiation therapy. I learn new words like Adriamycin, Cytoxan, *in situ*, HERC2 gene, injection port, sentinel node dissection, and nuclear injection. I come to understand the importance of brain scans, bone scans, organ scans, and blood tests. I become familiar with odds like ninety-eight percent recovery, five-year survival rates, and age demographics identifying me as a young "victim." I also learn that I'm young enough to take aggressive therapy and fight this thing successfully. I get numerous opinions in an attempt to assuage my fears. I'm looking for someone to tell me that there was some kind of mistake in my diagnosis. I find out later that those thoughts are normal. What's normal, I ask? Through it all, the fear is still there and the path is uncertain, but one thing is clear: my life is about to change—dramatically. And then there's the puppy.

I tell my husband that there is no way we can keep this dog. He's unruly, wild, and destructive. After all, Chaco is an English Cocker Spaniel bred for field work. And he's just plan nuts! We have to call the breeder and see if he will take the puppy back. My cousin offers to keep Chaco during the difficult days of my therapy. She has a big yard and two kids. Chaco would have fun. I think about the options and as my therapy starts, I also forget about the options as I become immersed in doctors, surgeries, medications, and my battle for survival. Chaco stays and slowly wins my heart.

Make no mistake, chemo is hell and I had a terrible time. When the chemo entered my system to kill the cancer cells, it killed a lot of other cells along the way. The pain was physical, emotional, intellectual, and as my hair fell out, it was visual. I slept and sometimes fell into a state of absolute despair. I'd lie in bed and question everything. I was pitiful, angry, tired, and didn't want to deal with anything. But then there was Chaco—a constant reminder of the wonders of life.

Chaco is blessed with the knowledge that the world is magic. His heart overflows with unconditional love. I'd reject him and he kept coming back—determined to help me fight. It's almost as though he'd look at me and say, "Get up. Don't give in. Let's go for a walk." He'd turn his head and look at me in a way that asked, "Wanna play?"

Sometimes he'd look at me with such love that I felt beautiful, again. And in his rare, quiet moments, he'd snuggle so close to me that I'd almost fall off the bed. I'd smile down at his sweet face and hug him closer.

It's been seven years. Statistically, I have reached the "free zone"—the cancer-free zone. I still think about it. The stalker in my past sometimes visits my dreams, even today. It was a hell of a fight and I've often thought that Chaco was sent to me as a guide through the battlefield. His steadfast love, spirit, and energy have filled my life in a way that's hard to describe. Oh, he still has his "puppy frenzy" moments, but they are fewer and shorter. I laugh as he runs around the house and quickly goes to lie down—pooped from the exertion, not my rejection. He still looks at me with longing when he wants to hit the trail or chase birds, but those walks are no longer the marathons of his youth, or mine. We've come a long way together. Oh, he still thinks the world is magic, and through him, so do I.

~Carla Andrews-O'Hara

# 98

# Snowball the Gross

*Biology is the least of what makes someone a mother.*
*~Oprah Winfrey*

Our ten-year-old dog, Heidi, shared a special bond with me. And we shared a disdain for Snowball—the Spitz-mix puppy given to my daughter Susie by her granny.

Snowball was given to Granny by her children after her old dog died, but this white bundle of fur was hyperactive compared to Happy. The kids didn't understand that Granny and Happy had grown old together. Granny didn't have the energy to keep up with, train, and nurture this pup. When we visited Granny, she said, "They love each other. I want to give Snowball to Susie." My husband never told his mother "no" and he wasn't going to start then. He brought Snowball and a happy Susie home.

The first week Snowball lived with us, we kept her penned in the laundry room at night. Snowball chewed a gaping hole in the sheetrock. Her black eyes sparkled and her black lips seemed to beam a proud smile.

Heidi didn't want a new puppy. No matter how many bowls we put out with food, Heidi thought they were all hers. We finally put Heidi's bowl on one porch and Snowball's on a porch on the opposite side of the house. Heidi lost weight running from porch to porch trying to make sure Snowball wasn't eating from either.

Snowball was smart though, and much younger, and she would wait until Heidi collapsed on the porch, exhausted, near her own special bowl. As soon as Snowball was confident Heidi was too tired to care, we would hear her chomping on the food in the bowl we'd designated for her. It took several months, but Heidi finally gave up trying to starve Snowball and even occasionally allowed her the luxury of sleeping on the same porch. They never bonded though, and I didn't think I would ever learn to like Snowball either.

Susie adored her. They were constant companions all summer. When Susie had to go to school in the fall, Snowball howled as the school bus pulled away with her best friend. When the bus disappeared in a cloud of dust, Snowball was on her own with no guide—or restraint. Boredom made trouble her companion. She gnawed young trees we'd planted and they died. "You gross and disgusting animal!" I spat one of the many times I tripped over the shell of a dead armadillo she'd found and left on the porch. This earned her the nickname "Snowball the Gross." Bob and I both became frustrated to the point of wanting to get rid of this bundle of trouble, but we felt trapped by Susie's affection for her.

The next year, Heidi and Snowball both became pregnant by the Collie next door. I worried about Heidi being able to bear the Collie pups, but let her do so. She and Snowball both swelled so big their bellies almost scraped the ground. Finally, in early August, Heidi had her litter. She'd never been a mother before and she surprised us by nurturing her pups immediately. She was also protectively aggressive toward Snowball when she waddled too close. Finally, a week later, Snowball had her puppies too.

Heidi reacted strangely to Snowball's pups. She kept trying to steal them away and nurse them with her own. At first, I thought she was confused and thought Snowball had stolen her pups, but I have often wondered if it wasn't something more. For a few weeks, this tug of war continued as Heidi sneaked Snowball's pups away and Snowball retrieved them. I found it intriguing that Snowball never got one of Heidi's pups—she always knew which were hers and only took those.

One evening after dinner when the heat was beginning to

subside, Susie went out to play. Snowball ran to greet her and Susie dismissed her as she climbed onto her bike. Heidi growled and barked—seemingly at Snowball. "Oh shut up, you ole grouch!" Susie commanded. But Heidi's hair raised and she bared her teeth as she growled and stood between her pups and Snowball. As Susie pushed the pedal down on her bike, Snowball leaped in front of her, nearly causing her to fall. Just behind Snowball was a huge rattlesnake. Its body coiled tightly and making a loud hissing sound, it snapped at Snowball. Susie screamed for Bob to get his gun. By the time he shot it, the snake had bitten Snowball many times.

Susie sobbed deeply as she and Bob lifted Snowball into the car and rushed to the animal hospital. The veterinarian gave Snowball shots and told Bob and Susie not to expect much. There was too much poison in Snowball's little body to hope for survival. He gave them some needles and medicine and sent them home.

We made her as comfortable as possible, but she heard her pups crying and so she cried too. Heidi too heard her former foe's pups crying. She continued her practice of finding Snowball's pups, mingling them with her own and feeding them all together. Snowball relaxed and slept when her pups quit crying.

The next morning, Susie begged me to let her stay home from school, but I thought it would be better to keep her mind off Snowball. She slowly boarded the bus and cried as they pulled away. Snowball let out a weak howl and my heart leaped with hope that perhaps she was getting better. I gave her the shots when they were due and stayed with her until she rested. Through tears of anguish and shame, I told her how grateful and proud I was that she blocked Susie from that snake. "I'm glad you were given to us. I'm sorry I called you gross." The vigil continued through lunch. After the noon shot, I stroked her until she closed her black eyes, and then went to clean house. Moments later, Snowball's scream pierced the air, and then she was dead.

Heidi raised Snowball's pups as her own. Susie kept the largest.

His name is Albert. He looks like his daddy but acts like his mother. I'm glad we still have Snowball with us through Albert.

~Joie Fields

# 99

# An Open Heart

*No one would choose a friendless existence on condition of having all the*
*other things in the world.*

*~Aristotle*

"**C**an you take Max?" the neighbor asked weeping. "You said you liked dogs, wanted a dog. We have to move and the new place doesn't allow them."

"But you've only had him a week," I said. Max sat attentively, taking in the scene.

The neighbor cried and nodded, stroking the puppy's head. "We've been transferred; no dogs allowed in the new place." Max looked at me expectantly. I agreed.

And so he moved in. Pillows were destroyed, shoes were eaten. I laughed at his antics. He was housebroken within days. But he wasn't a Max. He never came when called and there were three other dogs named Max on my lower Manhattan block. I got a baby book and read names to my new companion. "Aaron? Able? Armand? Wallace? William?" No response. "Spot? Fido?" Did he chuckle? Amused, I read the names of the authors from the books on my shelf. "Irving?" Nothing. "Buck?" Nothing. "King?" Nothing. "Aristotle?" His head turned with expectant eyes. I said it again, "Aristotle." He came to me. "Aristotle!" He nudged his wet nose toward my face, licking my nose.

Aristotle learned tricks quickly. He patiently taught me a few tricks, too. He balanced, hindquarters solid, paws in the air, bone balanced on nose. He waited for the command, flipped the bone in the air and caught it. He barked on command. He shook the hands of newcomers whether asked or not.

Aristotle was an excellent judge and jury. Those he liked treated me well. I learned quickly to avoid those he avoided.

Tennis balls were his passion. He'd chase and retrieve them until collapsing from exhaustion. He'd show off with tricks in front of crowds, conning younger, more athletic types to throw the ball, throw the ball, throw the ball in the parks around New York City.

Then one night a whimper came from the corner. Aristotle was sprawled on the floor, trying desperately to get up when I called. I quickly found the number of the vet. The after-hour operator forwarded my call to the all-night clinic. "Get here fast," the voice said.

I wrapped Aristotle's small shaking body in a towel and headed out for a cab. We arrived at the animal hospital and were met at the door. A man and woman in medical garb whisked Aristotle from my arms, motioning me to follow into the stainless steel room. The air was cool and smelled of antiseptic. Blood was drawn; tubes inserted; questions asked; and frowns made.

No, I hadn't seen him eat anything strange. No, we hadn't been to the country. Yes, he was current on all his shots. No, it couldn't be a reaction to a shot because the last one was several weeks ago. No, I hadn't had him since he was born. No, I didn't know where he was born. I got him from a neighbor who'd left town.

The days passed. I visited before and after work and cried, petting his soft golden head as those enlarged brown eyes desperately looked at me. He kept trying to stand, to follow me out, but his attempts were futile.

I'd made it to adulthood without having my heart broken by another, but here, with him, I could feel the pain of heartbreak.

The doctors, some of the best in Manhattan, didn't know what was wrong. They ran more tests, tried different drugs, attempted experimental treatments. I feared the medical bills. I had trouble covering my own rent every month; how would I pay for all of this? "We make choices," I told myself. "It will all work out."

Six days had passed, but Aristotle was no better. When I went in after work that night, the vet asked if I wanted to take him home. "I think we've done all we can do," the doctor said. He didn't look me in the eyes, but instead, looked into Aristotle's eyes. "He'll get better care with you over the weekend," the vet said.

"Will he...?" I choked back my tears. "If he's going to die, I don't want to take him home. Is he going to die?"

"I don't know," the vet said, but convinced me to take him.

I approached the desk to pay the bill and the young man behind the counter smiled warmly and said, "No charge."

"What? You've run all these tests. He's been here a week."

"We wanted to know what's wrong. We've never seen an animal sick like this. We know you can't afford all we've done; no one could. Just take him home and love him over the weekend."

Love? I'd never felt myself to be in love before. That's why I'd spent my life alone. I didn't know what love felt like. All this pain and worry? All this sorrow and grief? Is this what love feels like? We'd only been together a few weeks; doesn't love take longer? Can you really love an animal?

I pushed the furniture out of the way and we spent the weekend together on the living room floor. I stroked him and he nudged me. His big eyes looked deep into me. I hand-fed him food with the crushed antibiotics; he licked my hands clean.

I openly begged him not to die, not yet, not when I'd finally felt so deeply for another. I'd finally opened my heart to another soul; it couldn't be taken from me.

I awoke to a whimper. It was like that sound that started this ordeal. My heart filled with dread. Aristotle was standing by the door, begging to go outside. I quickly attached his leash, opened the door and he bound outside, barely making it to the street in time. He looked up at me and there was absolute relief in his eyes; was he mirroring me? It was a miracle, there's no other way to describe it.

When we walked into the vet's on Monday morning it was someone else's turn to cry. The doctors and technicians stopped what they were doing to see the miracle puppy prancing around the waiting room, showing off for everyone, as if nothing had happened. They took more blood and ran more tests for comparison. They never did find the source of the problem.

I knew what it was: Me.

Others may not understand, but I believe this was a test. This test proved I could love another. It proved my worthiness to posses this remarkable companion.

Love, I realized, is the simple willingness to share my life with others and to trust that we'll be there for one another no matter what happens. Aristotle helped me comprehend that love is an open heart, open to sorrow and to joy.

~Gregory A. Kompes

# The Appointment

*When a man's best friend is his dog, that dog has a problem.*
*~Edward Abbey*

The first time is always the toughest. I knew it would be terribly hard for my husband, Bob. All through the night before, he thrashed around in bed. At one point, I thought I heard him crying.

"It'll be fine, sweetheart," I said, snuggling with him.

"Maybe I should cancel the appointment," he said.

"No, honey, don't cancel it. You've already cancelled twice. You've got to go through with it someday, and tomorrow's just as good as any other time. I think you should just get it over with."

He finally got out of bed at dawn, having had no sleep. He knelt down beside our dog, Gracie, and kissed her on the forehead. "I'm sorry," he said tearfully.

"Bob, she's just getting groomed, for heaven's sake."

"But what if they hurt her?"

"Grooming is all they do. She's got all that matted fur. You've got to pull yourself together and be strong. You slept like a baby the night before my surgery."

"But this is different," he said caressing her. "She's not my wife. She's my dog."

At nine o'clock, he called the grooming place. "If she's in pain, you'll stop, won't you?"

I grabbed the phone and whispered to him, "You called them

yesterday and said the same thing." I apologized to the secretary. "My husband's a dork," I said.

Gracie gets tranquilizers when there's a thunderstorm because thunder freaks her out. Although she was very calm this morning, I said, "What about her pills?"

"That's a great idea." He went to the medicine cabinet and took one himself. Then he slept until her appointment time. After he dropped her off, he called me from his cell phone. "They said it'll take three hours," he said, sighing heavily.

"You're right near the pond," I said. "Why don't you take a walk?"

"Without my dog?" he said, aghast.

"Okay." I was trying to be patient. "Why don't you pick me up and we'll have lunch?"

"Without Gracie?"

"It's not like she sits with us at the table, Bob." He nixed lunch and came home, where he paced for three hours. Then he picked up our beautiful dog. That evening in the kitchen, he said, "I'm so glad it's over."

"Me too. You did great with this whole thing," I lied, holding up my arms for a hug. He raised his arms in return and walked past me to Gracie, where they sat on the floor together and embraced.

There's something very wonderful and tender about Bob's love for his dog. That night in bed, I reached across Gracie and put my hand on Bob's arm. "I love you," I said softly. I moved my hand above Gracie's head, which was resting on Bob's shoulder, and gently combed his hair with my fingers.

"I love you too. I don't know what I'd do without you," he said in sleepy tones. "But it's too early," he said, still in his dream state. "I'll feed you in the morning."

~Saralee Perel

# Best Dog in the World

*One's first love is always perfect until one meets one's second love.*
~Elizabeth Aston

Years ago, I owned the very best dog in the world.

I was a child when we got her. She was a graceful brown hound, a foundling who taught me that our pets are not purchased, but ordained.

She romped when I did and knew how to smile in that funny way that only some dogs have. She grew up with me, always there when I needed her. My grown hand still remembers the sleek bump on the top of her head and that gentle divot just past her nose that fit my index finger just perfectly.

She passed away during one of my college vacations. My heart broke then, and I knew that there would never be another dog like her, and there hasn't been. I was sure that I could never love another dog as much as I'd loved her.

Fortunately, I was wrong about that part.

My next dog came into my life when I was married. My husband traveled for a living, and I was often lonely. This dog grew into a lumbering Wolfhound and Sheepdog mix who taught me patience. He was a large, grizzled sentry, that dog. He rarely left my side until the children were born, and then he became their guardian, too. I can still feel that swirl of fur along his back and the weight of his chin when it rested in my lap.

When he passed away, my heart broke. As much as I had loved

that childhood dog, I had been wrong. This was the very best dog in the world. There would never be another dog like him, and there hasn't been. I was sure I would never love another dog as much as I'd loved him.

I was wrong again.

We got the next one, a loping black Lab-and-Terrier mix, when the children were little. He taught me the importance of adapting. He was everyone's dog from the beginning, and that was just as it should be. When he played tug of war with the children, he dragged them across the kitchen floor as they shrieked with laughter. He always seemed to sleep in the room of the child who needed his company the most.

These days his face is expressively gray, and he spends more time with me since the almost-grown children aren't around so much. The other day my oldest, home from college, played tug of war. We all laughed—just a little—as the dog was gently pulled across the kitchen floor.

He is, of course, the very best dog in the world. I will never forget that exquisitely soft tuft of fur behind his ears or the tickly feel when he nuzzles. There won't be another dog like him.

And that's okay, because we will never be at this point in our lives again.

Sometimes I've wondered why two species that get along so well should have such different life spans. It just doesn't seem right. And then I wonder if that's part of the lesson: To teach us that love itself has a spirit that returns again and again and never really dies.

It's amazing, in a way, how they bring to our ever-changing lives exactly what it is that we need at the moment. They make room for one another, this family of dogs who has never even met. And they fit—into our families, into our lives, into our memories, and into our hearts—because they always have been and always will be the best dogs in the world.

~T'Mara Goodsell

# Meet Our Contributors

**Mary M. Alward** has been writing professionally since 1989 and has been published in both print and online venues. She enjoys spending time with her grandsons, reading and gardening. Currently, Mary is taking a course with the Institute of Children's Literature and hopes to one day write children's books.

**Carla Andrews-O'Hara** earned a B.S. in Mass Communication and an M.A. in English. She is an advocate for life-long learning and works to promote education opportunities for adults. She spends her free time hiking, sailing, and exploring the great outdoors with her family and her two loving dogs, Kaibab and Chaco.

**Rae Armour** received her Bachelor of Physical Education in 1967 and taught high school for eight years. She is a gifted singer/songwriter/performer and opened for Faith Hill in Whistler in 2004. She is touring with her band AUGUST. She loves travel, golf and her dogs, Milo and Vallee. Contact her at aarmour@shaw.ca.

**Elizabeth Atwater** is a small town Southern gal whose love of reading as a young child turned into a love of writing at an early age. She is currently seeking an agent to help her get her books published. She can be contacted at eatwater@windstream.net.

**Joe Atwater** is a horseman who breeds, raises, and races Standardbred horses on his ranch in North Carolina. Horses have been an important part of his life since adolescence and they take up most of his time. The rest of his time is taken up by his devoted wife, Elizabeth.

**Nancy Berk, PhD**, is a clinical psychologist, author, and humorist. Her first book, *Secrets of a Bar Mitzvah Mom* (2005), illustrated her ability to pair self-help and humor. Nancy's next book is a survival guide for parents of college applicants.

**Marjee K. Berry** is a Christian writer with bipolar disorder whose writings are as varied as her moods. Her writings have been published in *More God Allows U Turns* and *Chicken Soup for the Teenage Soul on Love & Friendship*. She is proud of her four children and three grandchildren. Contact her at mkberry2@hotmail.com.

**Lil Blosfield** works as Chief Financial Officer for Child and Adolescent Behavioral Health in Canton, Ohio. She won First Prize in the 2008 *Chicken Soup for the American Idol Soul* story contest. She enjoys writing stories and poems inspired by her daughters, Amanda and Elizabeth. Lil may be contacted at LBlosfield40@msn.com.

**Dianne Bourgeois** is the author of *Pugs* (Animal Planet Pet Care Library). She wrote the humor column "Pug Tales" about life with Guinevere in *Pug Talk* magazine. She's the former editor of the *Pug Phoenix* newsletter for Pug Rescue of New England and authored its column "Pet Pug Corner."

**Elaine L. Bridge** worked in the woods on the west coast as a forester before becoming a stay-at-home mom to her three boys. Now living in Ohio she works part-time in a grocery store and is devoted to developing her relationship with God, caring for her family and writing inspirational material.

**Kristen Campbell Bush** received her Bachelor of Science in Communications from the University of Tennessee, and works in marketing for an insurance restoration contractor. Kristen has four dogs and four cats—all rescued. In addition to the pets, Kristen has a six-year-old daughter, Paige, who would love to become a veterinarian.

**Kristine Byron** is an interior decorator, writer of children's stories and is in the process of writing her first cookbook. She is looking to have her stories illustrated and published. Kristine enjoys cooking, entertaining and spending time with her grandchildren. You can reach her at rbyron14@aol.com.

**Janet Caplan** lives with her husband, one of her two daughters, plus two cocker spaniels, near Victoria on Canada's Vancouver Island. Janet writes memoirs and what she terms slice of life pieces. In addition to her writing, she enjoys walking with the dogs, hiking and photography.

**Laura Chesler** is a freelance writer who specializes in business collateral and features for print and online magazines. She loves reading, music and cooking, and quite by accident (and possibly with some cunning plotting on their end), her dogs are often the first to test her recipes. Contact her at laurachesler.com.

**Jeri Chrysong** resides in southern California with her faithful dog by her side. She enjoys writing, photography, travel, and the beach. Jeri has published other stories in the *Chicken Soup for the Soul* series, and is currently working on a book about her successful weight loss journey.

**Joseph Civitella, MscD**, is an ordained minister of spiritual metaphysics. He founded the School of LifeWork, has written the book, *Turning your Passion into a Profession* and the novel *Shadows of Tomorrow*, and recorded the CD "Soulace." He is currently working on a new book, *The Sacred and the Profane*.

**Courtney Conover** is a University of Michigan graduate and enjoys long distance running, Sunday mornings with a fresh newspaper, and doting on her mother's Bichon, Sir Meister. Courtney is currently working on her first novel. She and her husband, Scott, reside in suburban Detroit. Please e-mail her at: courtneyconover@yahoo.com.

**Sharon Love Cook** lives in Beverly Farms, Mass., with her husband and herd of cats (currently no dogs). She writes a humor column and draws cartoons for *The Salem News*. She is seeking a publisher for her humorous illustrated gift book about men and cats. E-mail her at Cookie978@aol.com.

**Tracy Crump** loves writing and has contributed to numerous anthologies, newspapers, magazines, and devotionals. She also enjoys presenting writing workshops including the popular "Stirring the Pot: Writing for *Chicken Soup for the Soul*" for groups at writers' conferences. Tracy can be reached at tracygeneral@gmail.com.

**Michele Cushatt** embraces writing as a catalyst to inspire people to live authentic and generous lives. A sought-after writer and speaker, her works have appeared in magazines, devotionals, compilations and almost daily on her blog, www.michelecushatt.com. You can connect with her at michele@michelecushatt.com.

**Elizabeth Cutting** is a writer, astrologer and seminar producer. She received her MBA from Northwestern University. When not writing or consulting the stars, she can be found foraging on a secluded Missouri farm with her Border Collie, Cara. Contact her at eacutting@aol.com.

Award-winning cartoonist **Roy Delgado's** cartoons appear regularly in the *Harvard Business Review*, *The Wall Street Journal*, *Barron's*, *Reader's Digest*, *Playboy* and over fifty national and international publications. He is the author of several books. You can reach him at roy.delgado@gmail.com.

**Lisa Plowman Dolensky** is a first generation University of Alabama graduate. Her creative nonfiction appears in *God Encounters*, published by Simon & Schuster's Howard Books (2009) and Tyndale House's *Life Savors for Women*. She celebrates twenty-three years of marriage and being mom to three miracles. Contact her at www.wingblots.com.

**Jane Marie Allen Farmer** works at both private and homeschooled children's enrichment facilities. She enjoys horseback riding and hiking. She and one of her four dogs, Leala, work as a pet therapy team. She received her BS in Wildlife/Fisheries Science, BFA in Art and MS in Education from University of Tennessee.

**Joseph Farris** is a staff cartoonist and cover artist with *The New Yorker* and works for many national and international publications. He also paints and his cartoons and paintings are in many collections including the Morgan Library and Museum in New York City. Contact may be made at: www.josephfarris.com.

**Joie Fields** is a freelance author, wife, mother and grandmother. Joie has written articles purchased by *Faith and Friends* and *War Cry* magazines, and *Seasoned Cooking* e-zine. She is author of the BibleStudyNotes group at Yahoo! Groups. She and her husband, Bob, have two children and two grandchildren. You may contact her at jffchayil@gmail.com.

**Carol Fleischman** is a regular contributor to *The Buffalo News*. Her articles cover a wide range of everyday events, from yard sales to wedding showers, but Carol's recurring theme is life as a blind person, especially the joys and challenges of working with guide dogs.

**Susanne Fogle** has written a weekly newspaper column, "Animal Tails" for the *Edwardsville Intelligencer* for ten years. She lives in Saint Charles, Missouri with her two dogs, one cat and a parrot. She may be contacted at Susannefogle@AOL.com.

**Erin Fuentes** received her B.A. from Converse College and enjoys working with the caregivers of Alzheimer's patients. She lives with her husband, daughter, Afghan Hound, a cat with two different colored eyes, and a feisty bunny. Erin has a collection of children's stories. Please e-mail her at erinc.fuentes@gmail.com.

**Linda Gabris** has instructed writing workshops and international cooking courses for over sixteen years. She has written a book, *Cooking Wild*, and hopes to have another book finished soon. Linda writes outdoor cooking columns and articles for magazines in Canada and USA. You can reach her at inkserv@telus.net.

**Ed Geib** is a patrol sergeant in a local police department in south central PA. He and his K-9 buddy, "Coal," love spending time on their boat on the Chesapeake Bay and traveling on the motorcycle (Coal rides in the sidecar).

**Nancy Lowell George** is a freelance writer in Richardson, Texas. Her essays have appeared in *Bark Magazine*, *The Christian Science Monitor* and *Guideposts*. Boone, a Lab-Shepherd mix puppy, recently joined her family. He shows great potential for material for future essays.

**T'Mara Goodsell** was literally raised with dogs since her parents often kept their Great Pyrenees puppy in her playpen. She is an active supporter of The Humane Society and a fan of mixed breeds. T'Mara has a degree in Education and lives with her two teenagers and dog near St. Louis, Missouri.

**Charmaine Hammond** received her Master's Degree in Conflict Analysis & Management from Royal Roads University, BC, Canada and is owner and president of Hammond International Inc. A professional speaker, facilitator and consultant, Charmaine is passionate about helping individuals and businesses reach and exceed their potential. Please contact Charmaine at charmaine@hammondgroup.biz.

**Kathy Lynn Harris** is a writer of novels, children's books, short stories, essays and poetry who lives high in the mountains of Colorado. Find out more at kathylynnharris.com or e-mail Kathy at kathy@kathylynnharris.com.

**Louis A. Hill, Jr.** authored three books and many articles. He earned a Ph.D. in Structural Engineering, designed bridges and buildings and joined the engineering faculty at Arizona State University. He retired an Emeritus Dean of Engineering from The University of Akron. He is listed in Who's Who in America.

**Marcia Hodge** works full time as an Oncology Data Specialist, while pursuing a career as a freelance writer. She enjoys reading, scrapbooking, and Swedish weave. Marcia has written numerous devotions and recently completed collaboration on a screenplay. She is currently working on a novel. Please e-mail her at hodgem@shands.ufl.edu.

**Veronica Hutton** received a Bachelor of Arts in English from Virginia Commonwealth University in 1994. She enjoys painting, reading, and raising her wonderful son. She continues writing, in the hopes of inspiring spiritual healing in others. Please e-mail her at veronicahutton@hughes.net.

**Robbie Iobst**, blessed wife of John, proud mom of Noah, and grateful owner of Scooby, lives in Centennial, Colorado. She is a freelance writer and speaker and her work has been featured in *Chicken Soup for the Tea Lover's Soul*. E-mail Robbie at robbieiobst@hotmail.com and read her blog at www.robbieiobst.blogspot.com.

**Gayle Mansfield Irwin** is the author of *Sage's Big Adventure*, an inspirational story about her blind Springer Spaniel. She conducts school and library speaking engagements. Her next children's book, *Sage Learns to Share*, is scheduled for publication in 2009. Visit www.sagestory.com for information. Gayle lives in Wyoming.

**Jennie Ivey** lives in Tennessee. She is a newspaper columnist and the author of three books: *Tennessee Tales the Textbooks Don't Tell*, *E Is for Elvis*, and *Soldiers, Spies, and Spartans*. She has published numerous fiction and non-fiction pieces, including stories in seven *Chicken Soup for the Soul* books. E-mail her at jivey@frontiernet.net.

**Daniel James** works in healthcare. He and his wife watch for lost dogs in the Denver, Colorado area.

**Carol Kehlmeier** is a former newspaperwoman and columnist. As a freelance writer, her work has been published in both secular and Christian publications. She is a wife, mother and grandmother writing from Westerville, Ohio.

**Sally Kelly-Engeman** is a freelance writer who has had numerous short stories and articles published. In addition to writing, she enjoys reading and researching. She also enjoys ballroom dancing and traveling the world with her husband. She can be reached at sallyfk@juno.com.

**Vicki Kitchner** has a Master's Degree in Special Education and holds a National Board Certification in Exceptional Student Education. Vicki and her husband, Skip, divide their time between Florida and North Carolina where they enjoy backpacking, adventure vacations, fitness and reading. Please e-mail her at vicki@hikersrest.com.

**Mimi Greenwood Knight** is a freelance writer living in South Louisiana with her husband, David, four kids and way too many pets. She has over four hundred published articles and essays in magazine, anthologies and on websites. Mimi enjoys baking, butterfly gardening, Bible study and the lost art of letter writing.

**Gregory A. Kompes** is a bestselling author, teacher, speaker, and self-promotion expert. Co-founder of the Patchwork Path series and Presenters & Programs, Gregory holds a BA in English Literature from Columbia University, NY, and an MS Ed. from California State University, East Bay. Visit him online at www.Kompes.com.

**Terri Lacher** is a retired executive assistant and mother of six, grandmother of fourteen. She grew up in the southwest, where she developed a love for storytelling and writing. Involved in many community activities, she now lives Center, Texas with her husband and Labrador retriever. Her e-mail address is btlacher@sbcglobal.net.

**Maxine Leick** earned a Bachelors degree in English Language Arts. She taught middle/high school English and speech in Nebraska for several years and does substitute teaching. Maxine's hobbies include cooking, baking, reading, and sewing. She rides and trains horses. Maxine enjoys working with teens and is involved in her community.

**Bobbie Jensen Lippman** is a prolific human-interest writer. She currently writes "Bobbie's Beat" for the *Newport News-Times*, Newport, OR. She has been a hospice volunteer for over thirty years. She lives with her husband, Burt, their dog Charley, and a shelter cat named L.S. (Lap sitter). She may be reached at Bobbisbeat@aol.com.

**Barbara LoMonaco** received her Bachelor of Science degree from the University of Southern California and has an elementary teaching credential. Barbara has worked for Chicken Soup for the Soul since February 1998 as an Editor and as their Customer Service representative. She is a co-author of *Chicken Soup for the Mother and Son Soul*. Contact Barbara at blomonaco@chickensoupforthesoul.com.

**Heidi Smith Luedtke** is a psychologist turned freelance writer who does her best work with toddler mayhem in the background and a dog snuggled under her desk. She currently resides in Alexandria, Virginia. Heidi's blog on parenting as a leadership experience can be found at www.LeadingMama.com.

**Kathy Lumbert** attended the University of Arizona. She currently works for the State of Colorado in the Community College system. Kathy loves dogs, reading, writing, drawing, painting and swimming. She is currently writing for The Presidential Prayer Team and has had numerous devotionals published for Family Life Communications.

**Natalia K. Lusinski** created her first newspaper, Nats Neat News Notes, at age ten. Since then, she has associate-produced a documentary for The History Channel, worked as a writers assistant on several TV shows, written many TV, film, and short stories, and dog-sat many a dog. E-mail her at writenataliainla@yahoo.com.

**Aaron M.** is a freelance writer and television producer in the Midwest. His lease forbids him from keeping a dog or cat in his apartment but he still keeps a box of Milk-Bones atop his refrigerator for when friends bring their dogs for a visit.

**Sharon Rice Maag** teaches fourth grade and Sunday School in Southeastern North Carolina. She won her first writing contest in third grade! Sharon simply loves writing, teaching, traveling, treasure hunting with her husband Doug, and, most of all, hanging out with their kids and grandkids!

**Jeff Mainard** received Bachelor of Arts degrees in English and Psychology from Portland State University in 1998. He is writing a novel about green living and how America will change with house conversions that generate enough food and energy to allow people to work at home. Please e-mail him at jeffmainard@hotmail.com.

**Tim Martin** is the author of four books and seven screenplays. He has two children's novels, *Scout's Oaf* (Cedar Grove Books) and *Fast Pitch* (Blitz Publishing) scheduled for publication in 2009. His work has appeared in several *Chicken Soup for the Soul* books. Tim can be reached at tmartin@northcoast.com.

**Alexis Joy May** is a middle school student in Texas. She is active in church and sports, and maintains good grades in the hopes of becoming a vet. She and her family enjoy several pets.

**Mary McCloud** received her Bachelor of Science in Nursing in 1983 and a Master of Science in Secondary Education in 1994. She works as a school nurse in Texas. Mary enjoys cooking, traveling, singing and writing devotionals and inspirational poetry. Please e-mail her at nursemccloud@yahoo.com or visit her website: www.marymccloud. wordpress.com.

**Beverly McClure** graduated cum laude with a Bachelor of Science in Education degree from Midwestern State University. She taught elementary school for twenty-two years before retiring. She now writes for children and teens. Three of her young-adult novels are published with more under contract.

**Marty McGovern** graduated from Colorado State University, taught English and music in Denver, and loves animals and photography.

**Jane Miller** helped her dog Sadie, now a certified therapy dog, to author *RUFF Times: A Ruff Writer's Journal*, available through their website www.ruffwriters.com. The website and journal were inspired by Sadie's visits to an assisted living home. Contact her via e-mail at Jane@ruffwriters.com.

**Michelle L. Miller, Ph.D.**, is the author of four books and is an award-winning producer and host of "Public Affairs Health Talk Radio" in Dallas, Texas.

**Susan Mires** has been a newspaper journalist for twelve years and is a business editor in St. Joseph, MO. She holds a degree in agriculture with a journalism minor from Northwest Missouri State University. She writes about the economy, country life and God's gracious touch in her life at www.susanmires.com.

**Jan Morrill** is the author of short stories and is working on her first novel. Her stories have been published in *Chicken Soup for the Soul* books and several anthologies. She spends her spare time writing and painting, and enjoys sailing and traveling with her husband. Please visit Jan at www.janmorrill.com.

**Joyce Anne Munn** is a retired educator. She serves on the national board of Christian Educators Association International, an organization for public school teachers. She volunteers at various places in her town and teaches Sunday school class. She loves traveling and playing with her two dogs and a cat.

**Stacy Murphy** received her BS from Texas A&M. She lives in East Texas with her husband and dogs (i.e. children). She writes about whatever moves her. She loves animals, movies and rocking chairs and is hoping to make a career out of what she loves most... writing. E-mail her at StacyMurphy100@aol.com.

**Christine Negroni** is a writer and a published author. She is not a dog person. Dillon came into her life at the request of her husband and four children. When Dillon went missing the whole family learned two important lessons; go after seemingly impossible goals and rely on the kindness of others.

**Dena Netherton** has degrees in music and education. A former music theater teacher, she has survived the trauma of directing both animals and children on stage. Now a freelance writer, she's authored three novels, several one-act children's plays, and children's songs and poems. Please e-mail her at brucedenakiri@aol.com.

**Marky Olson** and her husband live in Sammamish, Washington. She is a retired high school English teacher and is currently a business writer, corporate writing and public speaking teacher. The Olsons enjoy spending time with their two married daughters and two grandsons appreciating the wonders of the Northwest.

**Mark Parisi's** "off the mark" comic, syndicated since 1987, is distributed by United Media. Mark's humor also graces greeting cards, T-shirts, calendars, magazines, newsletters and books. Check out: offthemark.com. Lynn is his wife/business partner. Their daughter, Jen, contributes with inspiration, (as do three cats and one dog).

**Martha Penhall** has been part of UCLA Medical Center's People Animal Connection for ten years. She also volunteers for the Paws for Reading program. When not volunteering, Martha loves art, golf, the great outdoors and is writing *The Adventures of a Blind Wiener Dog* series. Contact her at mapenhall@earthlink.net.

**Ava Pennington** is a writer, speaker, and Bible teacher. She has published magazine articles and contributed to fifteen anthologies, including twelve *Chicken Soup for the Soul* books. She is also author of *A Year Alone with God - a 366-day devotional guide to the names and attributes of God*. Learn more at www.avawrites.com.

**Saralee Perel** is an award-winning nationally syndicated columnist and novelist. She is honored to be a multiple contributor to *Chicken Soup for the Soul*. Saralee welcomes e-mails at sperel@saraleeperel.com or via her website: www.saraleeperel.com.

**Kelly Carper Polden** is a communications professional with twenty years experience as a key contributor to a variety of businesses and non-profit organizations (www.kellycarpercommunications.com). She is also a freelance writer for numerous publications, and a first-time children's author of *Puppy Tales: The Adventures of Adam the Australian Shepherd* (www.amazon.com).

A native Oregonian, for nearly thirty years **Beverly A. Porter** has enjoyed life "southern-style" in Mississippi with her minister husband. She has taught on the elementary, secondary, and college levels, including ten years in academic administration. Bev enjoys writing memoirs, Christian fiction, and poetry.

The mother of three sons, **Caroline Poser** lives with her family in a small town in Massachusetts. She works full time as a software marketing professional and moonlights as an author and columnist. Contact her at www.CarolinePoser.com.

**Felice Prager**, owner of five cats, is a freelance writer with credits in local, national, and international publications. In addition to writing, she also works with adults and children with moderate to severe learning disabilities as a multisensory educational therapist. Please visit her website (www.writefunny.com) or her blog (www. writefunny.blogspot.com).

**Jennifer Quasha** is a published author of more than forty books. Her book, *The Dog Lover's Book of Crafts*, won the DWAA Best General Interest Book in 2002. Currently, she is a freelance writer and editor. Check out her website at www.jenniferquasha.com.

**Sarah Retzer** graduated as an Engineer with an English Literature minor in 1998. Currently, she is a Quality Manager in the aerospace industry. Sarah loves to spend time gardening, hiking, camping, practicing yoga, reading and writing. She aspires to become a full-time writer. Please e-mail her at s_retzer@yahoo.com.

**Bruce Robinson** is an award-winning internationally published cartoonist whose work has appeared in numerous periodicals including the *National Enquirer*, *The Saturday Evening Post*, *Woman's World*, *The Sun*, *First*, *Highlights*, and many others. He is also the author of the cartoon book *Good Medicine*. Contact him via e-mail at cartoonsbybrucerobinson@hotmail.com.

**Rachael Rowe** lives in Dorset, England and is a freelance writer who also works in healthcare. Her interests lie in travel, researching history and walking, particularly in the hills and along the coastline near her home.

**Kim Seeley** is a former English teacher and librarian who currently teaches disabled adults. She and her husband, Wayne, reside in Wakefield, Virginia, less than a mile from her grand-dog, Tyson, her daughter, and son-in-law.

**Sean Sellers** received a BA from the College of Architecture, Auburn University. Sean visited NYC as a teenager in 1982 thanks to a wonderful teacher. He never thought about writing anything until 9/11. Since 9/11 the structure of sentences has become a new frontier for him.

A native of Los Angeles, CA, **Al Serradell** is a recovering Public Relations executive who teaches Creative Writing while working as a Compliance Officer for the State of Oklahoma.

**Ann M. Sheridan** is the founder of Bimbo's Buddies (www.bimbos-buddies.org). She wrote *Dogs Get Cancer Too*, and has been published in *Chicken Soup for the Woman Golfer's Soul*. Ann resides in Long Branch, New Jersey. She enjoys writing, reading and walking Bambi, her Miniature Pinscher. You may contact her at ASheridan529@aol.com.

**Ryma Shohami** is a technical writer/editor who went on vacation to Israel twenty-five years ago and never left. She is married and has two beautiful daughters. Ryma loves books, music, and traveling, and is passionate about animal welfare. She dreams of swimming with dolphins in Hawaii.

**David Michael Smith** hails from Georgetown, Delaware where he resides with his wife, Geralynn, and their two children, Rebekah and Matthew. He has been published multiple times, and enjoys writing inspirational short stories. He graduated from the University of Delaware (Communications) in 1981. E-mail David at davidandgeri@hotmail.com.

**Mary Z. Smith** resides with her retired husband, Barry, ninety-two-year-old mother-in-law, Flora, and Rat Terrier, Frankie. They have four children, two of whom are biological and two who came to live with them. When she isn't writing for *Angels on Earth* or *Guideposts*, she can be found gardening or walking.

**Karen Starling** lives in Central Florida with her husband, three children, and nine dogs. She is a webmaster, and enjoys camping, reading, and watching her daughters show their Australian Shepherd dogs.

**Nancy Sullivan** enjoys multiple degrees and has written extensively over a long career in the disability arena. With one mystery novel near completion, she plans to write many more. Volunteering in animal rescue, Nancy delights in her own menagerie and is a Reiki Master Teacher. E-mail her at nancy.writes@sbcglobal.net.

**Brian Taylor** is the founder and Creative Director of book producer Pneuma Books and the designer behind the new look for *Chicken Soup for the Soul*. He has ghostwritten several chapters in *The Complete Idiot's Guide to Self-Publishing*. Still a kid at heart, he coaches baseball and likes to draw pictures. crdir@pneumabooks.com.

**Susan E. Tornga** lives in Southern Arizona and loves hiking in the desert. She is an ardent admirer of the women who settled the American West, a frequent topic of her writing. Follow her blog at susantornga.blogspot.com or e-mail her at susantornga.writer@comcast.net.

**Christine Trollinger** is from Kansas City, MO. She is a freelance writer whose short stories have appeared in various magazines and books of inspiration as well as newspaper columns. She is a widow, and a mother of three grown children, three grandchildren and two great-granddaughters.

**Ann Vitale** wrote three books for Mason Crest educational press and has several flash fiction and anthology pieces in print. She lives in northeast Pennsylvania, has been a dog trainer, breeder, 4-H leader, and a writing teacher and coach in several counties. Contact her at www.annvitale.blogspot.com.

**Pat Wahler** has been involved with animal rescue organizations since 1997. Her husband, dog, and cat have learned to deal with it. She writes a daily blog on critter-related stories and issues. Visit her at www.critteralley.blogspot.com.

**Beverly F. Walker** is a mother and grandmother who lives north of Nashville, TN, and enjoys writing, photography and scrapbooking pictures of her grandchildren. She has stories in many *Chicken Soup for the Soul* books and in *Angel Cats: Divine Messengers of Comfort*.

**Karen Adragna Walsh**, author of *Good Crazy: Essays of a Mad Housewife*, derives her craziness from husband Frank, daughter Kara and dog Tanner. Her story, "The Connection," appears in *Chicken Soup for the Soul: Living Catholic*. She's currently working on two children's books. Contact her at humormeso@aol.com, website: www.smatteringsbooks.com/KWalsh/index.html.

**Shirley Walston** has been a police reporter, truck driver, retail store owner and a missionary. She currently edits a magazine on the Big Island of Hawaii and travels whenever an opportunity arises. Read more about Luke and Kristal in her new book, *Kristal's Wedding*.

**Dallas Woodburn** is the author of two short story collections and a forthcoming novel. She has written more than seventy articles for publication. Dallas also created the Write On! For Literacy foundation and the publishing company Write On! Books. Please visit her website at www.writeonbooks.org.

**Susan Kimmel Wright** is a writer and writing teacher living in western PA with her husband, two dogs, four cats, four guinea pigs, one rabbit, and an elderly foster dog from the shelter where she volunteers with her youngest daughter. Contact her at floatingagainstthecurrent.blogspot.com.

# Meet Our Authors

**J**ack Canfield is the co-creator of the *Chicken Soup for the Soul* series, which *Time* magazine has called "the publishing phenomenon of the decade." Jack is also the co-author of eight other bestselling books.

Jack is the CEO of the Canfield Training Group in Santa Barbara, California, and founder of the Foundation for Self-Esteem in Culver City, California. He has conducted intensive personal and professional development seminars on the principles of success for more than a million people in twenty-three countries. Jack is a dynamic keynote speaker and he has spoken to hundreds of thousands of people at more than 1,000 corporations, universities, professional conferences and conventions, and has been seen by millions more on national television shows such as *The Today Show*, *Fox and Friends*, *Inside Edition*, *Hard Copy*, CNN's *Talk Back Live*, *20/20*, *Eye to Eye*, the *NBC Nightly News* and the *CBS Evening News*.

Jack has received many awards and honors, including three honorary doctorates and a Guinness World Records Certificate for having seven books from the *Chicken Soup for the Soul* series appearing on the New York Times bestseller list on May 24, 1998.

You can reach Jack at:

Jack Canfield
P.O. Box 30880 • Santa Barbara, CA 93130
phone: 805-563-2935 • fax: 805-563-2945
www.jackcanfield.com

**M**ark Victor Hansen is the co-founder of Chicken Soup for the Soul, along with Jack Canfield. He is a sought-after keynote speaker, bestselling author, and marketing maven. Mark's powerful messages of possibility, opportunity, and action have created powerful change in thousands of organizations and millions of individuals worldwide.

Mark is a prolific writer with many bestselling books in addition to the *Chicken Soup for the Soul* series. Mark has had a profound influence in the field of human potential through his library of audios, videos, and articles in the areas of big thinking, sales achievement, wealth building, publishing success, and personal and professional development. He is also the founder of the MEGA Seminar Series.

He has appeared on *Oprah*, CNN, and *The Today Show*. He has been quoted in *Time*, *U. S. News & World Report*, *USA Today*, *The New York Times*, and *Entrepreneur* and has given countless radio interviews, assuring our planet's people that "You can easily create the life you deserve."

Mark has received numerous awards that honor his entrepreneurial spirit, philanthropic heart, and business acumen. He is a lifetime member of the Horatio Alger Association of Distinguished Americans.

You can reach Mark at:

Mark Victor Hansen & Associates, Inc.
P.O. Box 7665 • Newport Beach, CA 92658
phone: 949-764-2640 • fax: 949-722-6912
www.markvictorhansen.com

**A** **my Newmark** is the publisher of *Chicken Soup for the Soul*, after a thirty-year career as a writer, speaker, financial analyst, and business executive in the worlds of finance and telecommunications. Amy is a *magna cum laude* graduate of Harvard College, where she majored in Portuguese, minored in French, and traveled extensively. She is also the mother of two children in college and two grown stepchildren who are recent college graduates.

After a long career writing books on telecommunications, voluminous financial reports, business plans, and corporate press releases, Chicken Soup for the Soul is a breath of fresh air for Amy. She has fallen in love with Chicken Soup for the Soul and its life-changing books, and really enjoys putting these books together for Chicken Soup's wonderful readers. She has co-authored more than two dozen Chicken Soup for the Soul books.

You can reach Amy and the rest of the Chicken Soup for the Soul team via e-mail through webmaster@chickensoupforthesoul.com.

# Thank You!

We owe huge thanks to all of our contributors. We know that you poured your hearts and souls into the thousands of stories and poems that you shared with us, and ultimately with each other. We appreciate your willingness to open up your lives to other Chicken Soup for the Soul readers. And we loved hearing about your fabulous dogs!

We could only publish a small percentage of the stories that were submitted, but we read every single one and even the ones that do not appear in the book had an influence on us and on the final manuscript.

Two long-time Chicken Soup for the Soul editors—Barbara LoMonaco and D'ette Corona—read all the stories and poems that were submitted for this book and created the manuscript. This book could not have been made without their expertise, their input, and their innate knowledge of what makes a great Chicken Soup for the Soul story. Barbara is our webmaster and also a fabulous editor, and D'ette is our assistant publisher and chief organizer and also a great editor. We also want to thank Chicken Soup for the Soul editor Kristiana Glavin for her assistance with the final manuscript and proofreading, as well as Leigh Holmes, who keeps our office running smoothly.

We owe a very special thanks to our creative director and book producer, Brian Taylor at Pneuma Books, for his brilliant vision for our covers and interiors. Finally, none of this would be possible without the business and creative leadership of our CEO, Bill Rouhana, and our president, Bob Jacobs.

# Chicken Soup for the Soul.

## Improving Your Life Every Day

R eal people sharing real stories—for fifteen years. Now, Chicken Soup for the Soul has gone beyond the bookstore to become a world leader in life improvement. Through books, movies, DVDs, online resources and other partnerships, we bring hope, courage, inspiration and love to hundreds of millions of people around the world. Chicken Soup for the Soul's writers and readers belong to a one-of-a-kind global community, sharing advice, support, guidance, comfort, and knowledge.

Chicken Soup for the Soul stories have been translated into more than forty languages and can be found in more than one hundred countries. Every day, millions of people experience a Chicken Soup for the Soul story in a book, magazine, newspaper or online. As we share our life experiences through these stories, we offer hope, comfort and inspiration to one another. The stories travel from person to person, and from country to country, helping to improve lives everywhere.

# Share with Us

We all have had Chicken Soup for the Soul moments in our lives. If you would like to share your story or poem with millions of people around the world, go to chickensoup.com and click on "Submit Your Story." You may be able to help another reader, and become a published author at the same time. Some of our past contributors have launched writing and speaking careers from the publication of their stories in our books!

Your stories have the best chance of being used if you submit them through our website at:

## www.chickensoup.com

If you do not have access to the Internet, you may submit your stories by mail or by facsimile. Starting in 2010, submissions will only be accepted via the website.

Please do not send us any book manuscripts, unless through a literary agent, as these will be automatically discarded.

Chicken Soup for the Soul
P.O. Box 700
Cos Cob, CT 06807-0700
Fax: 203-861-7194

# Chicken Soup for the Soul®
## Loving Our Dogs

Our 101 BEST STORIES

Heartwarming and Humorous Stories about Our Companions and Best Friends

Jack Canfield
& Mark Victor Hansen
edited by Amy Newmark

We are all crazy about our dogs and can't read enough about them, whether they're misbehaving and giving us big, innocent looks, or loyally standing by us in times of need. This new book from Chicken Soup for the Soul contains the 101 best dog stories from the company's extensive library. Readers will revel in the heartwarming, amusing, inspirational, and occasionally tearful stories about our best friends and faithful companions—our dogs.

978-1-935096-05-4

Classics for Dog Lovers